Mortality and Music

Bloomsbury Studies in Religion and Popular Music

Series editors: Christopher Partridge and Sara Cohen

Religion's relationship to popular music has ranged from opposition to 'the Devil's music' to an embracing of modern styles and subcultures in order to communicate its ideas and defend its values. Similarly, from jazz to reggae, gospel to heavy metal and bhangra to qawwali, there are few genres of contemporary popular music that have not dealt with ideas and themes related to religion, spirituality, and the paranormal. Whether we think of Satanism or Sufism, the liberal use of drugs or disciplined abstinence, the history of the quest for transcendence within popular music and its subcultures raises important issues for anyone interested in contemporary religion, culture and society. *Bloomsbury Studies in Religion and Popular Music* is a multidisciplinary series that aims to contribute to a comprehensive understanding of these issues and the relationships between religion and popular music.

Religion in Hip Hop, edited by Monica R. Miller,
Anthony B. Pinn and Bernard "Bun B" Freeman

Christian Metal, Marcus Moberg

Sacred and Secular Musics, Virinda Kalra

Mortality and Music

Popular Music and the Awareness of Death

Christopher Partridge

Bloomsbury Academic
An imprint of Bloomsbury Publishing Plc

B L O O M S B U R Y

LONDON · OXFORD · NEW YORK · NEW DELHI · SYDNEY

Bloomsbury Academic

An imprint of Bloomsbury Publishing Plc

50 Bedford Square	1385 Broadway
London	New York
WC1B 3DP	NY 10018
UK	USA

www.bloomsbury.com

BLOOMSBURY and the Diana logo are trademarks of Bloomsbury Publishing Plc

First published 2015
Paperback edition first published 2017

British Library Cataloguing-in-Publication Data

A catalogue record for this book is available from the British Library.

ISBN: HB: 978-1-4725-3451-4
PB: 978-1-3500-2689-6
ePDF: 978-1-4725-2680-9
ePub: 978-1-4725-2720-2

Library of Congress Cataloging-in-Publication Data

Partridge, Christopher H. (Christopher Hugh), 1961–
Mortality and music : popular music and the awareness of death / Christopher Partridge.
pages cm. – (Bloomsbury studies in religion and popular music)
Includes bibliographical references and index.
ISBN 978-1-4725-2680-9 (hb)
1. Popular music–History and criticism. 2. Death in music. I. Title.
ML3470.P36 2015
781.64′1588–dc23
2015018897

Series: Bloomsbury Studies in Religion and Popular Music

Typeset by Integra Software Services Pvt. Ltd.

For my father
George Aubrey Wright Partridge

Contents

Acknowledgements   ix

Introduction   1

1   Mortality and Immortality   9
    The obscuring of death and decay   9
    Immortality and the denial of death   14
    Words against death   19
    Strategies of immortalization   25
    Concluding comments   33

2   Death, Transgression and the Sacred   37
    The sacred, the profane, transgression and death   39
    Liminality and pissing people off   45
    Death and subcultural capital   47
    Death chic, youth culture and the romanticization of mortality   49
    The impure sacred   52
    Concluding comments   57

3   The Undead and the Uncanny   61
    Mortality and the uncanny   62
    Music and uncanny affective space   64
    Memory and *memento mori*   70
    Hauntology, spirit voices and exorcisms   73
    Can the world be as sad as it seems?   79
    Grotesque bodies   87
    Concluding comments   93

4   Morbidity, Violence and Suicide   97
    A vortex of summons and repulsion   98
    Thanatos, survival and *schadenfreude*   100
    Suicidal tendencies   105
    Disaffection, violence and death   117

The pornography of gore, violence and death   124
Living on death row   127
Concluding comments   134

5   Transfiguration, Devotion and Immortality   137
     A note on myth   138
     Transcendence and transfiguration   139
     Recorded immortality   145
     Pilgrims and dead rock stars   147
     Kinetic rituals   151
     Concluding comments   154

Notes   157
Bibliography   187
Index   211

Acknowledgements

As ever, I am indebted to my wife, Marcia, who is always more than happy to discuss popular music (if not death and dying) with me and to make suggestions of songs that I should listen to and books that I should read. Without her support, this book would be a poorer piece of work. I am also indebted to Sara Cohen of the Institute of Popular Music at Liverpool University for her comments. Likewise, an anonymous reader of the final draft made many helpful suggestions, for which I am grateful. Finally, I would like to thank Lalle Pursglove at Bloomsbury for her enthusiasm for the series in which this book appears and for her support for the book itself.

Introduction

Are you able to contemplate your death and the deaths of those closest to you?
Accepting the fact of death, we are freed to live more fully.
— Quaker Faith and Practice, *third edition (1994), 1.02.30*

All you that do this place pass bye,
Remember death for you will dye.
As you are now even so was I,
And as I am so shall you be.
— *A* memento mori *plaque in Ely Cathedral, England.*

In previous centuries, *memento mori* exhortations were hardly necessary. One's mortality was all too obvious. This, of course, is still the case in some parts of the world. My son reminded me of this when he emailed from northern India. He and his partner, travelling down from Nepal, had been disturbed when they had gone to help a man lying at the side of the road. Staring back at them with sunken, dark eyes, maggots and flies populating his mouth, they quickly realized that he was dead. Later, they had been shocked to find a partially immolated corpse (following a rather too brief encounter with a funeral pyre) floating in the Ganges next to where they were lodging. Presumably familiar with floating corpses, some local men joked among themselves as they attempted to disentangle the unfortunate cadaver from their boats' mooring ropes. While I am not claiming that these are everyday events in India, in societies where they do occur, reminders of mortality make carefully fashioned *memento mori* objects practically redundant. Likewise, for many of our forebears in the premodern West, life was brutal, short and precarious. Although only a few may have heard the daily chorus of peasants with carts of corpses yelling 'bring out your dead', as depicted in the film *Monty Python and the Holy Grail* (1975), exposure to death was quotidian.

Life is rather different in contemporary Western societies. Modernity has made the Grim Reaper's status as *persona non grata* very clear. As we will see in Chapter 1, death and decay are sequestered in hospitals,

hospices, mortuaries and cemeteries, and much cultural energy is expended
developing strategies to obscure and to sanitize the brutal facts of mortality.
But still, we are haunted by the inevitability of death. Indeed, this book is
almost certainly the product of my own sharpened awareness of mortality.
Since turning fifty, I have thought a lot about death and dying. I am not
melancholic, pessimistic or unhappy. I do not feel the urge to withdraw
to a darkened room to work through morbid scenarios of my own
dissolution. Nevertheless, I am increasingly aware of the precarious and
temporary nature of my existence. I am now closer to my death than I am to
my birth – and almost certainly much closer than I like to think I am. I am
aware that the few things that I have achieved in my life actually lack any
lasting significance, and that, at some point in the future, they and I will be
completely forgotten. Weeds will grow over my grave, which will eventually
crumble and be absorbed by the earth. Along with those people who mean
most to me, I will finally pass into nothingness: 'My name is Death, cannot
you see?/ All life must turn to me' (Incredible String Band, 'My Name Is
Death', *The 5000 Spirits or the Layers of the Onion*, 1967).

It is, of course, not only my own fragile mortality that haunts me. I am
who I am because of the web of relationships to which I belong. I am, as the
philosopher John Macmurray put it many years ago in his Gifford Lectures,
'a person in relation'.[1] As such, the vulnerabilities of other mortals directly
affect my experience of life and my sense of self. Hence, while it is true that,
as John Donne reflected, 'any man's death diminishes me, because I am
involved in mankind',[2] when close relationships are dissolved at death, I am
particularly diminished. Although I am currently in the fortunate position
of having grieved for only a very few close friends and family, when I have
grieved my own sense of impermanence has been increased. In recent years,
this awareness of the fragility of life and mortal vulnerability has been brought
home to me by my own father's dementia. Sadly, now in the latter stages of
the disease, the quiet, dignified, gentle, reserved man that I grew up with has
almost departed – and along with him any illusions I might have fostered
about the permanence of the self. Those fashionable, countercultural interests
of my youth, during which I had the luxury of viewing death and decay at a
distance to the sounds of The Fall, Joy Division, Bauhaus and dub reggae,
are gradually being replaced by a more intimate assessment of personal
extinction. At one time, the bell always seemed to toll for someone else. Now
it always tolls for me. A body that once thrived on late nights and excess
now aches and yawns more than it used to and enjoys an increasing bias
towards sedentariness. While this is not necessarily a bad thing, and while

theological notions of unending life are, I will argue, unbearable, I have a very clear appreciation that, as San Francisco's psychedelic revivalists Wooden Shjips remind us, 'Death's Not Your Friend' (*Vol.2*, 2010). Having said that, I am also acutely aware that for many people, including my father, the Reaper may very well arrive as the most welcome of friends.

The title of George Harrison's album *All Things Must Pass* (1970) is increasingly a *memento mori* challenge to me. While the words themselves struck me as profound when I first bought the album in the mid-1970s, now the music itself immediately draws me into reflection on the passing of days and the fact that 'there'll come a time when all of us must leave here' ('Art of Dying', *All Things Must Pass*, 1970). Of course, it is not the only album that has this effect. Numerous albums, songs, melodies and even musical phrases transport me to a moment in my past and to reflection on the passing of time. Indeed, it is this relationship between music and memory, which is indicated throughout and discussed specifically in Chapter 3, that is key to understanding popular music's significance for reflection on mortality.

While experiences such as the above are important, in that they add emotional texture and meaning to our lives, only the unwell and the foolish will spend much time reflecting on the fleeting nature of existence. Indeed, the contemplation of one's own impermanence is probably not possible for extended periods of time without becoming unhealthily morbid. As the psychiatrist Robert Wilkins has commented, 'the only reason that we are able to lead productive lives is because most of us, for most of the time, ward off such anxieties by marshalling our defence mechanisms. Psychodynamic forces such as denial and repression push down the disturbing reality of our own mortality into the eddying nether regions of our subconscious minds'.[3] This is an important point. While we quite naturally avoid serious reflection on the extinction of the self, nevertheless, its inevitability haunts us and fascinates us. We cannot but think of the terminus towards which we are progressing and which others have reached. As such, it needs to be dealt with. We do this in a number of ways that surface in social institutions and culture. Indeed, informing many of the ideas developed in this book has been the work of Zygmunt Bauman, for whom 'culture is the sediment of the ongoing attempt *to make living with the awareness of mortality liveable*'.[4] That is to say, much of the cultural work we do as humans and the value we place on that work relates to our awareness that life is short. Because we have not got much time, the time we have is precious and what we do in it is significant. There is, moreover, a niggling need to address the suspicion that (to quote the title of one of my favourite albums from the 1980s) *Life's Hard Then You Die* (It's Immaterial, 1986). If this is true, then existence seems absurd. There is, as Albert Camus discussed, a legitimate and necessary question as to whether life has meaning.[5] In short, mortality raises a number of important issues, which are routinely addressed in human culture. This book is a look at mortality through the lens of popular music culture. As such, it is a little different from other books on death and dying and, indeed, other books on popular music, in that it works at the interface of both.

While it hardly needs mentioning that throughout the arts the same ideas are articulated in more or less profound ways, nevertheless, I want to argue that, because of its peculiar ability to create affective space and, as such, function as a soundtrack to our lives, music is particularly powerful in drawing us into reflection on mortality. That is to say, it is often more than simply 'entertainment' (in the sense in which that term is colloquially and superficially understood). For many people, popular music is central to the construction of their identities, central to their sense of self, central to their well-being and, therefore, central to their social relations.[6] As such, it functions as a 'prosthetic technology', in that it modifies mood, increases performance, informs decision-making, creates emotional spaces within which meaning is made, evokes memories of significant relationships, and so on. Consequently, it has become central to the everyday personal lives of most people. To a large extent, I want to claim for popular music what Alain De Botton and John Armstrong claim for fine art, namely that it helps us 'to lead better lives – to access better versions of ourselves'. As such, it acts as 'a purveyor of hope', 'a source of dignified sorrow' and 'a guide to self knowledge'.[7] In short, it constitutes one of the principal ways in which we make living with the awareness of mortality bearable. Again, this makes it a very useful lens through which to examine the presence of that awareness in Western societies.

Moreover, because popular music is typically rooted within the liminal cultures of youth, within which death tends to be viewed at a distance, it often confronts the taboos of mortality with an uncompromising explicitness censured elsewhere in Western societies. Hence, to a large extent, we can view popular music's treatment of mortality through a Gothic lens, in that terror is viewed at a remove. More particularly, there is something of Edmund Burke's notion of the sublime here, in that death is viewed at a distance, and as such, it engenders a frisson of dread without immediate risk. From a position of safety, the listener can emotionally 'delight' in the excitement of contemplating the terror of death. For Burke, of course, 'terror is the ruling principle of the sublime'.[8] However, in Burkean aesthetics, terror and the sublime are not synonymous. That is to say, if we are actually threatened by that which is terrifying, we are unable to appreciate it aesthetically. Actual terror simply overwhelms our judgement, and as such, it is 'incapable of giving any delight whatsoever', it being 'simply terrible'. This is the position of the individual threatened with immediate annihilation. However, and this is key, 'at certain distances, and with certain modifications', terrifying events and objects 'are delightful'.[9] Indeed, 'delightful horror', is, he suggests, 'the most genuine effect and truest test of the sublime'.[10] For Burke, 'delight' is not 'pleasure' as such, but rather, it is the experience of being removed from the awfulness of the 'terror'. As will be discussed with reference to Julia Kristeva's notion of 'abjection', there is something both alluring and repellent about death and decay – but the allure can only be fully experienced at a distance. The point here is that this obsession with mortal vulnerability, which is central to the Gothic imagination, is comparable to the youthful treatment of death and gore in popular music. As such, while many of the discourses of depression, decay and death in popular music might (often with good reason) worry those of us who are older and concerned about the well-being of our children and the cultures shaping their minds, nevertheless, they are basic to the human condition. Consequently, they *can* function as healthy *memento mori* in societies that taboo the fundamental fact of existence that 'all things must pass'. As with eighteenth-century Graveyard poetry,[11] or Gothic, or cultural events and celebrations focused on death, such as the Day of the Dead in Mexico, popular music can provide a space within which we are able to reflect on mortality and, as such, come to terms with the inevitability of death and its implications. Indeed, because popular music is so close to the everyday subjective lives of listeners, it is able to create spaces within which they can express and think about what matters most to them. From reflection on oppression and aggression within hip hop, extreme metal and hardcore to meditations on depression and suicide within black metal, darkwave and goth music, spaces are created within which the often disturbing facts of mortality can be thought about and come to terms with.

Having said that, we will see that the relationship between mortality and music is rather more complex than simply being a sublime *memento mori*. On the one hand, for a small number of listeners, popular music is far from a 'delightful horror', in that there is some evidence to suggest that it might contribute to negative emotional states and self-destructive behaviours. On the other hand, influenced by hegemonic culture in the West, much popular music develops its own strategies for alleviating the effects of the awareness of personal extinction. For example, to return to George Harrison's declaration that 'all things must pass', this is, of course, actually a gentle introduction to reincarnation and, therefore, a denial of death and an articulation of the permanence of the self: 'I must be on my way/ And face another day.' Likewise, much reflection on mortality in contemporary Gothic-oriented music is embedded within narratives of the paranormal and the anomalous, which, typically influenced by a hegemonic Christian culture, resist notions of personal extinction. Again, more immediately, simply immersing oneself in the musical moment allows temporary escape from the haunting awareness of death. Hence, while the treatment of mortality in popular music functions very effectively as a *memento mori*, which can, in some cases, lead to negative emotional states, it can also operate as a strategy for alleviating the impact of the awareness of death.

Throughout the book, reference is made to music's ability to create 'affective space', the importance of which I have discussed more fully elsewhere.[12] Although what I mean by this will become increasingly apparent as the book progresses, and although I have briefly mentioned it above, it is perhaps worth saying a little more about the idea here. In recent years, there has been an appreciation of the significance of music's relationship to emotion.[13] Indeed, conceptualized as a device for the constitution of emotive action, we have seen that it can be understood as a 'prosthetic technology'. That is to say, in a number of complex ways, it is able to move us emotionally and physically. It immediately engages us as embodied beings. It evokes emotional states, which, in turn, guide thought, helping us to make sense of our lives, our relationships and who we are; through its engagement with emotion – and, relatedly, imagination and memory – it is able directly to organize the internal world of the listener. In other words, while, of course, music means more to some people than it does to others, generally speaking, it is able to create an 'affective space' – an emotional bubble – within which reflection occurs and within which we are encouraged to act in certain ways, from dancing to relaxing and from marching to meditating. This, of course, is why it is so effective in the manipulation of a viewer's response to scenes in a film. The significance of the non-cognitive dimensions of musical agency in relation to the discussion in this book is that popular music is able to evoke affective states within which we are drawn into reflection on life, on relationships and on the impermanence of both. Hence, not infrequently, at some level, music is able to encourage reflection on the significance of the finite self.

Finally, a few points need to be made regarding content and approach. First, this book is not a work of theology. I hope it will be useful to theologians in thinking through some of the issues discussed, but it needs to be borne in mind that it is written from a broadly cultural sociological perspective and is concerned very specifically with mortality and the human awareness of impermanence, rather than eschatological speculation about death and post-mortem survival or thinking about the presence of the divine in the arts. Second, as indicated above, it is also a little different from much sociological analysis currently done in popular music studies, in that the primary aim is to provide reflection on popular music's relationship to our awareness of mortality, rather than an analysis of particular genres, bands, artists and scenes. In short, the arguments developed in the following pages seek, on the one hand, to provide reflection on cultural responses to death and decay and, on the other hand, to contribute to our understanding of the social significance of popular music. Finally, while I have cast the net fairly widely, I have tended to focus on those genres that are conspicuous in their treatment of issues relating to mortality. However, it does not matter that some readers may be unfamiliar with some of the genres, bands and artists discussed. While they can, of course, spend a little time on YouTube familiarizing themselves with the music, again, the broad aim of the book is to provide an account of how a particularly significant area of Western culture articulates and manages the awareness of mortality. In the final analysis, I hope readers will be able to apply the arguments posited to genres, bands and artists with which they are familiar, as well as to the contemplation of their own impermanence.

1

Mortality and Immortality

The aim of this chapter is both to outline the shift in attitudes towards death and decay in the West and to introduce the cultural significance of our awareness of mortality. Although the discussion will provide some analysis of reflection on death and dying within popular music, the focus is on the wider cultural context. Hence, those narrowly concerned with popular music may conclude that the discussion in this chapter is a little too tangential to their interests and therefore wish to skip it. However, I encourage readers to bear with me because, inadequate though the discussion may be in many respects, its aim is to introduce the core issues addressed in the rest of the book. In short, it explores the implications of the universal human experience, articulated within the arts, that, on the one hand, we do what we can to avoid reflection on personal extinction, yet, on the other hand, we are haunted and obsessed by its inevitability. Hence, many of us approach our own death in much the same way that Rudolf Otto described the human experience of the 'the holy', namely as *mysterium tremendum et fascinans*[1] – a mystery that evokes both fear and fascination, both repulsion and attraction. Some grasp of the implications of this will facilitate a better understanding of the relationship between popular music and mortality unpacked more fully in subsequent chapters.

The obscuring of death and decay

The words of *The Book of Common Prayer*, 'In the midst of life we are in death', once carried a weight that they do not today. As explored in Gothic literature, adults were often haunted by memories of siblings and offspring who had not survived infancy. Many will have observed first hand the processes of death and decay. If not an everyday spectacle, it was certainly not uncommon.[2] As Philippe Ariès comments in his seminal – although not uncontested[3] – history of Western attitudes to death, it was 'always public'. Hence, he notes 'the profound significance of Pascal's remark that one dies alone, for at that time one was never physically alone at the moment of death'.[4] Indeed, such was public nature of death that some 'hygienically minded doctors of the late eighteenth century ... began to complain about the number of people who invaded the bedrooms of the dying'.[5] Likewise, 'in the early nineteenth century, when the last sacrament was being taken to a sick man, anyone could come into the house and into the bedroom, even if he was a stranger to the family'.[6]

Today, of course, the deceased receive a rather less intimate send-off, in that many of us would find the invitation to process past an open coffin in order to pay respects a macabre and daunting prospect.[7] Having said that, as the celebrated HBO series *Six Feet Under* (2001–2005) testified, 'open casket' viewings are still common in some Western cultures and serve an important function in the bereavement process.[8] However, while this is true, the series also beautifully illustrates Ariès' acerbic assessment of one of 'the most ridiculous and irritating aspects of the American ritual', namely 'the making up of the body and the simulation of life'.[9] Every effort is made by morticians, in their artistic constructions of exquisite corpses, to distance the bereaved from the reality of death and decay. While these processes can never be completely avoided, non-specialists in thanatology are now far less acquainted with the facts of death than they once were. As Kathleen Garces-Foley and Justin Holcomb discuss, 'families rely on ... death experts rather than traditional knowledge of how to respond to death .... Technological advances in embalming, cosmetic reconstruction, and casket materials are given precedence over religious concern for the journey of the soul, and the family relinquishes control of the body to the funeral home'.[10] Again, as memorably depicted in *Six Feet Under*, for some it is important to view the body 'after it has been made to look serenely asleep ... in order to have an authentic experience of death and farewell'.[11] This, of course, has meant that, as Jessica Mitford argues in her influential and cuttingly humorous critique of *The American Way of Death*, the funeral business has thrived as a result of the commodification of mortality. Indeed, funeral directors have played a significant role in the shaping of Western attitudes to death, the undertaker becoming a 'stage manager of the fabulous production that is the modern American funeral, the stellar role [being] reserved for the occupant of the open casket' – who, again, is cosmetically prepared to appear to be in a state of idealized sleep, rather than decomposition.[12]

Relatedly, as a result of the development of technologies of sanitation, it is difficult for many contemporary Westerners to imagine an everyday world in which the stench of disease, decay and excrement fills the nostrils. All that inhibits and hides putrefaction in modern societies, from modern preservatives and disinfectants to antibiotics and cosmetics, makes it hard for us to appreciate the close proximity to decay experienced by our ancestors.[13] In the thirteenth century, for example, Bonvesin de la Riva, in his *Book of the Three Scriptures*, was not alone in dwelling on the grotesque and vile nature of human life. Faced with the blood, bile and waste that naturally surround human existence, he concluded, quite reasonably, that there is nothing about embodied existence that is lastingly good and beautiful: 'the birth of man is of such a kind that he is engendered in nasty entrails by blood that is commingled of vileness and filth'.[14] The human condition is one that is shaped by the processes of decay and decomposition. 'After he is grown up and fully formed', observes Bonvesin, 'whether he be a male or a fine girl, he may be of fair and excellent appearance outside, but no one, either knight or lady, is fair inside'. He continues,

> There is no male or female of such beauty, whether small or great, queen or countess, that they are fair inside – this I boldly affirm. Instead they are vessels of filth and great nastiness .... The vessel is fair outside, but inside there is great rottenness. There is no food in the world, however precious it is, that does not rot inside as soon as it is hidden there. From the members of one's body, though they seem precious, issue no good fruit, only disgusting.[15]

Whether we can empathize or not with this view of embodied existence, it is nevertheless hard for us to inhabit the medieval mind, which was informed by much that we would not now be able to tolerate. Over the past 1,000 years or so, death has – as Ariès' study of the evolution of Western attitudes to morbidity and mortality demonstrates – shifted from the centre of Western culture, where it was accepted as a natural part of everyday life, to its edges, where, as far as possible, its grotesque reality is excluded from people's minds.[16] Consequently, nowadays, it is not unusual *not* to have had an encounter with a corpse. Even those who do, often because of the nature of their profession, rarely encounter the awful reality witnessed by our ancestors. It is obscured. As William Spellman puts it,

> where once the dying person found solace at home, surrounded by family and friends and in command of the goodbyes, more likely than not the experience

today comes at the end of costly treatments, all supervised by professional staff in charge of sophisticated life-sustaining machinery, the dying visited by, rather than living with, loved ones in a familiar setting....Death today is commonly at a distinct remove from life, very nearly clandestine, almost always unwelcome.[17]

The reasons for this shift towards what Ariès refers to as 'the invisible death'[18] are complex. That said, a few important social and cultural factors should be noted. First, as indicated above, there have been significant advances in the medical and sanitary sciences and a consequent increase in life expectancy. These have served to push ageing and death to the margins of culture as taboo subjects. Second, of wide-ranging significance has been the declining influence of institutional religion and its doctrines relating to death and the afterlife. With the decline in religious commitment, death as a theological construct articulated from the pulpit and meditated upon in devotional literature has slipped out of focus in Western culture along with the comforting belief in immortality. Finally, there has been a well-documented and much discussed turn to the self in the modern world,[19] which has led to an inflated view of the individual's uniqueness and significance. This is important because, for many, deprived of the hope of an afterlife, it is now too distressing to contemplate mortality as the absolute termination of the self. With the collapse of traditional religious frameworks, we are forced to accept that there is nothing unique or lastingly significant about my embodied self. In other words, death, the extinction of the self, seems to render life absurd and, as such, too difficult to face.

Having said that, although the turn to the self has exacerbated the situation, the shadow of death and the disturbing sense of meaninglessness it evokes have, of course, always pressed in upon human minds to some extent. The prospect of personal extinction, even in religious cultures, presented the enquiring mind with an unnerving question: What if our all too brief 'hour upon this stage' is all we have? Shakespeare makes the point forcefully in *Macbeth* (V.v.19–28):

To-morrow, and to-morrow, and to-morrow,
Creeps in this petty pace from day to day,
To the last syllable of recorded time;
And all our yesterdays have lighted fools
The way to dusty death. Out, out, brief candle!
Life's but a walking shadow; a poor player
That struts and frets his hour upon the stage,

And then is heard no more: it is a tale
Told by an idiot, full of sound and fury,
Signifying nothing.

His point, however, becomes acute in the modern period in which all we have is invested in the individual self and in the significance of the selves to whom we are intimately related. As Charles Taylor comments, 'one of the things which makes it very difficult to sustain a sense of the higher meaning of ordinary life, in particular our love relations, is death. It's not just that they matter to us a lot, and hence there is a grievous hole in our lives when our partner dies. It's also because they are so significant to us, they seem to demand eternity.'[20] But, for many of our contemporaries, eternity is an illusion and immortality an irrational wish (we will return to this point below).

Such issues bother us all. It is not surprising, therefore, that much existential contemplation has been evoked by musical reflection on individual meaninglessness in songs such as 'Dust in the Wind' by Kansas: 'all we are is dust in the wind … / All we do/ Crumbles to the ground …'.[21] Here, the writer, Kerry Livgren (who subsequently converted to evangelical Christianity), subverts the significance of the self so central to modernity and forces his listeners to consider the absurdity of an existence which ends conclusively in death. All our lives reach the same conclusion, and regardless of what we claim for ourselves and what we achieve, that conclusion is dust in the wind. We may, as explored in the film about the musician Nick Cave, *20,000 Days on Earth* (2014), establish an archive about ourselves, which collects everything that testifies to the significance (such as it is) of our 'hour upon the stage', in an attempt to extend that significance beyond our deaths, but that too will perish and be forgotten. Nothing is permanent – 'we are all dust in the wind'.

This is the problem faced by the modern, secular self. On the one hand, it has an inflated sense of personal uniqueness and significance, and, on the other hand, that uniqueness and significance is undermined by an inescapable commitment to the inevitability of its dissolution. The self – the construction and agency of which has been so important throughout our lives[22] – is, in the final analysis, as insignificant as dust in the wind: 'Out, out, brief candle!' This is the significance and affective power of the popular *memento mori* in the modern Western world. Whereas once a *memento mori* reminded the religious self of the inevitability of judgement and the need to live a life with the divine assize in mind,[23] now it reminds the secular self of its final insignificance and ordinariness: 'It's all sex and death as far as I can tell', sing Dead Can Dance.[24] But, if this is so, then, ultimately, what is the meaning of life?

Immortality and the denial of death

Hope springs eternal in the human breast;
Man never is, but always to be blessed:
The soul, uneasy and confined from home,
Rests and expatiates in a life to come.

(Alexander Pope, 'An Essay on Man', Epistle 1.95–98)

For the religious imagination, of course, existence is not simply sex and death. Theological anthropologies extend the self's significance beyond 'dust in the wind' by positing some form of afterlife. Hence, the words of committal at the burial of a body as commended in *The Book of Common Prayer*, 'earth to earth, ashes to ashes, dust to dust' – which refer to Genesis 3:19, 'you are dust, and to dust you shall return' – look beyond this material fact to the promise of resurrection. Indeed, in the quotation above, Alexander Pope reminds his readers of Augustine's famous declaration: 'You have made us for yourself, O Lord, and our heart is restless until it rests in you' (*Confessions*, I.7). As such, not only is the significance of the self secured and ultimate meaninglessness avoided, but real significance and meaning is waiting for us beyond death. It is this side of death that is found wanting. Can it be argued, therefore, that this is actually the point of the doctrine? In other words, is religion rooted in the denial of death? Is the prospect of personal extinction, which is so difficult for humans to comprehend, 'the raw material out of which theology created a future state'.[25]

This basic account of the origin of religion is a persuasive and influential one, not least because we can all feel the force of it.[26] The human being is, as François Dastur put it, 'that strange animal that *knows* that it must one day die. Nobody doubts that the feeling of a fundamental vulnerability is commonly shared by all living beings. But the human being is the only being that is aware of the ephemeral character of its existence. It knows that its existence cannot be indefinitely extended and that just as it had to begin, so, too, one day it will have to end.'[27] While we might avert our gaze from personal extinction, it haunts us. And, it is *personal* extinction that presents the problem. To think of someone else's death is not so problematic, awful though the prospect might be. Why? First, through media and the arts, we are presented with the fact of the death of other people in everyday life. It becomes part of our mental furniture at an early age. (The death of pets, of course, is also enormously significant in introducing us to the death of the other.[28]) Second, the death of another person is, while tragic, not the termination of one's own world, the cessation of an existence we have constructed. I can observe the death of another human being and make some sad sense of it within my own world. The situation, however, is entirely different when it comes to me and to the existence of my world. As Zygmunt Bauman put it, 'the death of others is an event in the world of objects "out there", which I perceive as any other event or object. It is *my* death, and *my* death only, which is not an event of that "knowable" world of objects. The death of others does not affect the continuity of my perception. The death of others is painful and shattering precisely because it does not do it.'[29] The core problem regarding personal extinction, therefore, is, as the theologian Herbert H. Farmer put it, 'even when I apprehend the world as thus independent of me and as the permanent object of knowledge for all selves, the world as so characterized is still my world and there wholly and solely through its relation to me. Whatever be the character of the world I know, I am, as the self knowing it … the absolute perspective-centre to whom alone the vast panorama is disclosed. If I vanish, everything vanishes.'[30]

Hence, I can experience the death of others in *my world*, but I cannot experience my own death because, by definition, it is the end of my experience. Everything has vanished. This, needless to say, is a distressing prospect for some people. Others may experience my death, but I cannot. I can only experience the passage to it. Indeed, even that approach to my extinction cannot truly be shared. This, of course, was what Pascal was getting at when he observed that 'one dies alone'.

This fact, of course, has not escaped popular musicians. It would be surprising if it had. For example, the thoughtful and provocative Scottish musician Malcolm Middleton (formerly of Arab Strap) forces his listeners, in typically blunt fashion, to face the implications of the inevitability of personal extinction: 'We're all going to die and what if there's nothing/ We'll all have to face this alone/ There's a *when* not an *if* inside everybody/ Mortal thoughts like this can make you feel so alone … . You're gonna die, you're gonna die, you're gonna die alone/ You're gonna die, you're gonna die, you're gonna die alone *all alone*' ('We're All Going To Die', *A Brighter Beat*, 2006). It might be argued, therefore, that theologies of the future state seek to offer protection from the psychological consequences of contemplating this awful fact, this lonely experience towards which we are all heading, this dissolution of the self. In other words, doctrines of personal immortality help us to live *as if* personal extinction and nothingness were not the case and *as if* we will not finally be alone. As the Tom Ramsey hymn, memorably sung by Johnny Cash, expresses: 'When I come to the river at the ending of day/ When the last winds of sorrow have blown/ There'll be somebody waiting to show me the way I won't have to cross Jordan alone/ I won't have to cross Jordan alone Jesus died all my sins to atone/ In the darkness I see he'll be waiting for me I won't have to cross Jordan alone' (Johnny Cash, *Hymns from the Heart*, 1962).

Quite reasonably, Ludwig Feuerbach, Karl Marx, Sigmund Freud, James Frazer and many others have made much of the denial of death and its relationship to doctrines of immortality. Freud's work in particular understands the origins of religion to be located within the human anxiety over death. As such, there is that which is psychologically necessary about the belief in immortality. Again, it would be odd if large-brained mammals had not evolved some way of dealing with such profound angst. Hence, Freud opines, illusory though it may be, it is difficult to dispense with – which, in some measure, accounts for the persistence of religion into the modern period. In other words, most of us are only able to get on with life because we can live *as if*, as Frank Sinatra might have said, there were no 'final curtain' to be faced.[31] As Richard H. Kirk of Cabaret Voltaire – a band which explored the dark recesses, obsessions and fears of human existence – commented when asked about the fear of death, 'there's a little nag at the back of my head which says, "I'm going to snuff it one of these days". I suppose everybody gets those; you just push it to the back of your mind and get on with it.' Fellow band member, Stephen Mallinder, agreed: 'we are all subject to an obsession with death, but it doesn't affect my day-to-day living particularly.'[32] It is this ability to live *as if* extinction itself were an illusion that Freud was referring to. That is to say, on the one hand, immortality is an illusion, but, on the other hand, living as if it were not, is a necessary component of the bedrock of our unconscious. Why is this? It is because it is not merely difficult to imagine one's own death, claimed Freud, but it is impossible: 'whenever we attempt to do so we can perceive that we are in fact still present as spectators. Hence … at bottom no one believes in his own death, or, to put the same thing in another way, that in the unconscious every one of us is convinced of his own immortality.'[33] The self cannot contemplate its own extinction.³⁴ This is why what he considers to be the illusions of religion are so necessary to so many people and so frequently rehearsed in popular culture. Again, Dastur's comments are worth noting here:

> ... death is an object of fear, and seems to be something we can face only to the degree that it is made relative and appears to have a hold over no more than a part of our being. It is Spinoza ... who declares: 'The human mind cannot be absolutely destroyed with the body, but something of it remains which is eternal.' He claims that although no immortality of the soul as a personal entity can be deduced from the eternal subsistence of the thinking essence of the mind, 'Nevertheless we feel and know by experience that we are eternal.' It is this experience of eternity at the very heart of duration that has always been opposed to the inevitable arrival of death, as a way of enabling death to be thwarted in advance.³⁵

In his attempt to make sense of this 'experience of eternity', Freud, in his 'Thoughts on War and Death', imagines that, while some distant ancestor living a short and brutal existence will have been painfully aware of the termination of life,

> he was nevertheless unwilling to acknowledge it, for he could not conceive of himself as dead. So he devised a compromise: he conceded the fact of his own death as well, but denied it the significance of annihilation – a significance which he had had no motive for denying where the death of his enemy was concerned. It was beside the dead body of someone he loved that he invented spirits, and his sense of guilt at the satisfaction mingled with his sorrow turned these new born spirits into evil demons that had to be dreaded. The [physical] changes brought about by death suggested to him the division of the individual into a body and a soul .... In this way his train of thought ran parallel with the process of disintegration which sets in with death. His persisting memory of the dead became the basis for assuming other forms of existence and gave him the conception of a life continuing after apparent death.³⁶

Hence, the reinterpretation of death as that which is other than the self's *terminus* is psychologically significant. It is hardly surprising, therefore, that, in both religious and secular cultures, it came to be constructed as sleep. As Marcus Aurelius put it in his *Meditations* (6.28), 'death is a rest from the solicitations of sense, and from impulse which pulls us around like a puppet, and from the vagaries of discursive thought, and from the service of the flesh.'³⁷ And, of course, in Christian cultures, there is a long tradition of death being understood as a state of dormancy. It is viewed as retiring to bed following a hard day's labour: 'in inscriptions next to the *hic jacet* (here lies) ... one often reads *hic pauset, hic requuiescit, hic dormit,* or *requiescat in isto tumolo* (here rests or sleeps or in this grave rests)'.[38] Such metaphors are, of course, rooted in biblical discourse about immortality: 'Many of those who *sleep* in the dust of the earth shall awake, some to everlasting life ... ' (Dan. 12:2); 'For if we believe that Jesus died and rose again, even so them also which *sleep* in Jesus will God bring with him' (1 Thess 4:14). In contemporary secular funeral culture, this discourse is continued: the body is 'laid to rest' in a 'slumber room' or a 'reposing room'.[39] Mitford recalls funeral directors who 'revamped the corpse to look like a living doll' and 'arranged for it to nap for a few days in the slumber room', as well as putting on 'a well-oiled performance in which the concept of *death* has played no part whatsoever – unless it was inconsiderately mentioned by the clergyman who conducted the service'.[40] Such discourses, constantly rehearsed in popular culture, support this belief that the existence of the self is no more threatened than when it sleeps. 'Sleep when I'm dead, you angels/ I'll sleep when I'm dead/ But until then/ Well, I should at least feel tired I think/ Before I lay me down to dream' (The Cure, 'Sleep When I'm Dead', *4:13 Dream*, 2008).

Similar general theories about the cultural denial of death and the significance of the belief in immortality have been advanced in other disciplines. The influential anthropologist, Bronislaw Malinowski, for example, made much of the value of the belief in immortality in human societies: 'of all the sources of religion, the supreme and final crisis of life – death – is of the greatest importance. Death is the gateway to the other world in more than the literal sense'. Indeed, he cannot avoid the conclusion that 'a great deal, if not all, of religious inspiration has been derived from it .... Man has to live his life in the shadow of death, and he who clings to life and enjoys its fullness must dread the menace of its end. And he who is faced by death turns to the promise of life'.[41] Viewed from this angle, religion appears to be a necessary and positive force within societies, binding communities together through its rituals and encouraging the belief in an existence that transcends death. Hence, for Malinowski, 'the belief in immortality ... is one of the supreme gifts of religion'.[42] Writing in 1925, on the basis of his anthropological work with the Trobriand Islanders, he observed that 'the savage is intensely afraid of death, probably as the result of some deep-seated instincts common to man and animals. He does not want to realize it as an end, he cannot face the idea of complete cessation, of annihilation'. So, he says, 'man reaches the comforting belief in spiritual continuity and in the life after death'. He continues:

> Yet this belief does not remain unchallenged in the complex, double-edged play
> of hope and fear which sets in always in the face of death. To the comforting voice

of hope, to the intense desire of immortality, to the difficulty, in one's own case, almost the impossibility, of facing annihilation there are opposed powerful and terrible forebodings. The testimony of the senses, the gruesome decomposition of the corpse, the visible disappearance of the personality – certain apparently instinctive suggestions of fear and horror seem to threaten man at all stages of culture with some idea of annihilation, with some hidden fears and forebodings. And here into this play of emotional forces, into this supreme dilemma of life and final death, religion steps in, selecting the positive creed, the comforting view, the culturally valuable belief in immortality, in the spirit independent of the body, and in the continuance of life after death. In the various ceremonies at death, in commemoration and communion with the departed, and worship of ancestral ghosts, religion gives body and form to the saving beliefs.[43]

In short, the denial of death is 'the result of a deep emotional revelation', something civilizing, rather than something primitive, irrational and destructive.[44] The rituals surrounding death and the rites of mourning are important life-affirming social events, and the religious framework that gives them meaning 'counteracts the centrifugal forces of fear, dismay, demoralization and provides the most powerful means of reintegration of the group's shaken solidarity and the re-establishment of its morale'.[45] Hope is secured for members of the community, who are bound together by death rites and the belief in the immortality of those of their number who have died. Because community and familial relationships are extended beyond this life into another sphere of existence, the sense of loss and societal depletion is assuaged.

Words against death

While there is much within contemporary Western culture that erodes intimations of immortality and rationalizes death as the inevitable decay of biological matter, as indicated above, the anxieties of the self are not so easily laid to rest. Many of us are, in our silent moments, faced with the struggle against meaninglessness. Indeed, as Albert Camus insisted, 'the one truly serious philosophical problem' – which is presented by the knowledge of mortality – remains 'whether life is or is not worth living...'.[46] As such, for many, a certain paraphysical farsightedness is a constructive response to the implications of death. Hope and longing urge us to gaze beyond the extinction of the self to some form of survival, some post-mortem experience of rest. This can be understood as a form of resistance to the affective impact of death.

Drawing on Maurice Bloch's notion of 'rebounding conquest', Douglas Davies has made much of the importance of 'words against death' in mortuary rites: 'the power of funeral rituals lies in the fact that death is directly faced, addressed, and, in one sense, experienced as a kind of transcendence'.[47] This, I think, points us in a helpful direction when thinking about the significance of discourses of death in popular music, which, again, function as *memento mori*. In other words, in facing the fact of death and in being forced to make sense of the death of a loved one, to interpret it in some more or less meaningful way, we enter into a discourse of resistance. It is through funerary rites, he says, 'that the shadow side of existence is confronted and not ignored. The ritual words and songs press significance upon the participants, who do not return to some prior "normal" state of life. They may never even be "happy" again, but they have touched "the depths" and survived'.[48] This touching of the depths, this facing the fact of personal mortality, is enormously significant, not least because a person has, 'in the new strength of bereavement ... the power to speak words of comfort to other people and, in so doing, speak words against death: words invested with significance because of what they have experienced in the face of grief'.[49]

With these ideas in mind, we can think about the idea of 'words against death' in two ways. First, although actually imagining personal extinction is, as Freud pointed out, enormously difficult, if not impossible, nevertheless, standing with the dead on the edge of the abyss, so to speak, and thus being forced to engage with the inevitability of death is of supreme existential importance. In this place, with the dead, we are forced to ask, as Camus put it, 'whether life is or is not worth living'. We are brought face to face with that which haunts us and causes us fear in our darker moments, but from which we naturally avert our gaze. However, it is in gazing into the abyss, in asking the difficult questions and in seeking meaning in the face of apparent meaninglessness, that some small moments of transcendence are possible. Here is the beginning of resistance to the fear of death. Second, of course, having stood in this place, we are in a position to stand by others who find themselves gazing into the abyss and pondering 'whether life is or is not worth living'.

Popular music, which has the power to move and to create affective spaces within which meaning-making occurs,[50] is a particularly effective carrier of words against death. For example, Michael Gira, in the song 'Rose of Los Angeles' (*I Am Singing to You From My Room*, 2004), recalls, 'looking down at my mother dying in a hospital bed':[51] 'Now wrapped within her wires/ The Rose of Los Angeles/ Now breathing through her mask....Her fingers soft but distorted/ Now reaching for the past'. More viscerally, following the sudden death of his son, Craig Minowa of Cloud Cult retreated to rural Minnesota, during which time he wrote a number of songs that he eventually shared on the band's first successful album, *They Live on the Sun* (2003). The album constitutes a collection of words against death. Minowa shifts between a yearning hope that his relationship with his son will continue – 'Grandma and Grandpa left this world together/ And now they're living somewhere on the sun/ I want to leave this world together/ And you and I will live up on the sun' ('On the Sun') – and the despair and anger of a bereaved man – 'Would you all believe I once had a baby?/ And I was married?/ Now, I'm alone .... Have I gone mad?' Then, on two of the songs, 'I'm not Gone' and 'Took You for Granted', he draws his son back into the world of the living through the sensitive inclusion of samples of his recorded voice. As he plays and as we listen, his son speaks.

Another profound articulation of grief is Public Image Ltd's 'Death Disco' (1979). A lacerating, bass-driven rendering of Swan Lake, it relates John Lydon's pain following the loss of his mother to cancer. Sung in his tortured, yearning vocal style, the song expresses the difficult, disorienting feelings that many young people will have experienced following the loss of a family member. 'Seeing in your eyes .... Told me in your eyes .... Watch her slowly die/ Saw it in her eyes/ Choking on a bed/ Flowers rotting dead .... Ending in a day .... Words cannot express.' Although, like Camus, no hope of immortality is contemplated, only the sad conclusion of 'flowers rotting dead', in articulating his grief, there is a sincere and constructive engagement with the fact of mortality, which, again, many will identify with. And those who have not grieved are introduced to something of the pain and confusion it will inevitably bring at some point in their lives.

Similarly, other work, such as that of Lou Reed or Peter Silberman of the band Antlers, has explored the emotional distress caused by cancer. In 2009, for example, Antlers released their moving concept album *Hospice*, which beautifully and sensitively relates the story of a friendship between a hospice worker and a patient suffering from terminal bone cancer. The trauma, the fear, the pain, the loss and the consuming sense of meaninglessness evoked are all carefully explored: 'In the middle of the night I was sleeping sitting up, when a doctor came to tell me ... that there was nothing that I could do save you ... ' ('Two – or, I Would Have Saved Her If I Could'). The music, which moves between the ambient and the anthemic, introduces the listener to an affective space within which something of the emotional turbulence caused by death and dying can be witnessed at a remove.

Likewise, Lou Reed, following the death of two of his close friends – the songwriter Doc Pomus and Kenneth Rapp ('Rotten Rita', who he had known since his time at Andy Warhol's Factory) – recorded *Magic and Loss*, a simple, stark and profound album that can be understood as a meditation on 'whether life is or is not worth living'. Like Gira, Lydon and Silberman, Reed touches the depths and survives. In this collection of moving, personal songs, he shares his experiences of observing the processes of decay and death and, finally, of bereavement. Although, inevitably, some have criticized such an idiosyncratic album – Robert Christgau dismissing it as dull[52] – such critics, I suggest, misunderstand its significance. *Magic and Loss* is a sharing of anguish, which offers no final answers, no comprehensive theories, but only reflection, some of which may be rather banal. But, it pretends to be nothing more than that and, as such, is so much more than that. These are simply one man's words against death, one man's thoughts as he stares into the abyss.[53] Certainly, for one bereaved person I know, the album was meditated upon as an evocative collection of profound thoughts that contributed to meaning-making during a particularly dark period. David Fricke of *Rolling Stone* articulates this significance beautifully:

> This is an album about death – and how to live with it. It is an eyewitness account, documented in compelling song, of a losing battle with cancer, the mourning after and the little miracles that, for the mourner, mark the beginning of the healing process. It will probably bum you out the first couple of times through. But it's worth your perseverance, because *Magic and Loss* is Lou Reed's most affecting, emotionally direct solo work since *The Blue Mask*, a stunning consummation of that album's naked guitar clamor, the hushed-chapel intimacy of the third Velvet Underground album and the barbed reportorial vitality of Reed's best songwriting. He offers no great moral revelations and no happy ever after, just big questions and some basic horse sense . . . . Yet the beauty, however dark, of *Magic and Loss* is in the asking – in the subtle, elegiac lift in Reed's stony sing-speak, the sepulchral resonance of his and Mike Rathke's guitars and the Spartan grace of the storytelling. Reed recounts the victim's harrowing odyssey of radiation treatments, chemotherapy and utter physical erosion with simple detail and then candidly traces his own pain train of confusion, self-recrimination and tentative, hopeful resolution . . . . Anyone who's been through this experience will know exactly what Reed is talking about. For anyone facing it for the first time, *Magic and Loss* can help with the starting over.[54]

As Fricke indicates, the sense of loss and longing, familiar to the bereaved, is achingly articulated throughout. Concentrated by the awful presence of cancer, his meditation is heavy with reflection on the degrading treatments used to resist it and his friend's gradual submission to it: 'I saw a great man turn into a little child/ The cancer reduced him to dust'; 'I saw isotopes introduced into his lungs/ Trying to stop the cancerous spread' ('Power and Glory'). Following his death, Reed records the significance of its impact on his world, which became immeasurably reduced and darkened: 'Now life is like death without living/ That's what life's like without you.... It's 'not fair at all ... forever dealing in hurt' ('What's good'). This rumination about the implications of death is particularly conspicuous in the song 'Cremation': 'Since they burnt you up/ Collect you in a cup.... Well the coal black sea waits for me, me, me/ The coal black sea waits forever/ When I leave this joint/ At some further point/ The same coal black sea, will it be waiting?' Here, again, is reflection on 'whether life is or is not worth living'. Are we simply carbon destined for nothingness? Perhaps! On the other hand, while he sympathizes with his deceased friend's conclusion that any speculation about immortality is little more than 'mystic shit' ('Sword of Damocles'), nevertheless, he cannot resist the urge to peer through the darkness of death to a farther shore: 'It seems everything's done that must be done/ from over here though things don't seem fair/ But there are things that we can't know/ Maybe there's something over there/ Some other world that we don't know about ... ' ('Sword of Damocles'). Indeed, in the song 'Magic and Loss' that hope becomes more concrete. As his friend passes through the flames of cremation, he imagines that 'there's a door up ahead, not a wall'.

Like the metaphor of sleep, this interpretation of death as a door, often informed by religious discourse, is a popular default position that resists the finality of death. Similarly, Buck Dharma (Donald Roeser) of Blue Öyster Cult, in his well-known song '(Don't Fear) The Reaper' (*Agents of Fortune*, 1976), although reflecting on his own death, is, as the song title suggests, persistently optimistic about post-mortem survival: 'All our times have come/ Here, but now they're gone/ Seasons don't fear the reaper/ Nor do the wind, the sun or the rain/ (We can be like they are).' More particularly, while 'Romeo and Juliet' may have died, they 'are together in eternity'. The song then speaks of embracing the Reaper as one who can escort us to another more desirable existence.

Again, Terry Jacks's version of the Jacques Brel song, 'Seasons in the Sun' (1973)[55] – originally about the pain of losing the love of an unfaithful wife – was rewritten as a personal reflection on the death of a close friend from cancer. As Jacks recalls,

> a really good friend of mine died. He had acute leukemia.... We were playing golf and he told me he's got six months to live. I said, 'Oh, come on.' And he said, 'No, there's no cure for what I've got' .... He was gone in four months. He was a very good friend of mine, one of my best friends, and he said I was the first one that he told. I remembered this song of an old man dying of a broken heart, and I liked some of the melody and there was something there. I rewrote the song about him and how he said goodbye to his friend and then he said goodbye to his father instead of his priest, and then he said goodbye to his girlfriend.[56]

Few people who hear the song forget it. The atmosphere of loss and longing it evokes, both musically and lyrically, is almost palpable. As I remember very well of my own teenage sister, who seemed to play it continuously, it led to much adolescent melancholy. 'Goodbye, my friend, it's hard to die/ When all the birds are singing in the sky.... We had joy we had fun/ We had seasons in the sun/ But the wine and the song like the seasons/ Have all gone.' While there is little in this song that echoes Lou Reed's hope that 'there's a door up ahead, not a wall', it creates an affective space within which to contemplate death and bereavement. Again, while there is no discussion of the processes of death and decay, sadness and reflection are evoked through its articulation of the ending of meaningful relationships, which are, of course, so central to our sense of self.[57] Hence, the song functions as both a *memento mori* and a *memento vivere* ('remember to live'). Recognizing the brevity of life can lead either to despair or to an appreciation of its value. 'Seasons in the Sun', although melancholic, does encourage the latter attitude. Because you too will soon die, you should appreciate life and find meaning in the quotidian moments of your existence: 'all the birds are singing in the sky'; 'spring is in the air/ Little children everywhere'; 'starfish on the beach'; 'Together we climbed hills and trees/ Learned of love and ABC's.'

Particularly evocative in this respect is My Chemical Romance's thanatological album, *Welcome to the Black Parade* (2006), which, conceived as a dark opera, articulates the reflections and sadness of a patient in the last stages of cancer. As Gerard Way, the singer, recalls, 'it wasn't the happiest time of our lives. We were questioning our mortality. I think it's a very human record under the bombast and the theatrics. The sound is very large and grand, but it's a very mortal record. It's an interesting record, because there's a lot of lyrics that examine ourselves – not just as a band, but as human beings.'[58]

This reflection on meaning and mortality is conspicuous in the central song 'Cancer': 'Turn away/ If you could get me a drink/ Of water because my lips are chapped and faded/ Call my aunt Marie/ Help her gather all my things/ And bury me in all my favorite colors .... Now turn away ... I'm awful just to see/ because all my hairs abandoned all my body/ Oh, my agony/ Know that I will never marry/ Baby, I'm just soggy from the chemo/ But counting down the days to go ... the hardest part of this is leaving you.' The overall point, however, is that such songs, often shaped around minor chords, at the very least, open up affective spaces within which to contemplate the significance of both mortality and life. Even the titles of instrumentals, such as 'Hey Cancer ... Fuck You!' by Years (*Years*, 2009), can function as 'words against death'. Overall, the basic point is that popular music matters, in that it has the resources to evoke contemplative spaces within which meaning-making is encouraged.

Strategies of immortalization

To repeat the principal point again, while it is difficult to avoid the fact that, as Epicurus famously put it, 'death is of no concern to us, for while we exist death is not present, and where death is present, we no longer exist',[59] nevertheless, it haunts us. It does so because, while I am never in a position literally to experience my own death, I am confronted by the deaths of others, particularly in my mourning for those close to me – as Michael Gira, John Lydon, Peter Silberman, Lou Reed and Terry Jacks articulate from their different perspectives. That is to say, while the encounter with death is not mine, I do feel the shock waves caused by a friend's or a relation's encounter with death. Dastur (quoting Alphonse de Lamartine) puts it well:

> Certainly, the death of a loved one is the announcement of 'my' death, since it condemns me to a desolation, the *experience* of which can be like the disappearance of all *Dasein*, of all ability to be *there*, like the melancholy revelation of the meaninglessness of my own being, for the fact that 'a single being is missing' is enough for it to seem suddenly that 'the entire world is emptied of its people'. The experience of such an 'emptying', of the melting of that horizon of meaning constituted by the world, can in no way claim to be a true assumption of death 'itself'.[60]

The impact of a loved one's death, 'the melting of the horizon of meaning' caused by death's intrusion into *our* world, is enormously significant. It is this universal awareness of the presence of death that haunts us. Indeed, this is what this book is about, namely, our awareness of mortality and our responses to that awareness. Hence, looking through the lens of popular music, the following pages are, to some extent, a reflection on Bauman's comment that 'culture is the sediment of the on-going attempt *to make living with the awareness of mortality liveable*'.[61]

Bauman's point is an interesting and complex one, in that it is rooted in the conviction that the awareness of mortality is what drives cultural production: 'if by any chance we were to become immortal, as sometimes (foolishly) we dream, culture would grind to a halt .... It was precisely the knowledge of having to die, of the non-negotiable brevity of time, of the possibility or likelihood of visions remaining *un*fulfilled, projects finished, and things *not* done, that spurred humans into action and human imagination into flight. It was that knowledge that made cultural creation a necessity and turned humans into creatures of culture.'[62] To some extent, this is simply the result of our desire to make a mark, to count for something and to acquire some level of immortality by inscribing our fleeting presence into the pages of history. However, it is also inspired by the sense of meaning bestowed by the knowledge of brevity and finality. The fact that life is short makes it meaningful; because our lives are limited, the meaning we invest in our various activities is increased, 'despite what we know about the limitations, the endemic brevity and ultimate futility of life's efforts'.[63] Death, in this sense, gives meaning to what we do in life. Life is precious because it is limited.

But, as Bauman indicates, this is all *despite* 'what we know about the limitations, the endemic brevity and ultimate futility of life's efforts'. Everything is subject to decay. This is expressed beautifully in Brian Eno's 'Golden Hours' (*Another Green World*, 1975): 'The passage of time/ Is flicking dimly up on the screen/ I can't see the lines I used to think I could read between/ Perhaps my brains have turned to sand .... Several times/ I've seen the evening slide away/ Watching the signs/ Taking over from the fading day ... '. Because we will, very soon, be separated from our health, from our memories, from our dignity, from all we have worked for, from all we have acquired, from all we have invested time and energy in achieving, there is a nagging sense that our significance as selves is little more than the fading of the light at the end of day. This is not something we can easily accommodate. This is why death becomes such a significant social problem. We simply cannot view is as the natural end to a biological organism. It is the end of our world, the dissolution of experience and meaning. As such, humans objectify death and invest it with enormous significance. 'Death is the last enemy to be destroyed' (1 Corinthians 15:26). Of course, such destruction is impossible. Just as death seems to render all human striving ultimately absurd, so the human aspiration to destroy death is, likewise, absurd. In the final analysis, we strive 'to deal with issues that by their nature cannot be dealt with – tackle what cannot be tackled, respond to challenges that pre-empt responses'. In summary, Bauman argues, our strategies are 'bound to be ineffective and ultimately defeated. Efforts known in advance to be vain pursuits of unreachable goals to avoid/postpone the disaster that couldn't be wished away, wouldn't go away, and couldn't be pushed away whatever one did or desisted from doing.'[64] In other words, 'strategies to defeat, postpone or disarm death', what he refers to as 'strategies of "immortalisation"', designed to cope with the fact of mortality', are not only bound to fail, but mortality itself is both 'definitely immune to all coping', and makes 'non-coping all but unthinkable and impossible.'[65]

The problem is that, although we cannot stare into the abyss of our own extinction, 'death *is*, is *real*, and we know it'.[66] Traditionally, of course, as we have seen, human culture has contrived to defeat 'the last enemy' by religious means, by imagining that the self's *terminus* will be circumvented in some way. In the modern period, although religious and paranormal belief in survival persists,[67] as Bauman shows, other strategies have evolved.

Before briefly unpacking these strategies, it should be noted that the drive towards immortality is motivated less by the long-term desire to live forever and more by the short-term desire to avoid extinction. While the two are logically related, the immediate problem of extinction obscures the more distant problem of eternal life, the actual experience of which would be one of hellish meaninglessness. Life has meaning because it is circumscribed. For example, with reference to Michel Houellebecq's 2005 novel, *La Possibilité d'une île* – which moves between the narratives of Daniel 1 and Daniels 24 and 25, who are neo-human clones of Daniel 1 – Bauman points out that, as Daniel 25 discovered, 'once the prospect of the end-of-time had been removed, and infinity of being had been assured, "the sole fact of existing was already a misfortune" and the temptation to voluntarily surrender the entitlement to further re-clonings and depart thereby into "simple nothingness, a pure absence of content" turned impossible to resist.'[68] We may not be able to face the fact of personal extinction, but this is far preferable to the prospect of unending existence and the meaninglessness that this inevitably entails. As David Byrne suggests in the Talking Heads' song 'Heaven' (*Fear of Music*, 1979), any pleasurable moment expanded infinitely loses any of its original significance and, indeed, becomes hellish: 'The band in Heaven plays my favorite song/ They play it once again, they play it all night long.' Again, 'When this kiss is over it will start again/ It will not be any different, it will be exactly the same.' Hence, without change and difference, 'Heaven is a place where nothing ever happens', and, of course, 'Its hard to imagine that nothing at all/ Could be so exciting, and so much fun.' As Bauman concluded, 'I guess that what we really yearn for when (if) dreaming of immortality, is prolongation of life and postponement of death, not "eternity." A prospect of "no end" is all too often no less odious a nightmare than the end itself.'[69]

Again, while death is what makes the life we have so significant, paradoxically, central to death's significance is the drive to explain it, to seek meaning in the face of it, and to develop strategies to avoid it. Death is, says Peter Kostenbaum, 'an influential self-concept. And it is this certainty about our eventual death and that of all other human beings that is the key to understanding our human nature … . Death – our own and that of others – explains what it means to be human (searching for meaning, immortality, freedom, love, and individuality), far better than psychological principles of sex and aggression, the biological instincts of survival and procreation, the utilitarian theories of happiness and approbation, or the religious ukase of God's will.'[70] In short, death invests our brief span of life with meaning, inspiring cultural production, the aim of much of which is to resist death, to avert our gaze from the abyss, and to reinterpret the inevitable. Hence, culture – and here we are particularly thinking of popular music culture – is the result of effort to find meaning in the face of extinction. As Ernest Becker argued, 'all man's creative life-ways, are in some part of them a fabricated protest against natural reality, a denial of the truth of the human condition, and an attempt to forget the pathetic creature that man is … . Society itself is a codified hero system, which means that society everywhere is a living myth of the significance of human life, a defiant creation of meaning.'[71] That is to say, human existence is fundamentally heroic, in the sense that it is a constant Sisyphean effort to transcend that which cannot be transcended. As Camus discussed in *The Myth of Sisyphus*, there is that which is fundamentally 'absurd' about human existence. Just as Sisyphus was condemned by the gods to spend each day ceaselessly rolling a large rock up a mountain, only to see it roll back down again under its own weight, so there is, he argued, a basic, unavoidable absurdity to existence. Human striving is as 'dust in the wind'. Yet, *and this is the point*, unlike animals, we are aware of this absurdity, and because we are aware of it, we are drawn into meaning-making, into grappling with existence, into rebellion against death. We develop strategies, as Bauman says, '*to make living with the awareness of mortality liveable*'.[72]

In his important and often overlooked book, *Mortality, Immortality and Other Life Strategies*, he begins by making the point that he does not intend to provide 'a study in the *sociology of death and dying*'. That is to say, he does not intend to examine 'the ways we treat people about to die and commemorate those already dead, the way we mourn the beloved and cope with the agony of bereavement, the rituals we devise to prevent the dead from disappearing from the world of the living too fast or without trace – and make their disappearance painless'.[73] Again, what he does furnish us with is an insightful discussion of attempts to make sense of mortality, which has unfortunately been misunderstood by some scholars, such as Douglas Davies and Jonathon Dollimore, who have focused on aspects of his observation that modern societies hide the reality of death in a way that previous societies did not.[74] While this is, of course, true, Bauman's principal aim is more penetrating. He seeks 'to unpack, and to open up to investigation, the presence of death (i.e. of the conscious or repressed knowledge of mortality) in human institutions, rituals and beliefs which, on the face of it, explicitly and self-consciously, serve tasks and functions altogether different, unrelated to the preoccupations normally scrutinized in studies dedicated to the "history of death and dying."'[75]

For Bauman, we have seen, 'culture is about expanding temporal and spatial boundaries of being, with a view to dismantling them altogether'.[76] It does this in two principal ways: 'the first activity of culture relates to *survival* – pushing back the moment of death, extending the life-span, increasing life expectation and life's content-absorbing capacity; making death a matter of concern, a significant event – lifting the event of death above the level of the mundane, the ordinary, the natural; directly or indirectly ... making the job of death somewhat more difficult'.[77] No longer is death a natural, quotidian event in which a self is extinguished. Rather, it is now a problem of the utmost importance; it is that which interrupts the continuation of our existence; it is something to be transcended. This 'making the job of death somewhat more difficult' lies at the heart of modernity. There is within modern culture a fundamental refusal to face death, which is manifested very clearly in its commitment to the omnipotence of medical science. This is, of course, also a point made forcefully by Michel Foucault in his *The Birth of the Clinic*, which provides a detailed description of the management of life and death at the end of the eighteenth century. In particular, he describes the processes by which the self becomes an object of science. Unlike pre-eighteenth-century medicine, which simply managed the effects of the Fall, there emerged a sense that science could manage bodies and control diseases.[78] Likewise, for Bauman, death has been 'deconstructed', 'redefined as the outcome of an essentially curable disease'.[79] This has led to a popular faith in the ability of science to produce solutions to the problem of mortality, which is not unlike the premodern belief in the abilities of the occult sciences. 'Lying (or not telling the whole truth) about its ultimate limits, surreptitiously substituting effective concerns with partial ailments for the (hopeless) struggle against the incurable malady of existence, medical science and the technology it spawns turns itself into a variety of magic. It promises ... what it cannot deliver, while diverting the attention from the idleness of promise through an ever more dazzling display of staggering surgeries, wonder drugs and awe-inspiring high-tech installations.'[80] As such, we are bewitched by the belief that each malady that marks our path to death can be cured.

These strategies of modernity are compounded by postmodern strategies, which deconstruct immortality. This is done in a number of ways, but perhaps most obviously in the identification of the self with, for example, work, reputation or love. The phrase 'Elvis lives' rarely speaks of his bodily resurrection or immortality – although, as discussed in Chapter 5, some may find that particular illusion meaningful – but rather of the continuation of his music beyond his biological life. Of course, the metaphorical extending of the self's significance is common in both religion and culture. Just as Rod Stewart considered his lover to be 'ageless' and 'timeless' ('You're In My Heart (The Final Acclaim)', *Foot Loose & Fancy Free*, 1977), so some have argued that the significance of Jesus needs to be understood as metaphorical rather than literal.[81] We express a person's significance for us, by imputing immortality to them. To repeat Taylor's point, 'because they are so significant to us, they seem to demand eternity'.[82] Although the conviction that people 'live on' in their work, or in their partner's memory, or in their children's love or in numerous other ways, is not a commitment to their literal immortality, it does contribute to a discourse that mitigates the impact and offense of death. Mortality is ameliorated by what Bauman refers to as an 'immortality-through-other-people's-memory'. In this sense, the quest for celebrity is a quest for immortality, in that it is hoped that one's 'fifteen minutes of fame' will be remembered, documented, inscribed into history, thereby extending the significance of the self beyond one's biological lifespan. For example, as indicated earlier in the chapter, to some extent, this quest for 'immortality-through-other-people's-memory' is explored by Iain Forsyth and Jane Pollard in their film about Nick Cave, *20,000 Days on Earth* (2014). At several points in the film, we are introduced to an intriguing archive devoted to Cave's life. Although there is an actual archive housed in a temperature-controlled room with sliding aluminium doors at the Melbourne Arts Centre, in the film, it is imagined in a dusty basement in Brighton, England. This is significant, in that there are moments in the film during which Cave reflects on the passing of time, the importance of memory and, implicitly, the processes of mortality. The archive is, therefore, invested with a particular significance. He is shown discussing and reflecting on even the most minor pieces of flotsam and jetsam that have been washed up during his 20,000 days on earth. Each piece represents a moment pregnant with meaning. As such, it is carefully explained and kept for posterity. In other words, significant moments of his life have been immortalized. His memory will fade and he will die, but his life, having been captured on photographs, films and a plethora of ephemera, will remain labelled and boxed in an archive.

More fundamentally, the desire for fifteen minutes of fame can be thought of as one of series of moments of intensive experience typical of contemporary life. That is to say, life is lived with mortality continually beyond the horizon; we become near-sighted, focusing on immediate experience; anticipating the next momentary episode; 'a happy life is one perceived as the perpetuity of new beginnings'.[83] 'Liquid modernity'/postmodernity has, for Bauman, led to a situation in which self-identity is increasingly fractured, fluid and frail. Our lives are chopped up into manageable, entertaining chunks of the ever-present, of the eternal now, of the immediately experienced, which serve to avert our gaze from the actual *terminus* of the self. And, of course, we can now take snapshots and 'selfies' of those moments, as if those frozen points in time define our lives and who we are. Postmodernity, 'instead of trying (in vain) to colonize the future … dissolves the future in the present. It does not allow the finality of time to worry the living; and it attempts to do it, mainly, by slicing time (all of it, every shred of it, without residue) into short-lived, evanescent episodes.'[84] In this sense, each moment is immortal, but, as he says, 'not here to stay'.[85]

> What we witness these days is immortality itself becoming mortal. But mortality stops being worrying if it comes together with a promise of raising the dead. The dread of death used to be brought home by the realization that one has but one life to live and that a chance missed is a chance that cannot be recovered. But that

truth is belied now by the offer to squeeze as many 'new and improved' lives into the lifespan as one can manage, and the advice that the quicker the successive lives are removed and replaced, the more of them will be packed in and so the volume of 'immortal experiences' will swell.[86]

Hence, we might think of postmodern life as a series of little deaths followed by distracting resurrections that absorb us. Nothing lasts and everything is temporary. Each moment is just as wonderful and just as banal as the next. In our fast-paced, download and dispose culture of consumption, we inoculate ourselves against macro mortality by injecting our lives with a series of micro mortalities and immortalities: replacing phones, replacing clothes, replacing cars, replacing relationships, replacing lifestyles and replacing identities. Indeed, to a large extent, the evanescence of postmodern life, composed of a series of deaths and resurrections, is something that listening to music itself perfectly illustrates. That is to say, it is an immersive experience that is enjoyed momentarily and then passes into history. It is unlike the visual arts in this respect. One cannot stand before it and ruminate; it can only be anticipated, experienced and then remembered. Hence, the fear of mortality is assuaged by continual anticipation of the next evanescent event, the next fifteen minutes of significance. Again, it is this continual process of resurrection that can be understood as immortality-in-the-present.

The overarching issue, of course, is that, as Bauman discusses, 'with eternity decomposed into…a movement of passing moments, nothing seems to be immortal any more'.[87]

> Nothing *can* be done forever. Knowledge I studiously master today will become thoroughly inadequate, if not downright ignorance, tomorrow. The skills I learn today by the sweat of my brow will not carry me far in the brave new world of tomorrow's technology and know-how. The job I won yesterday in fierce competition will disappear tomorrow….My prize possessions, my today's pride, will tomorrow become yesterday's taste and my embarrassment. The union which I have sworn to cherish and preserve will fall apart and be dissolved tomorrow at the first sign of my partner's or my own disaffection. Perhaps there will be a string of 'lifelong partners'.[88]

This celebration of the evanescent and focus on immediate gratification manifests in a series of disappointments and unfulfilled goals and relationships. Something of this sense of disappointment is conveyed in the song 'Once in a Lifetime' by Talking Heads (*Remain in Light*, 1981): 'You may find yourself behind the wheel of a large automobile/ You may find yourself in a beautiful house with a beautiful wife …. You may ask yourself, how do I work this?/ You may ask yourself, where is that large automobile?/ You may tell yourself, this is not my beautiful house/ You may tell yourself, this is not my beautiful wife .... You may ask yourself, am I right, am I wrong?/ You may say to yourself, "my god, what have I done?"' Throughout the song, there is a growing sense of anxiety and unease, as, one after another, the significance of what seemed to be important goals dissolve on their realization. I want a *large* car, I want a *beautiful* house and I want a *beautiful* wife, all of which are viewed as commodities and seem to lack meaning once acquired. Moreover, the music throughout is punctuated by references to the flowing of water and the passing of days. Indeed, although the song was popularly understood as a critique of suburban life – which, to some extent, it is – David Byrne, who wrote the lyrics, is clear that it is primarily a reflection on people 'being puzzled about the fact that they exist and they find themselves where they are'.[89] It asks its listeners to reflect on meaning within a Sisyphean existence. There is no transcendent horizon.

Concluding comments

'The cradle rocks above the abyss, and common sense tells us that our existence is but a brief crack of light between two eternities of darkness'.[90] With these words, Vladimir Nobokov distills the core existential theme with which this chapter has been concerned. How do we live with the awareness of mortality? How do we make sense of an existence that is little more than a 'crack of light between two eternities of darkness'? Approximately 155,000 humans die each day,[91] and we know that every morning we wake, we are a day closer to our own eternity of darkness. We all came from nothing and we will all return to nothing. Such considerations, whether we avoid them or dwell on them, inevitably shape the way we think about who we are and the meaning of our lives. It is hardly surprising therefore that human culture has been driven by the need to alleviate the emotional impact of the awareness of mortality. Throughout history, strategies have been developed which allow life to be understood as meaningful and death as vulnerable to it. Significant industry has gone into the creation, dissemination and defence of discourses that imagine the self as protected from, or immune to dissolution. As the theologian Paul Tillich put it, 'the temptation not to accept finitude, but rather to lift oneself to the level of the Unconditioned, the Divine, runs through all history'.[92] Traditionally, religious narratives have transformed death into a moment in the continuing history of the self, a period of sleep from which the individual will awaken, a passage to another existence in which there is no *terminus*.

Similarly, beyond traditional religious discourses, strategies have evolved within modern and postmodern cultures to obscure the inevitability of the final day. The instrumental rationality of modernity has led to a deconstruction of mortality, in which death is pathologized, interpreted as the unnatural culmination of a series of biological problems that require technical solutions. Modernity, in short, 'deconstructed a mortality one cannot overcome into a series of afflictions that one can'.[93] Just as some are comforted by the promise of eternal life, so many others are bewitched by the rather pathetic hope that medical science will provide an increasingly sufficient stream of remedies to continually postpone the final breath. Some are even bewitched by the fantastical notion that they can be cryogenically frozen until the divine powers of medical science have reached their apotheosis, at which point they will be thawed and immortalized. Comforted by this exaggerated estimate of human technology, some reason that, *for now*, we need not consider the processes of decay that will eventually claim us. After all, science may save us.

Postmodernity deconstructs immortality into 'immortality-through-other-people's-memory' of our achievements or our impact on their own short lives. The postmodern life is also an episodic life, which deconstructs immortality through the provision of a series of small deaths and resurrections made available within a consumer culture. The continual acquisition and disposal of objects, relationships, commitments and identities distracts us from the inevitability of the 'mortality one cannot overcome'.

Moreover, as we have noted, the very idea of immortality is itself problematic. On the one hand, as Bauman (quoting Elias Canetti) put it, 'How many people will find it worthwhile living once they don't have to die?'[94] As Tillich argued many years ago, while 'nothing is more difficult than to accept the last impassable border', and while 'everything finite would like to extend itself into infinity', what is not contemplated is the fact that 'an infinity of the finite could be a symbol for hell'.[95] Indeed, inconsiderately burdening humans with immortality was one of the crimes for which Sisyphus was condemned to his hellish existence. He tricked Thanatos (the personification of death), chaining him up deep in the Underworld, in Tartarus, thereby removing death, the result of which was chaos and misery. Not only is meaningful life without death difficult to contemplate, but, to put the same point differently, the significance of death for a meaningful life needs to be appreciated. Again, there is something about Terry Jacks's 'Seasons in the Sun' that functions as a *memento vivere*, evoking a sense of the significance of a limited lifespan. As Spellman says, 'our personal journeys are significant precisely because they are framed by a beginning and an end. We craft our significance – singularly and in the company of our fellows – between these universal bookends. Without them we lose the sense of urgency, the deadline that propels us to live in a meaningful manner while we are able'.[96] In many respects, the message of *memento vivere* is nowhere better summed up than in the words and the tune of a song composed by a man dying on a cross next to Brian Cohen, the reluctant messiah in Monty Python's *The Life of Brian*: 'For life is quite absurd/ And death's the final word/ You must always face the curtain with a bow .... So, always look on the bright side of death/ Just before you draw your terminal breath .... Life's a piece of shit/ When you look at it/ Life's a laugh and death's a joke, it's true...' (*Monty Python Sings*, 1989). Written by Eric Idle, there is something profoundly Camusian about this song. As such, for many years, it has consistently been among the most popular funeral songs, often *the most popular*.[97] While not avoiding the Sisyphean absurdity of existence that many of our contemporaries tacitly acknowledge, it functions very clearly as a *memento vivere* for the bereaved in a way that many funeral songs do not.

Overall, the aim of this chapter has been to draw the reader's attention to the social and cultural significance of 'the presence of death as a *ghost* haunting the *totality* of life'.[98] Thanatological concerns are, as Farmer said of philosophical problems generally, 'rooted at some point in contrarieties which are latent in the everyday experience of ordinary people and which either operate there, below the surface, as unconscious and fluctuating determinants of consciousness, or, more rarely, emerge into explicit awareness'.[99] Popular *memento mori* grow out of this everyday experience of being haunted by the awareness of death, they reflect our concerns about ultimate meaninglessness and, as such, they remind us that we too must die. Popular music in particular does this in a number of ways, many of which, as we will begin to see in Chapter 2, exploit the transgressive potential of death and decay as taboo discourses in the modern world.

2

Death, Transgression and the Sacred

The treatment of death within popular music is typically playful: 'Dress sexy at my funeral my good wife/ Wink at the minister/ Blow kisses to my grieving brothers' (Smog, 'Dress Sexy at My Funeral', *Dongs of Sevotion*, 2000). It is also typically transgressive. We will see, for example, that artists often enjoy exploiting the notoriously complex confluence of thanatos and eros in Western culture – sex and death: 'I love the dead before they're cold/ They're bluing flesh for me to hold' (Alice Cooper, 'I Love the Dead', *Billion Dollar Babies*, 1973). Indeed, some artists, particularly those associated with the industrial scene, such as Michael Gira (the main creative force behind the bands Swans and Angels of Light), have made a career out of exploring sex, violence, death and the relationship between them. (We will explore the cultural significance of this relationship below.)

Typical in this respect was one of the more notorious 'death-rock' acts of the 1980s and 1990s, namely the absurdly transgressive and influential Los Angeles band, Christian Death. From the release of their influential *Only Theatre of Pain* in 1982, through numerous line-up changes and increasingly controversial albums, such as *Sex and Drugs and Jesus Christ* (1988), *Sexy Death God* (1994), *Pornographic Messiah* (1998) and *Born Again Anti Christian* (2000), they constructed an aesthetic that explicitly provoked conservative Christian culture. Central to this aesthetic was not merely adolescent blasphemy, but also discourses organized around sex and death that focused very keenly on challenging Western Christian theology and morality. 'Incurable disease on the day of rest/ I go walking on water in a sea of incest/ I've got the image of Jesus embedded in my chest ... Jesus, won't you touch me? Come into my heart/ Where the hell are you when the fire starts? ... Satan is by far the kindest beast' ('Spiritual Cramp', *Only Theatre of Pain*, 1982).[1] That the founding member Roz Williams – born Roger Alan Painter in 1963 in Pomona, California – was brought up in a conservative Southern Baptist family is hardly a coincidence. It is not difficult to trace his interests back to a liminal adolescent mind shaped by an early exposure to

theological understandings of death as 'the wages of sin' (Romans 6:23), the
macabre price for salvation (e.g. Luke 22:39–23:56) and 'the last enemy to be
destroyed' (1 Corinthians 15:26). He is not alone of course. For example, it is
also not difficult to trace Alice Cooper's fascination with mortality back to
his religious upbringing in the Church of Jesus Christ. Indeed, it is surprising
how any young mind subjected to the injunctions in hymns and sermons
to 'sacrifice' oneself, to be 'washed in the blood of Christ', or to be 'bathed
in the blood of Lamb', or to be plunged in 'the crimson flood' manages to
struggle into adulthood unscathed. Of course, some do not. As Jason Bivins
discusses, the scars of a 'religion of fear' can run deep.[2] Of the several ways in
which theologies of gore and death might work their way out in the lives of
individuals and in contemporary culture, a fundamentalist religio-politics is
one and Christian Death is another: 'Accept the gift of sin .... The price of red
death/ Is the price of true love .... More blood on your surplice/ More blood
for the price of red death/ Nailing you to the wall/ Nailing you to the Spanish
mystic....Blood on our hands/ Blood/ Blood/ Blood' ('Cavity – First
Communion', *Only Theatre of Pain*, 1982). Again, the relationship between
these lyrics and the sermons and hymns to which the young Williams was
exposed is a conspicuously direct one. Although, in a 1994 interview, he
indicated that he frequently failed to fully understand the meanings of his
songs 'until years later', he was always clear that they were directly informed
by a reaction to his upbringing: 'You're told there's this wonderful God and
this beautiful heaven for you when you die. You're also told that death is a
horrible thing and you know you should be afraid of it and live in fear of
it...'.[3] His response was a fascination with transgressive notions of death
and decay, most of which were viewed through a contemporary Gothic lens.[4]
Indeed, not only did he lift his stage name, 'Rozz Williams', from a gravestone
in a cemetery he frequented, but, tragically, on 1 April 1998, he slipped a
noose around his neck, 'accepted the gift of sin', and embraced the 'the final
enemy' – he committed suicide. In subsequent chapters we will see that, not
only is death a common theme in popular music, but Williams is not the only
artist to have embraced it in an act of suicide.

The discussion in this chapter makes a number of simple points. First,
the articulation of death and decay in popular music culture is rooted in
transgression. Second, as such, it can be understood in terms of liminality
within youth subcultures. Third, discourses of transgression are themselves
significant, in that they engender affective spaces within which meaning-
making can occur. Fourth, because Christian theological ideas have been

central to constructions of the sacred, the profane and mortality in Western culture, it is those ideas that have provided the core themes for discourses of transgression. More specifically, mortality in popular music occulture is theologically nuanced. For example, because, particularly since Augustine, sex in the West has tended to be associated with sin, and, 'the wages of sin is death' (Romans 6:23),[5] together sin, sex and death have provided a well-equipped playground for liminal subcultures to enjoy. Hence, returning to our thoughts in Chapter 1, the activities and discourses that have evolved within this playground, while typically ludic in character, nevertheless challenge taboos and explore profane space in important ways. Finally, the unnervingly transgressive exploration of mortality within popular music cultures functions as a *memento mori* in modern societies.

The sacred, the profane, transgression and death

As I have discussed elsewhere,[6] music's universal power to move, to agitate, and to control listeners, to shape their identities, to structure their everyday lives, to define and to demarcate, to challenge and to construct hegemonic discourses, is central to its relationship with the sacred and the profane. In particular, it is because of this relationship that popular music is able to operate as 'edgework'[7] at the boundary of the sacred and the profane. It is perhaps odd, therefore, that analyses of the sacred and the profane have been something of a blind spot in popular music studies. To some extent, this is simply a reflection of certain blinkered discourses within academia,[8] including the dominant ideological positions informing much critical theory. Having said that, the work done by theorists of popular music, from the Frankfurt School to Birmingham University's Centre for Contemporary Cultural Studies, has always impinged very directly on 'the sacred'. Some readers may be a little surprised by this comment, largely, I suspect, because they fail to make an important distinction between 'the sacred' and 'religion'. While religious discourses are, of course, centrally concerned with articulations of the sacred, the two are not synonymous. That is to say, following Émile Durkheim, we can understand the sacred as relating to the articulation of what people perceive to be absolute or non-contingent. Whether embedded within religious discourses or not, the sacred concerns those ideas which are understood to be set apart from the rest of social life and which exert a profound moral claim over peoples' lives. Understood in this way, 'religions' constitute a particular way of articulating the sacred, usually with reference to the supernatural, mortality and immortality. That is to say, deities, demons, life, death, heaven and hell become part of the rationale for submitting to and enforcing the claims of the sacred. Hence, following Durkheim, we might think of religion as 'a unified system of beliefs and practices relative to sacred things, that is to say, things set apart and surrounded by prohibitions – beliefs and practices which unite its adherents into a single moral community ...'.[9] But, the important point to note is that communities unified around a system of beliefs and practices relative to sacred things *need not be* 'religious' – in the sense in which that term is commonly understood. All human communities are organized around notions of the sacred. They all align themselves with core values considered absolute and binding. Hence, the sacred needs to be understood primarily in terms of the ways people relate to and experience that which is considered to be 'set apart' from everyday life in some absolute sense. Whether we think of human rights, the protection of children, the freedom of speech or the value of 'life', there is a sense of that within society which is set apart and non-contingent.

To press this point a little further, there are particular moral assumptions that are believed to be so fundamentally self-evident, so essential to civilized social life, that they are beyond question, and the violation of them elicits a sense of revulsion and a demand for some form of restitution. In other words, the sacred is organized by cultures into specific, historically contingent, manifestations. These manifestations or 'sacred forms' comprise, as Gordon Lynch puts it, 'constellations of specific symbols, thought/discourse, emotions and actions grounded in the body. These constellations of embodied thought, feeling and action recursively reproduce the sacrality of the sacred form and constitute groups who share these discourses, sentiments and practices.'[10] Hence, sacred forms are historically contingent expressions of particular cultures, the products of particular histories, contexts and communities, rather than being ontologically fixed. Our approaches to dignity, dying and death, for example, constitute particular sacred forms. As James Green comments, 'in no society do people simply leave the dead as they are and unceremoniously walk away.'[11] The end of a person's life demands recognition. The dead demand respect. Because of this, the judiciary establishes laws to ensure that due respect is given to the dead, and religions formulate rituals to mark death as a rite of passage. Being culturally relative, sacred forms change over time according to the shifting contours of the social contexts in which they are constructed.[12] What is sacred in one culture is not sacred in another and often changes from one generation to the next. Hence, Western notions about death and dying are not universal. Other cultures approach the corpse differently. As Diana Eck says of funeral rituals along the Ganges, 'death, which is elsewhere polluting, is here holy and auspicious'.[13]

This brings us to another obvious, but important point. We cannot think of the sacred without also thinking of the profane. The construction of the sacred is also the construction of the profane. Just as lines and boundaries divide, so the sacred needs to be understood in a relational or oppositional sense. To quote Mary Douglas's influential study, *Purity and Danger*, 'sacred things and places are to be protected from defilement. Holiness and impurity are at opposite poles'.[14] Concern with purity and pollution arises in societies as a way of constraining members to conform to social norms, to adhere to the sacred. Therefore, again, social and cultural constructions of the sacred are tied to constructions of the profane, in that the latter is constituted as a threat to the former. Certainly, few cultures would not consider a corpse – the embodiment of death – to be, in some sense, polluting and, as such, profane.[15]

Concerning the nature of the profane, not only is it constructed as a threat to the sacred, but it accrues a transgressive charge relative to the strength of the sacred: the stronger the sense of the sacred, the greater the revulsion evoked by that which threatens to profane it. Indeed, the revulsion – the sense of profane threat – occasioned by the transgression of a sacred form, such as the abuse of children, the violation of a human right, the desecration of a corpse or the denial of life, can be so powerful that it can lead to moral panic and, for some members of society, sanction extreme levels of violence and even the ending of a life. The threat of profanation must be expunged in order to limit the pollution of society. There must be a restoration of the authority and integrity of the sacred.

We are now in a position to begin to understand why liminal minds, focused on transgression and the formation of identities over against mainstream society, might find death and decay appealing. While much popular music reinforces hegemonic constructions of the sacred, such as particularly traditional notions of femininity and sexuality,[16] it is also frequently characterized by discourses and sonic environments that are transgressive. Typical is the pornography of gore and the celebration of death in extreme metal. Mortician's 'Intro/Defiler of the Dead' from their 1995 *House by the Cemetery* EP is a good example of this embrace of profane discourses around death: 'Necrophile, corpses pile/ Mummified, mother lies/ Skull soup bowls/ Nipple belts/ Hearts in pans/ Eyes in cans'. Likewise, Death's album *Scream Bloody Gore* (1987) explores a similar intriguingly transgressive terrain: 'Pain, growing stronger/ Life, exists

no longer/ Welcome, to a world of pain/ Death and despair' ('Denial of Life');
'With chainsaw in hand/ Your death I demand/ Slicing through your fat/ My
awaited gore attack' ('Sacrificial'). Again, almost any song from the creatively
indelicate oeuvre of Cannibal Corpse could be cited: 'Lying there cold after a
torturous death/ Your life ended fast you took your last breath/ Dead in a grave,
your final place/ The maggots infest your disfigured face/ Pus through your
veins takes the place of blood/ Decay sets in, bones begin to crack/ Thrown six
feet down left to rot/ Brains oozing black down the side of your broken neck'
('A Skull Full of Maggots', *Eaten Back To Life*, 1990). Ozzy Osbourne's removal
of a bat's head with his teeth, Mayhem's ornamental use of pig and sheep
heads impaled on stakes during concerts and Alice Cooper's staged lynching
of himself and impaling of babies are all transgressive precisely because they
present society with that which it (for a number of very sensible reasons) shuns
as profane and polluting. Often composed at the liminal edges of hegemonic
culture, on the rejected periphery, popular music's very existence, from folk to
jazz to dubstep, has always constituted a threat to the sacred centre. Not only
does it play with rejected discourses – such as those of mortality in Western
culture – but, as popular music, it does so with a peculiarly effective ability
to engage the emotions and the subjective life.[17] This, of course, is largely
why, on the one hand, popular music matters socially and, on the other hand,
why conservative religion – the traditional gatekeeper of the sacred – worries
about it. There is, of course, little that is sophisticated or culturally insightful
about much of this music, but its very existence and its appeal to young people
does raise a number of interesting issues.

Concerning the relationship between religion and the sacred, I want to
make two general points. First, not only does the temptation to 'cross the line'
between the sacred and the profane lie at the heart of the human condition,
but one of the primary functions of religion has been the managing of this
temptation. Consequently, second, while, strictly speaking, the meaning of the
term 'transgression' simply refers to the act of 'stepping across' a boundary, its
core meaning in the West has always been nuanced along Augustinian lines.
That is to say, it has tended to suggest trespass, the breaking of some law or code
of behaviour, an offense against the sacred. In other words, it has been shaped
by the Christian understanding of sin, which, Augustine tells us, is to 'wilfully
transgress the commandment of the Lord'.[18] It is this that gives it its power
and its appeal. What might be understood as a basic evolutionary impulse to
push at boundaries and adapt to new cultural conditions has been understood

theologically in terms of a fundamentally profane bias within the human condition, interpreted as a 'fallen' nature: 'all have sinned, and come short of the glory of God' (Romans 3.23). From the outset, Christian theology has taught that the human desire to transgress boundaries consistently overrides respect for them. As Walter Brueggemann remarks of Genesis 3:1–7 (the story of Adam and Eve), 'the prohibition which seemed a *given* is now scrutinized as though it were not a given but an *option*. The serpent engages in a bit of sociology of law in order to relativize even the rule of God. Theological-ethical talk here is not to serve, but to avoid the claims of God .... The givenness of God's rule is no longer the boundary of a safe place. God is now a barrier to be circumvented .... The *prohibition* of 2:17 is violated ....'[19] It is, however, more than this, in that it is not simply that the prohibition becomes optional, but, again, that the very act of identifying something as taboo invests it with enormous attractive power. Hence, the cultural force of the story of the Fall and the narrative of sin and redemption, which has shaped Western thinking, is its identification of the charged relationship between taboo and transgression that lies at the heart of the human condition. That which is prohibited is attractive. (We will return to this point in the following chapters.) For a religion to identify something as profane simply increases its appeal. The forbidden fruit is the sweetest: 'I really don't care about the wrong or right/ The fruit is forbidden but it's sweet and it's ripe/ I think I'm gonna pick me some and take me a bite' (Everlast, 'Die in Yer' Arms', *Love, War and the Ghost of Whitey Ford*, 2008).

Central to this discourse is the religio-cultural relationship between sin and death. That is to say, so significant is sin as the rejection of the sacred that it is aetiologically linked to death: 'but you must not eat from the tree of the knowledge of good and evil, for when you eat from it you will certainly die' (Genesis 2:17); 'just as sin entered the world through one man [Adam], and death through sin, in this way death came to all people, because all sinned' (Romans 5:12). Pollution leads to death. The life–death binary is a sacred–profane binary. This, of course, invests death with a peculiar transgressive significance, which, again, was influentially developed in Augustine's theology. In his interpretation of the story of the Fall (Genesis 1–3), because Adam disobeys God, humanity is condemned to 'a life and death like that of the animals.'[20] At this point, Augustine binds sex and death together with sin. That is to say, we must procreate like animals because we must die like them. Again, the argument is that these ideas have shaped Western culture and, as such, determine the way we think about sex and death. Because the first human transgressed, the human race was profaned and, as such, became subject to death. Humans became mortal. Hence, because humans die, they are required to have sex to continue their existence. But in having sex, an unnatural, profane act (it being the direct result of disobedience to God), they pass that mortality on to their offspring – the doctrine of 'original sin'. In summary, for Augustine and much subsequent Western culture, birth, sex and death are directly related as the result of human transgression.[21] Consequently, some of the most emotionally charged constructions of the profane and transgression in the West tend to be related, in some way, to sex and death. Whether we are aware of it or not, we all carry Augustinian baggage. It is simply part of the way we Westerners think! Again, this helps us to understand the transgressive appeal of sex and death in popular music.

To develop the above points a little further, the subject of death is taboo, not simply because (a) it reminds us of our own extinction, nor just because (b) corpses are a threat to our health if not attended to, but also because (c) it is heavy with negative religio-cultural meaning. In fact, all three are related in the Western construction of life as sacred and death as profane. Hence, that which is culturally considered profane is discursively linked to death and the processes of decay. The term 'decadence', for example, which refers to a state of moral or cultural decline typically characterized by excessive indulgence in pleasure (understood as profane), has its roots in French term *décadence*, which is taken from the medieval Latin *decadentia*, which refers directly to 'decay'. Unrestrained pleasure, immorality, sin, decay and death are related. Mortality and the process of dissolution are saturated with negative theological meaning. Hence, again, those looking for weighty transgressive discourses are culturally drawn to those of death and decay. Moreover, these discourses are particularly powerful when they are explicitly linked to the purity of the sacred through religious discourse. It does not take Westerners seeking symbols of transgression long to find their way to that profane confluence. It is culturally instinctual. For example, bearing this in mind – and returning to the points made at the beginning of this chapter – it is hardly surprising that there is a particular focus on Jesus in cultures shaped by Christian constructions of the sacred. Along with Christian Death, band names include Rotting Christ, Dead Jesus, Corpse ov Christ, Corpus Christi, Aborted Jesus, Jesus Corpus, Impaled Nazarene, Nailed Nazarene, Nazarene Decomposing, Impaled Christ, Mangled Christ, Aborted Christ Childe, Severed Savior, Christ's Flesh, Amputated Christ, Behead Christ, Christ Dismembered and so on. The list, of course, could be a rather long and tedious one.

Liminality and pissing people off

The term 'liminal' has been used several times in this chapter because it is a useful concept for understanding not only popular music subcultures, but also their particular attraction to transgression. The term, as it is used here, refers directly to the work of the anthropologist Victor Turner, who, following Henri Junod and particularly Arnold Van Gennep, analysed rites of passage and developed a theory of the ritual process as a movement from structure through antistructure and back again to structure; from order, through disorder, and back to order. Central to this process are the existentially meaningful periods of 'antistructure'. These periods he described in terms of liminality, core to which is transgression – the crossing of 'thresholds' (*limen*).[22] This stage of a rite of passage may be temporary and brief, or it may be extended indefinitely, as in the case of those who live in religious communities or hippie communes beyond the norms and structures of society.

> The attributes of liminality or of liminal *personae* ('threshold people') are necessarily ambiguous, since this condition and these persons elude or slip through the network of classifications that normally locate states and positions in cultural space. Liminal entities are neither here nor there; they are betwixt and between the positions assigned and arrayed by law, custom, convention, and ceremonial. As such, their ambiguous and indeterminate attributes are expressed by a rich variety of symbols in many societies that ritualize social and cultural transitions. Thus, liminality is frequently likened to death, to being in the womb, to invisibility, to darkness, to bisexuality, to the wilderness, and to an eclipse of the sun or moon.[23]

Liminality is typical of subcultures (to which we will return below). It identifies a temporary period of 'acceptable disorder' when conventional structures are suspended and questioned; everyday values and behaviours are challenged; transgression is not merely tolerated, but celebrated; socially problematic ideas and taboo subjects are explored. Emilie Bresson of the French Doom metal band Monarch puts the point succinctly: 'we prided ourselves on pissing people off'.[24]

I have used that quotation from Emilie Bresson to provoke those readers who might not yet grasp the importance of analysing the work of artists whose declared intention is to piss others off. Surely, this is simply vulgar and unworthy of serious consideration. My argument is simply that a statement such as this constitutes the tip of a large social and cultural iceberg. Responsible cultural analysts need to be persistent in asking why so many people in our society are pissed off and why they want to piss others off. Once those questions are asked, large issues requiring many volumes of analysis begin to emerge. This book is a small contribution to such work.

Positively, the convictions and activities of liminal *personae* present an opportunity for wider society to examine itself, to reflect upon its values and to establish what it wants to protect as sacred. In the West, liminal cultures have challenged core sacred forms, such as those related to traditional Christian morality, secularity and war. In this way, each generation engages critically and positively with the presuppositions and values of a previous generation. However, negatively, liminal cultures are often – sometimes with good reason – perceived to constitute a profane threat to constructions of the sacred and, therefore, to social order. However, the point here is that, as Turner argued, whether one examines the tribal rituals of the Ndembu in northwestern Zambia or sits down with Jack Kerouac's largely autobiographical 1957 novel, *On the Road*[25] – the defining text of Beat culture[26] – the *limen* is a universally significant period, typical of youth cultures, during which, so to speak, one slips through the looking glass into a 'realm of pure possibility'. Within this liminal space, established meanings collapse: 'in this gap between ordered worlds almost anything may happen. In this interim of "liminality", the possibility exists of standing aside not only from one's own social position, but from all social positions and of formulating a potentially unlimited series of alternative social arrangements.'[27] Again, whether one considers the androgyny explored by many musicians or the meditations on suicide, death and decay in the lyrics of industrial and extreme metal bands, or the violent resistance to Christian hegemony in black metal, or the angry nihilism of punk and hardcore, or the opposition of folk and rock musicians to the Vietnam war, through disorder and the inhabiting of subjunctive worlds, idealism and the possibility of change emerges. This possibility is made available to them by the perception of a temporary release from social and cultural structures.

As Dunja Brill comments, 'the notion of transgressing common social norms and style codes' is a 'core ideal' within subcultures,[28] which, it is argued here, can be understood as liminal. Indeed, although we have spoken of liminal cultures and subcultures, Turner spoke of *communitas*, which emerges 'where structure is not'. This is not 'community' as such (which is why he uses a different term), but rather the spontaneous coming together of like-minded liminal personae. New symbols and discourses are generated within *communitas*, largely through art and spirituality, rather than legislative and political structures.[29] Again, this is demonstrated perfectly within popular music cultures. New ideas, symbols, styles and discourses are manifested within tribal allegiances to particular genres of popular music. Hence, music consistently emerges as the *vox populi* of a generation, challenging taboos and embracing transgression.

Concerning the fascination with mortality in contemporary Western liminal cultures, this is immediately evident from a brief survey of the names of bands and artists: This Mortal Coil, Funeral for a Friend, Dead Can Dance, Shroud of Bereavement, Burial, Autopsy, Ulcerate, Impaled, Dismember, Exploding Corpse Action, Napalm Death, Dead Baby and so on. Again, an album such as *Danse Macabre* (2001) by the American post-punk band The Faint is, we have seen, not alone in its explicit reflection on murder and decomposition: 'I feel a warm resistance/ Beneath the outer layer/ What once moved living organs/ Leaks through a thin veneer .... Not breathing one more breath .... And I caused your violent end' ('Posed to Death'). Similarly, another song imagines a suicidal person's final thoughts: 'As I lay to die, the things I think/ Did I waste my time? ... All we want are just pretty little homes ... I don't want to regret what I did .... Agenda suicide ...' ('Agenda Suicide', *Danse Macabre*, 2001). More visceral and graphic analyses of mortality can be found in Nick Cave's work, which is suffused with references both to personal and to collective death, as well as the search for redemption.[30] Such liminal treatments of mortality are quite distinct, sometimes refreshingly distinct, from those treatments common in modern Western societies, which seek to taboo it.

Death and subcultural capital

In our everyday negotiations with what Pierre Bourdieu has theorized as 'cultural capital',[31] we establish what is 'in' or 'out' through a continual articulation of signs of distinction, such as sartorial, gastronomic, literary, artistic and musical tastes. The application of this notion of cultural capital to youth subcultures has been influentially developed by Sarah Thornton in her study of club scenes in the late 1980s and early 1990s.[32] Although a little dated now, it is still replete with good sociological common sense. While Bourdieu was keen to map cultural capital back onto class distinctions, Thornton shifts the focus to subcultures – which often transcend class allegiances.

> Subcultural capital confers status on its owner in the eyes of the relevant beholder .... Subcultural capital can be *objectified* or *embodied*. Just as books and paintings display cultural capital in the family home, so subcultural capital is objectified in the form of fashionable haircuts and well-assembled record

collections (full of well-chosen, limited edition 'white label' twelve-inches and the like). Just as cultural capital is personified in 'good' manners and urbane conversation, so subcultural capital is embodied in the form of being 'in the know', using (but not overusing) current slang and looking as if you were born to perform the latest dance styles.[33]

Being 'hip' or 'cool' (or whatever the current, local term is) describes one's relationship to subcultural capital, in that it identifies who is 'in the know' regarding what is authentic and niche. To some extent, of course, this can be understood in terms of the construction of the authentic *sacred* over against the inauthentic *profane* – the Other, which is allied to 'mass consumption' and the mainstream. Hence, in much the same way that all communities evolve in accordance with their constructions of the sacred over against that which they consider a profane threat, so subcultures erect boundaries in order to distinguish themselves from the Other, from that which is perceived to threaten their authenticity and erode their subcultural capital. That is to say, subcultural boundaries are porous and, as such, vulnerable to the influence of the mainstream. What was once underground and steeped in subcultural capital eventually succumbs to the mainstream and, as such, loses that capital. Take, for example, dubstep, the core ideas of which were, arguably, initially experimented with in 1999–2000 by the British producer El-B (Lewis Beadle). They were then developed in South London by producers such as particularly Digital Mystikz and promoted by the pioneering BBC DJs John Peel and then Mary Anne Hobbs. At this point, the subcultural boundaries began to show signs of erosion. The genre began to go mainstream. In 2006, Burial (William Emmanuel Bevan) produced his self-titled, critically acclaimed debut album. This was quickly followed in 2006 by another well-received, eponymous debut album by Skream (Oliver Dene Jones). From this point on, the genre quickly found its way on to mainstream dance compilations and eventually into the work of artists such as Britney Spears ('Hold It Against Me', 2011) and Taylor Swift ('I Knew You Were Trouble', 2012). Within a decade, what was once underground, subversive and dark became commercial, mainstream pop. This sanitizing and mainstreaming of subversive genres and subcultural identities is a constant process. As such, it puts pressure on subcultures to evolve and, in many cases, to become more transgressive or subversive in order to maintain a perceived authenticity over against the commercial, mainstream, inauthentic Other.[34] As Thornton discusses, subcultures are continually engaged in a process of policing the boundaries in order retain subcultural capital. There is a constant classifying and reclassifying of tastes as legitimate and a demonizing of those considered illegitimate. This accounts, to some extent, for the race to the bottom when it comes to the treatment of gore and death. Ozzy Osbourne might be primetime viewing, and heavy rock might be used to sell cars, perfume and insurance, but few Western companies will want to promote their brands with songs about necrophilia, decomposition and mutilation. *In liminal subcultures, authenticity is established at the extremes.*

The argument is that youth subcultures typically tend to distinguish themselves from the mainstream and to establish authenticity through alliances with increasingly transgressive signifiers and discourses. The relationship to the profane is key to the maintenance of authenticity and subcultural capital. And few discourses in the West are more able to distinguish young people from mainstream Western culture – including much pop music culture – than those relating to mortality. Because, as we have seen, death and dying have been removed from the everyday experience of most late-modern people, tidied away in hospitals, nursing homes and 'chapels of rest', for a subculture to bring mortality back out into the cultural daylight, so to speak, distinguishes it very clearly from hegemonic forms of the sacred in the West. Indeed, in a culture in which other taboos, such as sex and even pornography, are being eroded, death is one of the few transgressive discourses left for liminal minds to explore in their attempt to attain subcultural capital.

Death chic, youth culture and the romanticization of mortality

It is important to remember that, distasteful though some of these ideas may be, we are not here thinking of the psychopathology of serial killers, grave robbers or necrophiles, but of discourses that, generally speaking, have their origins in vibrant, healthy, hormonally charged youth cultures. This appeals to perfectly normal adolescents! This is significant because they are the discourses of those immersed in life and at some distance from death. Nevertheless, as discourses around mortality, they function perfectly as transgressive gestures. Not only do they distinguish subcultures from an older generation and from the mainstream constructions of the sacred policed by that generation, but there is an obvious sense in which, as *youth* subcultures, they are in a position to play with that older generation's taboos about mortality. As indicated in the Introduction, there is something fundamentally Gothic about this embrace of death by those not threatened by it. Typical is the song 'Live Fast, Die Young' by the US hardcore band, Circle Jerks: 'I don't want to live to be thirty-four ... live fast, die young!' (*Group Sex*, 1980). First, this brutally distinguishes one generation from the next; second, in choosing death over ageing, it privileges, even sacralizes youth; finally, the celebration of mortality transgresses a core sacred form. Again, perhaps the most obvious articulation of this death-before-decrepitude discourse is The Who's song 'My Generation' (1965). Pete Townsend – who wrote the lyrics and, as if to emphasize the point, drove a hearse at the time[35] – is happy to sneer, 'I hope I die before I get old'. (Now an old man, he is, of course, a little more sensitive to the ageing process than he was in the *joie de vivre* and *jouissance* of his youth.[36]) However, the point here is that, for a number of reasons, it is hardly a surprise that liminal youths play with discourses of death as a transgressive gesture.

Unsurprisingly, 'death chic' within popular music subcultures is linked very clearly to sexuality – to eros/life. That is to say, discourses of mortality are less related to death and more related to the immediate and vital preoccupations of youth. Indeed, there is an explicit sexualizing of mortality. As Lauren Goodlad and Michael Bibby comment of goth culture, it is oriented around 'romantic obsessions with death, darkness, and perverse sexuality'.[37] Again, Karen Macfarlane's analysis of Lady Gaga's use of contemporary Gothic themes discusses a series of photos in which she is 'both the vampire and its victim: neck, mouth and hands smeared with blood, mouth opening in pain and/ or orgasmic passion'. Again, 'sex and death overlay each other ... to create ... a "fabulous monstrosity".'[38] Death is sexy. Hence, as we will see in Chapter 3, within these subcultures, funereal garb, a cosmetic deathly pallor, images of decay, infirmity and a melancholic aesthetic are all used to accrue subcultural capital. The processes of mortality excite and attract. As Fred Botting says of contemporary Gothic, its 'illusions of mortality and the sexed body emphasize bloody corpses, ripped flesh and oozing wounds'.[39] Indeed, the popularity of the vampire within liminal cultures is, of course, directly related to such discourses around sexy death. However, the argument is that these discourses are able to function in this way only because they are articulating the experiences of the virile and the healthy, rather than those of the old, the sick and the dying. The closer one gets to death, the more taxing it is to convey its sex appeal.

This last point is an important one. The subcultural fascination with mortality is expressed and enacted in the absence of the stench of decay, the disintegration of the body, the bereaved family and crippling depression. In other words, death chic merely constructs a simulacrum of death. The perception of decay can be described in terms of what Jean Baudrillard has referred to as a hyperreality,[40] an imagined state for the 'darkly inclined',[41] with little sense of what that darkness might be. Far from being the embrace of mortality, we might think of such transgressive subcultural gestures in terms of an attempt to overcome the knowledge of human mortality. That is to say, the brutal reality of death and the dissolution of the self are romanticized and sexualized in some popular music cultures, particularly those drawing directly on the discourses of contemporary Gothic. It is, as such, a thoroughly modern gesture. Only in a culture in which the terror of death is kept at a distance from life, in which antiseptics and antibiotics arrest decay, could such discourses evolve and become chic. Again, as noted in the Introduction, *actual* terror occasioned by the prospect of imminent annihilation simply overwhelms our judgement and, as such, it is, as Edmund Burke argued, 'incapable of giving any delight whatsoever', it being 'simply terrible'. Death cannot be chic for the person about to die. However, and this is central to Burke's understanding of the sublime, 'at certain distances, and with certain modifications', terrifying events and objects 'are delightful'.[42] It is this 'delightful horror' that is 'the most genuine effect and truest test of the sublime'.[43] Indeed, as we have seen, for Burke, 'delight' is not 'pleasure' as such, but rather it is the experience of being removed from the awfulness of the 'terror'. Death and decay can be treated playfully because they are romanticized notions. Likewise, only in a broadly secular culture, in which the undead, the demonic, hell and the afterlife are transgressive fictions, rather than postmortem certainties, can the dead and the undead be treated as cultural resources. Certainly, for many young people, the prospect of finding out whether they are fictions or not is, again, at some psychological remove.

Finally, as indicated above, the ludic embrace of death by youth subcultures is, in some respects, like a child in a playground mocking a bully at a distance. The mocking is only possible because of the distance. As the distance is reduced, the situation changes significantly. This raises an interesting issue regarding ageing in subcultures. It is a little surprising that the reception of discourses of death and decay has not been addressed in studies of ageing and popular music. Andy Bennett's work is perhaps the most significant in this area, but it does nothing to address this important complex of issues, which are, after all, so central to the ageing process. Essentially, the position he takes is an example of 'the modern strategy' for dealing with mortality identified by Bauman. That is to say, Bennett's premise is that, 'in the context of late-modernity, ageing is no longer regarded simply as a slow and inevitable process of bodily decay and deterioration. On the contrary, it is often regarded as a time of personal growth and even rejuvenation.' He continues, 'improving standards of health and the availability of treatments to enable those with long-term illnesses and age-related disabilities to lead relatively normal lives have given individuals higher levels of expectation that they will be able to have the sort of life they choose in middle age and later life.'[44] While this is obviously true, it sidesteps the problem of our knowledge of mortality and the reception of popular music – much of which is the voice of transgressive youth cultures – by those who are aware that their lives are far nearer to their conclusion than their beginning and by those who have seen loved ones suffer and die. This will inevitably alter their perception of discourses of death and decay. They are also, as we will see in Chapter 3, made aware of the passing of time, in that music is linked very closely not only to emotion but also to memory.

The principal thesis here, however, is that, unlike many older people, youth cultures can play romantically with notions of death and decay because they are little more than notions. They are transgressive, boundary-crossing gestures, which cease to be authentic when performed by those beyond youth. As one gets older, succumbs to disease, worries about cancer, has organs removed and attends funerals, the significance of the discourse changes. For youth subcultures, much of the treatment of death and decay is not that of Lou Reed's *Magic and Loss* or John Lydon's 'Death Disco', both of which, we have seen in Chapter 1, are the articulation of grief as a result of the impact of cancer on close friends and family. Again, it is, I suspect, difficult to cultivate a sense of 'death chic' with a terminal illness, a serious heart condition or just plain middle-aged decrepitude.

The impure sacred

As we have seen, for the liminal mind, there is something almost *de rigueur* about transgression, about allying oneself with the Other and about forming an identity around the profane. As one goth put it, 'most people in the Gothic scene want to distinguish themselves from the world of the average, where there is not a lot of place for imagination and deviation from the norm.'[45] Consequently, it is little surprise that subcultures tend to construct meaning around, to quote another goth, 'liking what other people find hideous or disgusting' and 'loving things that other people couldn't love'.[46] While such thinking is to be expected in the *communitas* of subcultures, in that it is simply a manifestation of a liminal and transgressive desire to identify oneself as standing over against the mainstream, there is, as indicated above, more that can be said about *the experience* of transgression and its relationship to the sacred that helps to explain its significance and appeal.

First, it is worth noting that the very term 'sacred' introduces a fascinating complexity. The English word 'sacred' is derived from the Latin *sacer*, which has a more nuanced meaning than simply 'holy' or 'consecrated'. Unpicking these strands of meaning, which informed Durkheim's thought, William Pickering identifies three: first, *sacer* can refer to that which is 'holy, consecrated, as in a holy place or sacred art'. Second, it can refer to the 'inviolable', to that which 'cannot be broken'. Third, and importantly for this discussion, *sacer* can also refer to that which is 'damned, cursed, profane, bloody'.[47] This is because *sacer*, as well as meaning holy and consecrated, also suggests 'accursed or horrible, as something devoted to a divinity for destruction, and hence criminal, impious, wicked, infamous'.[48] This complexity, which Durkheim articulates, has led to the development of two distinct traditions in the interpretation of his thought, one of which is concerned with the 'pure sacred' and another which is concerned with the 'impure sacred'. As Lynch puts it, 'the focus on the "pure" sacred addresses sacred forms *as* cultural structures, exploring not only the content of specific sacred forms, but also the circulation, reproduction, and contestation of these structures through social life. By contrast, the focus on the "impure" sacred conceives of the sacred in terms of experiences and states that arise precisely through the *suspension* or *transgression* of cultural structures.'[49] Hence, needless to say, in focusing on affective states, the impure sacred is a little more amorphous and difficult to grasp, in that it identifies significant moments of illumination derived from intense experiences, which are both transgressive and transitory. Orgasm, searing pain, shock, revulsion, fear and induced altered states can all evoke experiences of the impure sacred.

It is clear, therefore, that in approaching the impure sacred, we are approaching particular affective spaces, created within moments of transgression, that engender meaning-making. Apollonian prohibition which carefully separates the domains of the sacred and the profane is actively, even aggressively transgressed in the Dionysian pursuit of a significant experience. 'Sex and drugs and rock and roll/ Is all my brain and body need/ Sex and drugs and rock and roll/ Are very good indeed' sang Ian Dury ('Sex & Drugs & Rock & Roll', 1976) in what is little more than a good summary of a life devoted to experiences of the impure sacred. Indeed, while one could mention a number of transgressive philosophies and activities for which culturally rejected and extreme behaviours are important, many of them have some presence within the liminal world of popular music. From the rejection of received Christian morality to the explicit fascination with the Satanic, from a flirtation with sex and violence to pornography and explicit misanthropy, from the smoking of marijuana to experimentation with psychedelics and opiates and from a concern with mortality to the embrace of decay and death, there is an overthrowing of convention, a challenging of taboos, a disruption of order and a suspension of sacred forms in creative acts of transgression and the pursuit of states of ecstasy.

As we will discuss in Chapter 4, the power and the impact of discourses oriented around sex, drugs, violence and death are, moreover, increased through the prosthetic effect of loud and disorienting sonic environments.[50] For example, some bands, such as Swans, Sunn O))) and Boris or musicians such as Merzbow (Masami Akita) and Pharmakon (Margaret Chardiet), have experimented with high volume, immersive noise and teeth-grinding dissonance, which Others a normative relationship to music. Indeed, because of this, the sonic experience can be unnerving and disorienting in ways that alter perception and mood. Hence, although Paul Hegarty is correct in his observation that such encounters with sound have the effect of 'taking individuals out of themselves by forcibly rooting them in bodily experience',[51] actually, sonic transgression does more than this. It engages the emotions, through a sonic assault on the body, in very particular and often uncomfortable ways, which, in turn, lead to the construction of affective spaces within which meaning-making occurs. For example, it is interesting that Chardiet/Pharmakon, commenting on her significantly entitled album *Abandon* (2013), describes her motivation to make 'noise music' as 'something akin to an exorcism where she is able to express, her deep-seated need/ drive/ urge/ possession to reach other people and make them feel something specifically in uncomfortable/ confrontational ways'.[52] There is an all-consuming, emotionally significant possession of the person by sound, which Chardiet describes in terms of hypnosis.[53] It is, in effect, a pre-cognitive, embodied response to an aggressive and disturbing sonic impact, the effect of which can evoke a transgression of cultural structures. 'Noise music is something that affects the listener in a guttural way first', insists Chardiet. 'It gives you a physical response or it gives you a sort of involuntary reaction...I think that when you listen to pop music or rock music, your brain immediately makes connections with other bands or artists that you've heard, so you immediately sort of put it in this genre context, which is very analytically based. With noise music or more extreme forms of music, rather than trying to place it in a category or relate it to something you've heard before or sort of guess what the point of it is, you're forced back on this very physical, guttural, instinctual reaction...'.[54]

And, of course, when such music is directly linked to transgressive occulture, the effect is often profound, and new ways of thinking about normative values are suggested. There is something about radical, subversive negativity, about the exceeding of constraint and the transgression of taboo, that engenders profound experiences and shifts in perception.

Studies of transgression in recent years, from Foucault's work to the more recent analyses of Peter Stallybrass, Allon White and Chris Jenks, have found Georges Bataille's insights concerning the impure sacred provocative and inspiring. As well as being a follower of Durkheim's nephew and protégé, Marcel Mauss, Bataille became interested in the avant-garde and surrealism.[55] These interests, along with his brief early flirtation with Roman Catholicism, stimulated a fascination with the nature of the sacred. Early in 1937, with Roger Caillois, he formed the short-lived neo-Durkheimian group, the *Collège de Sociologie*, 'a transgressive, subversive group of marginal adepts who attempted to recreate and reinvoke the power of the sacred and of the mythic as effervescent, quasi-religious elements outside the official political arena'.[56] Like the periodic demonization of the often imagined excesses of popular music cultures, Bataille's group 'attracted a wild and sometimes dark reputation for its interest in the extreme faces of such collective effervescence and experience of the sacred. There was even a rumour circulating among some of those close to the group that they intended at one point to carry out a human sacrifice'.[57] This interest in the extremity of human experience, in sacrifice and death, was the result of a deconstruction of older structuralist binaries of the sacred and the profane. Rethinking the meaning of *sacer* as not simply holy and consecrated but also 'accursed or horrible ... criminal, impious, wicked, infamous',[58] Bataille explored what he referred to as 'the accursed share'.[59] He was interested in the analysis of extreme states associated with the profane, such as experiences of nausea, sickness, pain and anguish. They concerned him 'precisely to the degree that they are uncontrollable, in so far as they shatter the composed rationality of the isolated individual'. In other words, 'that which is revolting, shocking, that which disarms predictable patterns of thinking and feeling, that which lies at the unhallowed extremes and unavowed interstices of social, philosophical or theoretical frameworks, are the objects of Bataille's fascination. Encounters with horror, violent disgust, that miraculously transform into experiences of laughter, intoxication, ecstasy, constitute ... inner experiences that overwhelm any sense of the distinction between interiority and exteriority'.[60]

These 'inner experiences' he understood in terms of mystical or transcendent encounters, in which there is a going beyond or outside of oneself: 'states of ecstasy, of rapture, at least of mediated emotion … an experience laid bare, free of ties … '.[61] Such experiences describe well the moments of antistructure celebrated within liminal cultures, moments during which hegemonic constructions of the sacred are suspended.

A conspicuous countercultural example of this is the recreational use of adrenochrome,[62] which, according to Hunter S. Thompson in *Fear and Loathing in Las Vegas*, 'makes pure mescaline seem like ginger beer'.[63] However, this is not an easily acquired substance, in that 'there's only one source for this stuff … the adrenaline glands from a *living* human body'. A person has to be sacrificed in order to extract adrenochrome. 'It's no good if you get it out of a corpse.' That is to say, only through an act of extreme profanity, only through the complete suspension of the sacred, can an individual achieve the desired altered state. Extreme states can only be experienced by means of extreme acts of transgression. While there is, of course, no scientific evidence for the psychedelic effects of adrenochrome,[64] the profane takes on the weight of the sacred in such experiences. Just as the taking of life in sacrificial rituals evokes the sacred, so, it is believed, does extreme transgression. Indeed, as if to emphasize the profanity of adrenochrome, Thompson tells us that his fictional dose had been acquired from 'one of these Satanism freaks'.[65] That is to say, he explicitly links it to religio-cultural constructions of the profane. Its significance as a drug and its profanity are directly related. Unsurprisingly, therefore, along with much else that relates to the profane appreciation of mortality, adrenochrome has found its way into the liminal spaces of popular music culture as a signifier of extreme transgression-oriented psychedelia. 'High tide/ Wide eyed/ Sped on adrenochrome … . Panic in their eyes/ Rise/ Dead on adrenochrome', sang Andrew Eldritch of The Sisters of Mercy ('Adrenochrome', *Some Girls Wander By Mistake*, 1992). The drug's signification has similarly inspired other artists, from the pop-punk of the The Groovie Ghoulies (*Appetite for Adrenochrome*, 1989) to the techno-dub of the Children of Dub ('Adrenachrome', *Chameleon*, 1996) and the ambient rock of Emeralds ('Adrenochrome', *Just Feel Anything*, 2012). In brief, the relationship between mortality, profanity and experiences of the impure sacred is a relatively common theme within liminal cultures. (Industrial music and culture has, we will see, made much of this relationship.)

Clearly, this broadly Durkheimian approach to the sacred is a difficult one, in that the concept simultaneously has two apparently contradictory meanings, one which relates to sacred forms as cultural structures around which social life is oriented, and one which is focused on the experience of transgressing those structures. For Bataille, 'whatever is the subject of a prohibition is basically sacred', whereas, normally, we tend to think of that which is prohibited in society as profane.

> The taboo gives a negative definition of the sacred object and inspires us with awe on the religious plane. Carried to extremes that feeling becomes one of devotion and adoration. The gods who incarnate this sacred essence put fear into the hearts of those who reverence them, but men do reverence them nonetheless. Men are swayed by two simultaneous emotions: they are driven away by terror and drawn by an awed fascination. Taboo and transgression reflect these two contradictory urges. The taboo would forbid the transgression, but the fascination compels it. Taboos and the divine are opposed to each other in one sense only, for the sacred aspect of the taboo is what draws men towards it and transfigures the original interdiction. The often intertwined themes of mythology spring from these factors.[66]

'The taboo would forbid the transgression, but the fascination compels it.' As noted earlier in the discussion of Augustine and Christian constructions of sin and the profane, we are drawn to taboos and to the experience of transgressing them. (We will return to this experience of attraction and repulsion when we discuss abjection in Chapter 4.) This brings us directly to those experiences encouraged by the liminal relationship with death and decay. There is a perception of something important and personally significant in standing over against the mainstream, in embracing what has been prohibited, in giving oneself to the Other. Liminal meaning-making can take place in the affective spaces constructed around transgressive discourses and within the experiences of dissonance and high volume.

Concluding comments

What Roland Boer says of Nick Cave's work is true of a number of artists across a range of genres from industrial and punk through to goth and extreme metal: 'unlike the tendency to compartmentalize death in our (post)modern world, to sequester the elderly into compounds known as "retirement villages", to block death through the frenzy of consuming commodified trash, to separate death from life, and for rock singers to favour lust and love, in all its triumphs, frustrations and disappointments, Cave is refreshingly, if at times scandalously, direct'.[67] Like Bataille, popular musicians, far from evading the taboos that circumscribe our short lives, not only transgress them, but seek meaning in their transgression.[68] Hence, while the treatment of mortality in popular music is often little more than a ludic gesture, a simulacrum of mortality, created in the youthful absence of death and decay, it does have cultural significance. This significance is related to the fact that it is crudely explicit in a way that few modern discourses are. Because it conspicuously celebrates that which society abhors and profanes, it disturbs a number of sacred cows. One need only acquaint oneself cursorily with the obsessions of grindcore and death metal to realize just how explicitly crude this can be.[69] Carcass's *Reek of Putrefaction* (1988) is a particularly salient example, its track titles providing an indication of its lascivious devotion to gore: 'Genital Grinder', 'Regurgitation of Giblets', 'Maggot Colony', 'Vomited Anal Tract', 'Fermenting Innards', 'Excreted Alive', 'Foeticide', 'Feast on Dismembered Carnage', 'Splattered Cavities', 'Psychopathologist', 'Burnt to a Crisp', 'Pungent Excruciation' and so on. The carnivalesque and transgressive nature of Carcass's challenge to Western strategies for obscuring the reality of mortality is evident in the lyrics of their evocatively entitled celebration of body-snatching and cannibalism, 'Exhume to Consume' (*Symphonies of Sickness*, 1989): 'My culinary necromancy/ Scrutinised then brutalized/ My forensic inquisition is fulfilled ... I devour the pediculous corpse/ Whetting my palate as I exhume/ The festering stench of rotting flesh/ Makes me drool as I consume.... Ulcerated flesh I munch/ Rotting corpses are my lunch/ On bones I love to crunch.' Such eloquent lyricism is fundamentally related to popular music's role as the voice of liminal culture. It functions as a prosthetic technology, creating affective spaces within which the impure sacred is evoked, liminal meaning is made and personal and social identities are constructed.[70]

Liminal youth cultures are situated beyond 'their mundane structural context'. They are – to quote Turner's observations of the Ndembu of Zambia – 'in a sense "dead" to the world', in that they are separated from normative sacred forms.[71] Indeed, it is largely because liminal culture operates beyond normative cultural structures, that it 'has many symbols of death'. Mortality offers a primary transgressive discourse. Liminal personae in tribal societies, Turner says, 'may be classed with spirits or painted black .... They are also "polluting" ... because they transgress classificatory boundaries. Sometimes they are identified with feces; usually they are allowed to revert to nature by letting their hair and nails grow and their bodies get covered with dust'.[72] Without wanting to get too carried away with superficial anthropological comparisons between the Ndembu and the modern West, it is interesting to note that in both societies blood, excrement, decay and death signify impurity and their liminal cultures explicitly invert this signification in their transgressive behaviours. They identify themselves with religio-cultural symbols of impurity. That is to say, there is something universal and very human about the relationships between (a) death and decay, (b) transgression and the profane and (c) the foci of liminal subcultures. Western culture may have increased the transgressive charge of taboos relating to mortality through its development of strategies for obscuring evidence of death and decay, but these relationships are widely acknowledged throughout all human cultures.[73]

Having said that, bearing in mind the discussion in Chapter 1, there is something peculiarly significant about much Western popular thanatology. Because of the way death and decay are obscured in the modern West, they have become particularly profane. As the sociologist Archie Hanlan put it, while himself dying of cancer, 'dying … is the real pornography of our time – the dirty business that is to be shunted out of the way, the dying patient who is to be shoved off in a ward where he won't offend or bother other people'.[74] Along with the fact that, culturally, our understandings of mortality have been negatively informed by a long history of Christian theology, contemporary strategies to hide evidence of mortality from a secular self that is unable to face extinction have led to a profound tabooing of death. Again, it is this that accounts for its increased appeal to modern liminal subcultures, which, located at some conceptual and chronological distance from the Grim Reaper, are happily and comfortably able to taunt him and to exploit his transgressive potential: 'The coffin is sealed on your rotten corpse/ You lie in darkness, death corrodes your face/ You are rotting, maggots in your coffin' (Napalm Death, 'Maggots in Your Coffin', *Leaders Not Followers*, 2000). In this way, as liminal discourses, they both disturb and contest prevailing sacred forms and provide *memento mori* in societies that struggle to face mortality.

Finally, it is also worth noting here that, while gore and death (which will be discussed in Chapter 4) have an obvious transgressive appeal, this does not mean that the songs therefore lack serious intent. For example, Impaled, much of whose work has focused on the abuse of medical procedures, have provided thoughtful criticisms of the US health-care system: 'Ticking off the subjects in a queue of the damned/ Fungible commodities to hoodwink and scam/ Devouring our meds as your body wastes away/ The side effects are cancer, rotten gums, and decay/ You can't control the nausea or diarrheic shit/ We have a pill for that but it will cost you quite a bit/ The tumours are spreading and they won't go away/ Poisons are injected to keep them at bay/ To counter the poison, we have here a pill/ We can't make you better if we don't make you ill' (Impaled, 'You Are the Dead', *The Last Gasp*, 2007).

The Undead and the Uncanny

No tradition or sensibility has done more to inspire popular thanatology than the Gothic. From Horace Walpole's 1764 novelette *The Castle of Otranto* through to Gothic rock, imaginations have been drawn to boundary-crossing themes, ambivalent discourses, perverse religion, occult knowledge, hauntings, revenants, dark secrets, profane sex, death, decay and Romantic constructions of the past. Peering through the cracks of the everyday into the dark recesses of human experience, Gothic occulture is rooted in liminality, transgression and the impure sacred. 'Gothic reveals the shadow within, the skull beneath the skin.'[1] From its inception, the Gothic has, as Patrick McGrath comments, 'disturbed and subverted all that is certain, singular, rational, balanced, established. Its *raison d'être* is transgression. It identifies limits so as to assault them.'[2] As such, it is hardly surprising to find it flourishing in the liminal spaces of popular music culture, encouraging reflection on death and decay. Of course, as discussed in the Introduction and Chapter 2, this is typically done in that type of Romantic, Gothic way that can only be undertaken at a distance. Articulated within postsecular youth cultures, it offers a safe approach to sublime ideas and experiences that disturb us. As such, it can be understood in terms of a largely modern strategy for dealing with mortality. Drawing on religious strategies that have lost much of their theological cogency and cultural weight, it suggests that death is not final. It is a permeable boundary, a state from which one can return. It is not the terminus of the self.

As we have seen, within much 'Gothic popular music', the graveyard, the funereal and decay are treated as fashionable interests for the acquisition of subcultural capital by those who give themselves, if only sartorially, to darkness: 'The bats have left the bell tower/ The victims have been bled/ Red velvet lines the black box/ Bela Lugosi's dead/ Undead, Undead, Undead' (Bauhaus, 'Bela Lugosi's Dead', 1979). This is quite different from some of the music we have already discussed. For example, while it is arguable that some of Lou Reed's work that can be considered Gothic, particularly during his time with the Velvet Underground, this is less the case with *Magic and Loss* (1992). While the album refuses to submit to hopelessness, it articulates his reflections on the cancer, chemotherapy and eventual loss of two of his close friends as a mundane, tragic struggle. This is not to say that contemporary Gothic discourse is, by comparison, trivial and wholly detached from the brutal reality of death and decay. It is not. But, it is an approach that is allied far more closely to religious strategies for coping with mortality. (Hence, to some extent, it can be framed theoretically in terms of the postsecular.)

While this chapter is anchored to the Gothic, its interests are far broader than 'Goth' music and subcultures. That is to say, it is *both* concerned with the Romantic articulation of death and decay in popular music *and also*, perhaps more significantly, with the way music is able to recover the past, to haunt the present, to summon revenants and to awaken the undead in our memories. Of course, much of this is framed using the standard genre conventions with which academics and devotees are frequently preoccupied: graveyards, Victoriana, haunted houses, vampires, moonlight, mist, gloom, the flamboyant funereal, neo-medievalism and the antique futurism of steampunk.[3] However, although, of course, such tropes will be mentioned, the point to keep in mind is that, in this chapter, the Gothic is a lens through which to look at the way popular music is able to create 'affective spaces' within which we are drawn into reflecting on mortality in a way that conflates loss and longing, life and death and mortality and immortality. 'Gothic forces its readers, viewers, and listeners to identify the ghosts that haunt them ... .'[4] This is essentially what I mean when I refer to 'popular music Gothic' (as opposed to 'Gothic popular music'/'Goth music'). In the final analysis, although we will be exploring a number of ideas, such as particularly the construction of 'affective space' and 'the uncanny', I want to argue that popular music Gothic is able to function as a *memento mori*. It coerces us in gentle and brutal ways to reflect on the passing of time and the inevitability of our own terminus – although, again, it does this in a way that protects us from the full impact of the awareness of death.

Mortality and the uncanny

In a recent discussion of 'Gothic music', Isabella van Elferen makes use of the broadly psychoanalytic notion of the 'uncanny'. Uncanny sounds, she says, 'pervade Gothic. Hollow footsteps and ghostly melodies haunt the heroines of

Gothic novels.'[5] This is interesting, in that, again, uncanny sonic environments immediately introduce a safe modern strategy for dealing with mortality. To return to Zygmunt Bauman's helpful analysis, 'culture is precisely about *transcendence*, about *going beyond* what is given and found before the creative imagination of culture set to work; culture is after that permanence and durability which life, by itself, so sorely misses. But death (more exactly, the awareness of mortality) is the ultimate condition of cultural creativity as such. It makes permanence into a task, into an urgent task, into a paramount task ... .'[6] The Gothic use of the uncanny can be understood as an attempt at that task. It is a cultural strategy for dealing with our impermanence, for transgressing the inevitability of that final boundary between being and nothingness. As with religion, it introduces us to intimations of transcendence and the beyond. If death is, to quote Bauman again, 'a *ghost* haunting the *totality* of life',[7] Gothic exorcizes or, at least, tames that ghost with intimations of the self's permanence. It is this, I suggest, that helps us to understand the social and cultural significance of the uncanny, which has become a useful and popular lens through which to read the Gothic,[8] and which is so powerfully evoked by sound.

Drawing on Freud's well-known 1919 essay, 'The Uncanny' (*Das Unheimliche* – 'unhomely'),[9] the concept has become a broad, flexible and increasingly popular one in contemporary cultural theory.[10] There is no doubt, says Freud, that the uncanny 'belongs to the realm of the frightening, of what evokes fear and dread'.[11] These feelings are unnerving because they emerge from a confluence of the familiar and unfamiliar. More specifically, we experience the uncanny when that which is familiar suddenly becomes unfamiliar. 'The uncanny is ghostly', says Nicholas Royle. 'It is concerned with the strange, weird and mysterious, with a flickering sense (but not conviction) of something supernatural. The uncanny involves feelings of uncertainty, in particular regarding the reality of who one is and what is being experienced ... . The uncanny is a crisis of the proper ... .'[12] Notions related to the ghostly, the weird, and the supernatural are, of course, those of enchanted worlds. It is hardly surprising, therefore, that Freud understood this common feeling of the uncanny in terms of 'infantile complexes which have been repressed, or when primitive beliefs are once more revived by some impression, or when primitive beliefs which have been surmounted seem once more to be confirmed'.[13] That is to say, the uncanny identifies dark and primal fears that lie not far below the surface, those insecurities regarding the impermanence of the self. The uncanny tends to concern, says Freud, 'anything to do with death, dead bodies, revenants, spirits and ghosts', for 'in hardly any other sphere has our thinking and feeling changed so little since primitive times or the old been so well preserved, under a thin veneer, as in our relation to death'.[14]

The uncanny is primarily used in Gothic discourse as a strategy of defamiliarization through the creation of disturbing affective spaces. Imagine, for example, that you are lying in bed, relaxing in the darkness, thinking about the day and surrounded by everything that is homely and familiar. Gradually, the silence is disturbed by the faint sound of steady breathing. Barely audible though the sound is, it seems to fill the room. A familiar space is defamiliarized, the everyday is haunted and the homely is made *unheimlich*. The use of the uncanny, while frightening, also functions as a life strategy for dealing with mortality; the Gothic re-enchants death and the dead through its use of the uncanny. Death cannot be the end of the self, because selves from the past are revealed in the present. The whisper of air, the creak on the stair, the metronomic tick of a clock marking the passing of time and the barely heard voices all defamiliarize and enchant. As such, the boundary between the known and the unknown is eroded. Hence, on the one hand, the Gothic evocation of the uncanny functions very directly as a *memento mori*, in that it exposes the fear of death, which is a more or less repressed part of our mental furniture. That which is hidden away in our culture, locked deep in our unconscious, is exposed. We are brought face to face with mortality: the bleak graveyard, the cemetery statues of mourning angels and the house haunted with memories of the departed. On the other hand, as Gothic peers through the cracks of the everyday into unfamiliar haunted spaces, it introduces us to the possibility of immortality. The very revenant itself, that which frightens and disturbs, also meets our fear of mortality with the suggestion of immortality. It is that intimation of the permanence of the self in Gothic that functions so effectively as a modern strategy for dealing with the self's impermanence.

Music and uncanny affective space

Music, as an invisible, spectral manipulator of emotion, resurrecting memories and creating mood, has a unique prosthetic ability to evoke the uncanny. This is why van Elferen makes much of the notion in her discussion of Gothic music: its 'capacity to stretch time and space and to dissolve subjectivity ties in with Gothic's distortions of reality and the self, and music-inducted transgression is an important factor in the genre's performativity'. In particular, 'the immersion in Gothic music can move listeners into the liminal spaces of Gothic, between past and present, between God and the devil … Gothic music is a journey into the uncanny.'[15] But, what does that mean? What does it mean for an individual to 'journey into the uncanny'?

In order to understand the dynamics and the significance of popular music Gothic, I want to briefly introduce a few points that I have developed elsewhere regarding music's unique power to construct 'affective space'.[16] This term is an important one, in that it refers to music's prosthetic ability to manipulate emotion and, thereby, to create internal worlds within which meaning is constructed. This is the key to the power of the sonic uncanny. Music is able to unhinge and to disturb because, first, it has a fundamental relationship with emotion, and, second, human emotionality is directly related to meaning-making and to what Jürgen Habermas has referred to as the individual's 'lifeworld' – the latent, taken-for-granted core values, beliefs and understandings about who we are, how we relate to others, what the world is like and how we fit into it.[17]

But, how does music create meaningful affective spaces? Like all technologies, music is often affectively linked, 'through convention, to social scenarios, often according to the social uses for which it was initially produced – waltz music for dancing, march music for marching and so on'.[18] In other words, music often contextualizes and gives meaning to situations because of what might be thought of as its 'intertextual' relationship to compositional conventions. That is to say, it creates affective spaces shaped by feelings, which have been evoked by memories of previous times when the music has been heard. Of course, certain melodies, rhythms, beats and so on are composed with particular activities in mind, so that, even if we have not heard the music before, we know how to respond affectively. While this raises a number of issues,[19] it is important to note that our emotional investment in a piece of music is directly related to its meaningfulness.

In referring to intertextuality, we are thinking, in general terms, of the ways in which 'a text', as a signifying practice, to quote Julia Kristeva, 'presupposes the existence of other discourses …. This is to say that every text is from the outset under the jurisdiction of other discourses which impose a universe on it.'[20] Thinking of music as 'text' – a coherent set of signs, which can be read for meaning – it is clear that it is influenced by other texts, discourses and affectively significant moments. For example, one person I spoke to when researching an earlier book related to me a sense of the uncanny occasioned by Gregorian chant. She had travelled to an old theological seminary to run an art workshop. She arrived the previous evening and although it was twilight, prior to settling down for the evening, she decided to walk around the cloisters. As she did so, through the silence, she heard a faint chanting, which she described as both beautiful and 'eerie'. When I asked why she thought it was 'eerie', she immediately replied that it reminded her of the film *The Name of the Rose*, which, based on the book by Umberto Eco, is set in a shadowy Benedictine monastery in Northern Italy in 1327 and relates the story of an investigation by a Franciscan friar into a series of mysterious deaths. This memory of unease, which she related to the Gregorian chant in the soundtrack to the film, shifted her into an uncomfortable affective space. It was, she recalled, 'creepy'; it 'made my heart race'. Tranquility was transformed into unease. Music that is regularly used to relax and evoke contemplation now provoked a sense of the uncanny. The intertextual relationship between the music, the cloistered setting and the monks was, to paraphrase Kristeva, subjected to the jurisdiction of another discourse (*The Name of the Rose*), which imposed a universe upon it.[21] The result was an affective space defined by the eerie and the creepy.

It is worth noting, of course, that, although used for relaxation and spiritual contemplation, the relationship between Gregorian chant, haunted space and the Gothic runs deep within Western occulture. This makes it very useful for those musicians wanting to evoke the medieval uncanny. As the central tradition of Western plainchant,[22] it is culturally associated with a particular form of devotion and a particular ecclesiastical setting. As such, it is difficult to detach it from that context when we hear it. Hence, we respond accordingly, in that, again, because it is a gentle form of music associated with the sacred, the affective space it creates is, for many people, calming and 'spiritual'. This is evident in, for example, many of the chant-based pop releases by Gregorian (Frank Peterson). But, there are, of course, usually more meanings conveyed than simply relaxation and spirituality. Readings of Gregorian chant will typically include feelings of reverence, informed by, perhaps, Gothic notions of medieval ecclesiastical life and processions of chanting, cowled monks. This, of course, is why some contemporary esoteric groups make liberal use of cowls and liturgical chant in seeking to construct affective spaces conducive to the perception of sacred gravitas. For example, the soundtrack to a video of a ceremony of the esoteric Order of the Solar Temple seized by police in Quebec following a mass suicide included Gregorian chant and showed members performing their rituals in cowls.[23] Similarly, in popular culture, the gravity of occult ritual is often conveyed visually with cowls and candles and aurally with liturgical chant. Indeed, it is because of these affordances that it is used to great effect in films such as Roman Polanski's *The Ninth Gate* (1999) and Stanley Kubrick's *Eyes Wide Shut* (1999). The soundtrack to the latter, for example, includes Jocelyn Pook's haunting 'Masked Ball' (*Flood*, 1999), for which Romanian liturgical chant was sampled and played backwards.[24] Again, just as cowls and candles are used in music videos by bands wanting to evoke a sense of Gothic gravity,[25] so Gregorian chant is employed for similar reasons. Of course, again, intertextuality is key here. That cowls and chant are used in film, that they articulate a Gothic sensibility and that they are linked to esoteric ritual is highly significant, in that musicians are now able to use them in the knowledge that their meanings are relatively stable. These meanings are explicit in the use of chant on, for example, 'The Song of the Sibyl' by Dead Can Dance (*Aion*, 1990) or 'First Prayer' by the black metal band Deathspell Omega (*Si monvmentvm reqvires, circvmspice*, 2004). Particularly interesting is the confluence of the religious, the uncanny and the erotic – as explored in Kubrick's *Eyes Wide Shut*. These texts work particularly powerfully together, as is evident in the distinctive ways chant is used by Shaggy on 'Church Heathen' (*Intoxication*, 2007) and, most evocatively, Enigma on 'Sadeness' (*MCMXC a.D.*, 1990), the latter being one of the most internationally successful records of the 1990s.[26] Although 'Sadeness' is a piece of music conspicuously linked to the Marquis de Sade, including sexually suggestive female vocals, the meanings Gregorian chant possesses are still powerfully present. Hence, when juxtaposed with that which would typically, in a Christian culture, be considered profane, the effect is powerful, creating a particularly evocative dissonance, which, in turn, creates a sense of transgression and the uncanny.

Having said that, it is also important to understand that, to a significant extent, the range of available meanings is limited by the 'interpretive communities' to which one belongs. In other words, as Stanley Fish has argued, readers' subjective responses to texts and the meanings evoked are, in the final analysis, shaped by interpretive communities, rather than either the text or the reader.[27] Such communities are made up of those who share 'the interpretive strategies' which are always, wittingly or unwittingly, brought to texts. Subcultures, for example, will guide the interpretation of their members. Fans of goth music and black metal, for example, are likely to read chant in a very particular way. We listen to songs in distinctive ways, determined by the interpretative communities to which we belong. For one person, a song may seem profane and polluting, while, to another, it appears profound and exciting. Hence, the affective spaces created by the music will depend to a large extent on the interpretative community to which a listener belongs.

Bearing the above points in mind, it is hardly surprising that, for example, the affective spaces and the meanings evoked by music can shift significantly between cover versions by different artists, who in themselves carry meanings which influence the listener's interpretation. Take, for example, the song

'Personal Jesus' by Depeche Mode (*Violator*, 1990). Originally, the song is about personal relationships and the way in which one partner can be significantly dependent on the other. In this sense, one partner becomes 'the savior', 'the confessor' and 'the Jesus', of the other partner. This particular use of theological terminology empties it of religious meaning and reflects the secularizing currents in Western societies. However, the meaning of the text shifted radically when it was covered in 2002 by Johnny Cash (*American IV*), a well-known convert to evangelical Christianity from a famously chequered past, and then again in 2004 by Marilyn Manson (*Lest We Forget*), whose misanthropic rhetoric and criticisms of Christianity are also well known. Sung gently to an acoustic guitar and piano by the Christian Cash in old age, 'Personal Jesus' is sacralized, becoming a touching devotional song by a man not too far away from a meeting with his maker. Sung by Marilyn Manson, accompanied by raw, aggressive guitar riffs and pronounced heavy bass and drums, it drips with irony and profane meaning – all of which is made explicit in the video, which is conspicuously Gothic in its careful mixing of sacred and profane imagery.

Finally, music can also have a conspicuous intertextual relationship to sonic structures evident in the natural and social worlds. For example, echo can give the impression of space, as in Bauhaus's goth classic 'Bela Lugosi's Dead', and lightly playing the keys of a glockenspiel or brushing crotales can communicate the impression of a stream, a gentle breeze or, depending on the other musical and cultural texts involved, the ghostly. Apparitions, hauntings and intimations of the occult are, for a number of cultural reasons, often evoked through the use of recordings of creaks, howling wind, thunder, rain or a tolling church bell. The use of dissonance and electronic effects reminiscent of wind whistling and moaning is very movingly, if disturbingly, used on Bass Communion's album *Loss* (2006), which implicitly references bereavement and the paranormal continuity of lost selves. Perhaps most evocatively, however, such effects are carefully used on Black Sabbath's genre-defining classic, 'Black Sabbath' (*Black Sabbath*, 1970), inspired by the novels of Dennis Wheatley. I remember first buying this album in the 1970s. Before placing the needle on that initial track, the construction of affective space within which I would hear the record had already begun. The sacred-profane ambiguity of the name 'Black Sabbath' and the cover of the album – an eerie photograph of an old mill, haunted by a strangely profane figure dressed in black – indicated very clearly the occult context within which this album should be interpreted. I still remember my heightened feelings about that album, which translated into a perception of it as being *more than* just a record. Fetishized, it had more significance than that. As the first song begins, almost immediately a very particular affective space is created: the sound of torrential rain, a rumble of thunder, and the tolling of a church bell. The use of the church bell as a signifier of religion is an interesting one. The church, the graveyard, the funereal and Christian doctrines of the afterlife both challenge the final termination of the self and provide the raw material for inversion into explicitly profane spiritual discourses. Hence, not only does the album immediately draw the listener into a particular affective space oriented around mortality, but the intertextual affordances are all profane. The spectral figure on the cover, the church bells, the thunder and the rain are joined by the opening slow, dissonant heavy riff, which confirms the uncanny, ghostly and occult nature of the album. Gothic, as van Elferen notes, 'revolves around the suffocating spaces, the hauntings, and the psychological destabilization of the ghost story. Empty spaces like deserted ruins, bleak landscapes ... spooky spaces haunted by various types of spectres'[28] all evoke the uncanny and, we have seen, deconstruct mortality (in their suggestion that death is not the end of the self). There are few album covers and opening tracks that demonstrate this better that Black Sabbath's eponymous debut. The first chord confirms the presence of the profane. Oriented around the dissonance of the 'Devils interval',[29] the riff gradually softens and the thoughts of a clearly disturbed and anxious mind, evocatively articulated by the young Ozzy Osbourne, make clear the *unheimlich* nature of the space into which we have been invited: 'What is this that stands before me?/Figure in black which points at me .... Satan's sitting there, he's smiling .... Oh no, no, please God help me.' This is classic Gothic, in that it immerses the listener in the ambiguities of immortality: the hope that we will not terminate at death; the fear of what is beyond death; the dark threat of the profane; and the return of the undead. Again, an affective space is evoked, which both evokes fear and reinforces discourses of immortality.

Dissonance and discordant sounds have been widely used in popular music and film to evoke unease, as in the frenetic high-pitched guitar in 'Voodoo Dolly' by Siouxsie and the Banshees (*Juju*, 1981) or, most memorably, the dramatic stabbing of strings in their upper registers in Bernard Herrmann's score for Alfred Hitchcock's 1960 film *Psycho*.[30] Similarly, natural sounds, such as the cawing of crows and ravens – because of the birds' associations with carrion, decay and death, and, consequently, their widespread religio-cultural connections with mortality and the paranormal[31] very quickly create a sense of the uncanny. For example, Lurker of Chalice (Jef Whitehead/Wrest) begins his 'Piercing Where They Might' by gently drawing the listener into an unsettling space, signified by samples of ravens cawing, prior to his washes of brooding, ambient black metal (*Lurker of Chalice*, 2005). Again, equally evocative are the melancholic, slightly uneasy affective spaces created by Grouper (Liz Harris) – listen to *Dragging a Dead Dear Up a Hill* (2008) and *The Man Who Died in His Boat* (2013). She explains how her recordings 'often sound as though they've been made against a vast mountainscape: voice and instruments – muted piano, spider-strummed guitar or growling drone – are steeped in reverb and delay. "When you have reverb and smeared-out sounds there's an implied expansiveness. My music is partly about making a sound that reflects an actual physical space that's wide and empty." '[32]

The overall point is that, because of intertextuality, whether we think of the use of strings in *Psycho*, the cawing of ravens, Gregorian chant or the steady bass drum beats reminiscent of ritual that are frequently used by occult-oriented musicians, such as Black Widow (e.g. 'Come to the Sabbat,' *Sacrifice*, 1969) and Demdike Stare (e.g. 'Forest of Evil (Dawn)', *Tryptych*, 2011), music is a powerful technology for creating affective space and evoking the uncanny. Hence, while we may read particular meanings into specific pieces of popular music because of their associations with moments within our own histories, the same pieces also convey meanings as a result of their associations with ideas in wider culture, as well as associations that have formed within the interpretive communities to which we belong. In this sense, Simon Frith is correct to insist that 'we are not free to read anything we want into a song'. Rather, 'the experience of pop music is an experience of placing: in responding to a song, we are drawn, haphazardly, into affective and emotional alliances with the performers and with the performers' other fans,'[33] as well as with wider interpretive strategies. This is why, as indicated earlier, van Elferen is quite right when she claims that 'the immersion in Gothic music can move listeners into the liminal spaces of Gothic, between past and present, between God and the devil … Gothic music is a journey into the uncanny'.[34] And this is true, not just of 'gothic music', but of all music.

Memory and *memento mori*

There is a growing body of research demonstrating that the relationship between human memory and music is a rather special one. As Matthew Schulkind discusses in a recent thoughtful article on the subject, although more work needs to be done to establish conclusively whether memory for music is as singular as some of us like to think it is, nevertheless, 'the unique structure of musical stimuli strongly suggests that memory for music is indeed special.'[35] Certainly, as David Hesmondhalgh has discussed, it is indisputable to most of us that music is 'powerfully linked to memory ... . It allows us to remember things that happened, how we felt, and what it is like to move, dance, and feel to a certain set of sounds, rhythms, and textures.' It has, in short, a peculiar ability 'to get stuck in our minds'.[36] Hence, says Schulkind, 'given the ubiquity of music, it is not surprising that cultural beliefs have emerged regarding its power.'[37] That is to say, the vast majority of us can provide our own examples of music's exceptional power to evoke memories and instantaneously to place us at some point in our past. There are even 'numerous anecdotal claims in the popular media regarding the special effect that music has on memory in patients suffering from dementia'.[38] Indeed, there is actually more than anecdotal evidence to suggest that musical intervention has a positive effect on the autobiographical memory of dementia patients.[39] Again, as Michael Thaut discusses, 'musical memories often appear to stay more intact and accessible to recall than nonmusical memories in disorders affecting memory functions.'[40] While there are a number of reasons why this might be the case, it is likely that 'the affective context in which most musical materials are learned may ... contribute to more resilient memory functions, since emotional context enhances learning and recall'.[41] Unsurprisingly, therefore, 'music is used to trigger emotionally laden memories of past events as sources of reflection on life'.[42] Although Schulkind shows that, as we get older, memory struggles with the particular details of popular music (such as lyrics and song titles), this does not undermine the point I want to make here. It matters little whether we can remember all the words or titles of songs, because music has an ability to create similar affective spaces to those created when it was first heard, and consequently, it is able to resurrect similar meanings and emotions.

In short, 'sounds are', as David Toop says, 'woven with memory'.[43] This is, I suggest, largely why music is so intimately related to the uncanny, in that it is able to transform the everyday by shifting us into affective spaces that feel both familiar and unfamiliar. Because it has a peculiar ability 'to get stuck in our minds', almost immediately on hearing a familiar piece of music we enter a very particular emotional space that often merges our past and present. In this sense, music is able to haunt us by drawing us back through our personal histories to relationships with the lost and to places long forgotten. For example, quite unexpectedly, on hearing a piece of music, we can experience those who have died returning to us in sometimes profound and disturbing ways. Whenever I hear 'Handsworth Revolution' by Steel Pulse (*Handsworth Revolution*, 1978), I am immediately transported back to the late 1970s and to memories of a close friend who died several years ago. Likewise, I was recently moved by a beautiful short documentary for which the musician Emily Levy sorted through a number of mix-tapes compiled for her by her late brother, Gus.[44] The pieces of music were discussed with close friends and clearly had the effect of evoking significant moments in their shared histories. As such, Gus was made present in the affective spaces created by the music. He was in a sense immortalized in his choices of music, through which he had shared something of who he was. That is to say, as emotional beings, the everyday and the mundane can be transformed simply by the introduction of a piece of music or a song, which stimulates memory and draws us into particular affective spaces.

More than this, however, not only can we think of music as a medium for 'the returned', the revenant, but, because music is able to evoke powerful emotional responses through its peculiar ability to summon the past, the affective spaces it evokes often function as reminders of mortality. Particularly, as we get older, they become, in a very powerful sense, *memento mori*. Alela Diane's gentle psych-folk song 'Take Us Back', using traditional Gothic tropes, evokes this sense of music's bewitching ability to summon the past, as she remembers old friends and thinks about beginning again – 'take us back … the fiddle's cry is an old sound/ A lonesome bow/ Creeks and moans of empty houses are songs like fallen rain …. Muted voices, just beyond/ The silent surface of what has gone' (*To Be Still*, 2009). A piece of music can evoke memories of childhood and youth, of liminal identities we once valued, of places that have changed, of love and loss and of those friends and family who are no longer with us. These produce powerful and meaningful affective spaces, within which we are very quickly drawn into reflection on the passing of time and on our own impermanence. Brought back to us in the music, the departed speak to us: *memento mori*, 'remember that you too will die'.

Of course, there has been much discussion concerning those intrinsic qualities of music that elicit profound emotions, what Leonard Bernstein referred to as the affective theory of musical expression – 'why is the minor "sad" and the major "glad"?'[45] Hence, as I have discussed elsewhere,[46] music per se, because of its close relationship with emotion, can evoke contemplative states in which we reflect on significant autobiographical moments and relationships. In other words, we do not need to have formed a previous relationship with a piece of music for it to evoke a meaning-making affective space that draws on memories, conflates past and present, summons revenants and functions as a *memento mori*.

Hauntology, spirit voices and exorcisms

We have seen that music per se, regardless of whether or not it is 'Gothic music', has the ability to evoke the uncanny and to draw us into reflection on mortality. This is essentially Toop's thesis in his eclectic book *Sinister Resonance*. All sound, primarily because of its immaterial and fleeting nature, is 'a haunting, a ghost, a presence whose location in space is ambiguous and whose existence in time is transitory. The intangibility of sound is uncanny – a phenomenal presence both in the head, at its point of source and all around – so never entirely distinct from auditory hallucinations. The close listener is like a medium who draws out substance from that which is not entirely there. Listening, after all, is always a form of eavesdropping.'[47] Indeed, as indicated above, what van Elferen says of 'Gothic music', which she understands in a very particular sense, is actually equally applicable to music per se – to sonic environments per se. It can, she says, 'take listeners to where formerly opposed binaries of time, space, and being collapse. Immersed in these twilight zones, they find themselves *within* Gothic spectrality, and that means within a profoundly dislodged temporality as well as ontology.'[48] The word 'Gothic' need not be used here, as all music is similarly efficacious. Hence, as we have already noted, while 'the uncanny' is central to van Elferen's understanding of the significance of *Gothic* music, almost any composition, depending on the context and a person's autobiographical relationship to it, can evoke powerful feelings of the *unheimlich*.[49] Music, regardless of the genre, can instantaneously defamiliarize the everyday. Having said that, there are, of course, certain techniques and tropes in popular music that have a very specific relationship with the Gothic uncanny. These, I want to suggest, are related in some direct way to our reflection on mortality.

The use of overdubbed voices, for example, evokes the uncanny, giving the listener the impression of eavesdropping a conversation from another time. The music in a very particular way feels haunted by the presence of other human wills. It is not just sound. There is a sense of intentionality and a perceived desire to communicate that appears to press through the music into the listener's personal space. A thoughtful recent example of this in contemporary lo-fi electronica is 'DMT' by the young Orlando musician XXYYXX (Marcel Everett). A slow, brooding, bass-heavy beat – reminiscent of the dark sonic environments created by British dubstep producer Clubroot (Dan Richmond) on *II-MMX* (2010) – is beautifully overlaid with indecipherable vocal samples. It is as if the listener is experiencing waves of siren singing from the spirit world washing over the everyday. A similar, but far more haunting effect is produced by the Norwegian composer Biosphere (Geir Jenssen) on his album *Man With a Movie Camera*, commissioned by the Tromsø International Film Festival in 1996 and released as a bonus disc with the album *Substrata* (2006). The whole album is sepia tinted, haunted by noises and voices sampled from old films and other times. No matter how ethereal the music, the eerie sound of disembodied voices immediately suggests transgression and evokes the uncanny. Of course, to some extent, all recorded singing is experienced by the listener as disembodied. In Chapter 5, we will see that this is particularly significant when it comes to listening to the music of dead musicians. However, the point here is simply that some music uses vocal samples in a very particular way in order to evoke the ghostly. As such, it goes beyond the standard recording of the human voice, which simply brings to mind an embodied singer. Rather, the everyday is defamiliarized, and we are gently coerced into a haunted affective space. Matt Elliot, a master of mortality music, does this particularly well through the use of sepia-tinted voices from the past. For example, the singing on the beautifully melancholic remix of Yann Tiersen's 'La Dispute' (Third Eye Foundation, *I Poo Poo on Your Juju*, 2001) seems to gradually possess the music as it progresses. Towards the end of the track, the 'spirit voices' begin to haunt the affective space created, constantly repeating the same words: 'So you say the world is lonely'; 'You are alone.' Gradually, the melancholic melody is dominated and disturbed by these thoughts, before the voices fade back into silence, leaving only the music and an uncanny feeling of sadness and solitude. Likewise, wailing and screaming create a disturbing sense of the uncanny on 'Corpses as Bedmates' (Third Eye Foundation, *Ghost*, 2006). Similarly, David Tibet's work with Current 93, much of which is embedded in esoteric signification, uses layers of spoken voices to shift listeners into an occult world. On the album *All the Pretty Horses* (1996), which is essentially a series of reflections on religion and mortality, 'Twilight Twilight Nihil Nihil' gradually introduces the listener to a number of competing voices. While the album is not difficult to listen to (and certainly one of the more accessible releases from Current 93), it is unnerving and disturbing. It alters perspectives and creates an ambiguous affective space within which the uncanny is almost tangible. Again, the very suggestion of disembodied communication creates a slightly disturbing affective space, which guides one very quickly to reflection on the ghostly and, therefore, to thoughts of mortality and immortality. Indeed, any suggestion of sound from beyond the grave is a challenge to the silence of nothingness, a strategy for resisting the inevitability of personal dissolution.

There is a useful overlap here with certain aspects of Jacques Derrida's thinking regarding 'hauntology'.[50] Of course, he was not particularly interested in paranormal phenomena per se.[51] As Fredric Jameson has commented, hauntology 'does not involve the conviction that ghosts exist or that the past (and maybe even the future they offer to prophesy) is still very much alive and at work, within the living present: all it says ... is that the living present is scarcely as self-sufficient as it claims to be; that we would do well not to count on its density and solidity, which might under exceptional circumstances betray us'.[52] This is precisely the point that I want to make here. The uncanny introduces into the modern world the idea that we would do well not to count on the density and solidity of the living present, which might under exceptional circumstances betray us. What is in the past might very well not remain there, because death might not be the terminus of the self.

The sense that this might be the case, on the one hand, evokes unease and, on the other hand, suggests hope. Notions of the ghostly and intimations of the beyond lengthen the human horizon. Our terminus, just a few short years away, has its finality compromised. For Derrida, hauntology replaces its near homonym ontology; it subverts the priority of being and presence; it undermines the stability and certainties of modernity with the figure of the ghost as that which is neither present nor absent, neither deceased nor living. As Colin Davis has commented, 'Derrida's spectre is a deconstructive figure hovering between life and death, presence and absence, and making established certainties vacillate'.[53] Developing this pregnant idea, which many others have done in the service of their own theories,[54] there is an important sense in which hauntology refers to 'an essential unknowing which underlies and may undermine what we think we know'.[55] This is why the terminology of haunting, ghosts, spectres and the supernatural is so evocative in the discourse of deconstruction. Music is particularly effective in this respect. Sound and silence communicate very well this intimation of the uncanny, this suspicion of an essential unknowing about our existence. Music, in other words, has a peculiar ability to deconstruct dominant readings of 'reality'.

As both van Elferen and Toop discuss, even in literature, much use is made of sonic environments to evoke the uncanny. 'Through sound, the boundaries of the physical world are questioned, even threatened or undone by instability.'[56]

This is why music, says Toop, 'was a reminder of the transience of life in the didactic vanitas genre of seventeenth-century still life paintings'. He continues:

> Adriaen Coorte's *Vanitas Still Life in a Niche* of 1688 shows a glass half-filled with wine, pipe and tobacco, dice, a watch, playing cards, an oil lamp with smoldering wick, an empty shell, a pochette (a small bowed string instrument…) and a music book. A skull serves as a paperweight; upper teeth clamped on the cover of the book, whose dog-eared corners artfully rise to beguile scholars of the future with glimpsed fragments of notes on staves. Even the pneuma of the music, transient, yet so easily resuscitated through notation, is destined for the silence of the tomb. Though imbued with sufficient vitality to overpower such morbidity, music, along with silence, is uncomfortably close to death – a shocking and shaping of the air, then suddenly gone.[57]

Hence, again, sound *and the lack of it* are able to evoke reflection on mortality and the meaning of life. Just as sound terminates in silence, so being ends in nothingness. This is why sound and silence are able to be used to great effect in film and literature for evoking the uncanny, as, for example, has been masterfully done by authors of the classic English ghost story, such as M.R. James and, more recently, Susan Hill. Susan Hill's subtly complex story, *The Child's Hand*, is a good example:

> …as I stood in the gathering stillness and soft spring dusk, something happened. I do not much care whether I am believed. That does not matter. I know. That is all…
>
> I know because if I close my eyes now I feel it happening again, the memory of it is vivid and it is a physical memory. My body feels it, this is not only something in my mind.
>
> I stood in the dim, green-lit clearing and above my head a silver paring of moon cradled the evening star. The birds had fallen silent. There was not the slightest stirring of air.
>
> And as I stood I felt a small hand creep into my right one, as if a child had come up beside me in the dimness and taken hold of it. It felt cool and its fingers curled themselves trustingly into my palm and rested there, and the small thumb and forefinger tucked my own thumb between them.[58]

Here, the references to stillness and silence are carefully used to create an affective space within which is introduced the encounter with a transgressive presence that questions mortality and sanity. In the 'gathering stillness', in which 'the birds had fallen silent', there was not even 'the slightest stirring of air'. That silence is pregnant with the uncanny, with references to death and nothingness. Something is not quite right, unhomely, unfamiliar. We have been introduced to an 'essential unknowing which underlies and may undermine what we think we know'.[59] Sound, silence and the spectral are very closely related. And, as noted above, the move from sound to silence is particularly evocative of the move from being to nothingness, from activity to emptiness, from life to death. Only the revenant emerges from such dead silence.

In this hauntological sense, we might return to think of the use of voices to evoke the uncanny. I do not want to stretch the analogy too far and inadvertently slip into pretentious nonsense, but there is a sense in which overdubbed voices in music can be read as a form of 'electronic voice phenomena' (EVP), the spirit communication some believe to be decipherable within white noise. Popularized by the Latvian academic and parapsychologist Konstantīns Raudive (1909–1974), during the twentieth century, spiritualists came to believe that the dead were able to communicate, not simply through sensitive mediums, but also through new technologies, such as the radio.[60] By carefully listening to background noise and interference, voices from the spirit world could be deciphered. (Of course, this again introduces the idea that musicians who have died are, through the medium of recording technology, able to communicate with listeners and to reach new audiences. We will return to this in Chapter 5.) Indeed, that there is this uncanny resonance with mediumship and the spectral has led some musicians to explore the relationship in their music. As well as the numerous lyrical and titular references to the paranormal in popular music, some have sought to construct haunted spaces that reflect EVP and even incorporate recordings of claimed paranormal phenomena. Again, a good example is Bass Communion's *Ghosts on Magnetic Tape* (2004), which is a collection of darkly ambient compositions directly inspired by the idea that the dead might be able to communicate. Layered washes of rumbling, bass-oriented ambient sound are permeated by eerie sonic effects: creaks, clicks and crackle. This is then intensified and made almost claustrophobic by the interruptions from the imagined spirit world: a haunting piano, dated orchestral music and mournful opera singing taken from antique 78 rpm records. Barely decipherable voices, eerie breathing and numerous layered effects conspire to create a very particular sense of the uncanny. As Steve Wilson (the musician behind Bass Communion) describes:

> I collected some source material from recordings of old 78 rpm records that I found in my parent's attic. So I was playing these records and I couldn't even play them at 78. I was having to play them at 45....So what I was getting off the record was hardly any of the music at all. It was almost all the surface noise and the crackles from the record because they were so old and so scratched.

Those crackles and this...ghostly sound of the music coming through from underneath the crackle created something in my mind. It almost felt like the dead trying to communicate through the noise, which led me on to that whole concept of ghosts trying to communicate with the living world through the medium of recorded music or recordings.[61]

In so doing, Wilson was able to evoke an affective space within which the boundaries between the past and the present, and between the beyond and the mundane, appear to have collapsed. The living and the dead seem occupy the same space. That which should be deceased and in the past has slipped its cold hand into ours.

Similarly, and no less viscerally is the recording of actual exorcisms, the cardinal example of which is perhaps 'The Jezebel Spirit' from one of the most significant albums of the post-punk period, *My Life in the Bush of Ghosts* (1981). Composed by Brian Eno and David Byrne, the album, as Cary Wolfe says, has an 'uncanny effect ... on almost everyone who hears it'.[62] 'Jezebel Spirit' includes a recording of a ritual carried out in New York by an unknown exorcist, samples of which are layered 'like disembodied ghosts over a shape-shifting bed of electronics and "found" percussion coaxed from garbage cans and ashtrays'.[63] As the voice of the exorcist confidently challenges the unclean spirit – 'out Jezebel, out, in Jesus' name' – a disturbed woman breathes heavily as the undead Princess of Tyre (see, 1 Kings 16–21) resists the process of deliverance. A profane biblical figure who, we are told, was thrown down from a window, trampled by horses and eaten by dogs had, according to the exorcist, returned and entered a woman in New York. While, of course, nowadays, few would find the bizarre beliefs informing such rituals credible, nevertheless, 'The Jezebel Spirit' introduces classic Gothic tropes relating to mortality and spectrality. It suggests what we instinctively want to believe. The self is permanent. Dead flesh in a coffin cannot be the end of me.

Another, more recent example of the use of exorcism is Rihanna's video for 'What Now' (*Unapologetic*, 2012). Although the song has no Gothic content as such, it being typical of the relational lyrics one would expect from Rihanna, she was very clear that she wanted to make the video 'kinda eerie' and 'very creepy'. As she put in an interview at the time, 'everyone's probably expecting a narrative type of video or a love story of some sort, or something really soft and pretty'. However, what she actually produced was a video that drew directly on her experiences of witnessing possession and exorcisms while growing up in Barbados: 'We would go to church and sometimes it would happen in church .... In the middle of a ceremony, somebody would just get up screaming and spinning out of control.... It's really like ... you can't control it, night and day.... They'd speak in a different voice.'[64] (Although not a believer in spirit possession myself, having witnessed such behaviours, I remember well the uncanny atmosphere evoked – a familiar person in a familiar setting with an unfamiliar voice.) In religious contexts, such experiences immediately suggest the ingress of the ghostly into the everyday. Using double-exposure, the video very effectively communicates what can only be imagined in deliverance culture, namely, the presence of two beings within a single person, the living and the dead in communion, the sacred and the profane in the same space.

Such discourses, of course, are central to Gothic, not least because it is 'an anti-historicising language, which provides ... the critical means of transferring an idea of the otherness of the past into the present'.[65] Although, anthropologically speaking, not all spirit possession can be construed as a conflation of past and present, nevertheless, within Gothic, possession through haunting is exactly this, a transference of the otherness of the past into the present. As is clearly articulated on both 'The Jezebel Spirit' and particularly *Ghosts on Magnetic Tape*, the past haunts the present and, as such, places a question mark against secular constructions of mortality. Our lives are not bookended by nothingness. Hence, again, discourses of the uncanny, while unnerving, are also life strategies for dealing with mortality. The power of the revenant, the force of that which has returned, that which has slipped its cold hand into ours, lies in the fact that mortality is faced, addressed and transcended. The experience of the uncanny turns our eyes towards death, towards the dissolution of the self, while suggesting that we can look through it into the unknown beyond where the self's permanence is assured.

Can the world be as sad as it seems?

Having discussed the general notion of 'popular music Gothic' in terms of popular music's ability (like all sonic environments) to evoke the uncanny and to encourage reflection on mortality, this section focuses more closely on 'Gothic popular music', on music that is shaped around contemporary Gothic tropes and betrays a preference for minor keys, descending melodies and foregrounded bass. Although, because contemporary Gothic has been so ubiquitously hybridized, it is somewhat artificial to restrict it to a particular movement, subculture or genre of music;[66] nevertheless, it does identify a particular 'field of discourse'[67] within which there are a number of core themes and musical ideas that make the concept a useful one.

Central to the Gothic field of discourse is reflection on the nature of mortality. Whether we think of the anthropomorphic personification of death as a bisexual goth girl in Neil Gaiman's graphic novel, *Death: The Time of Your Life,*[68] or the studied morbidity within much darkwave and industrial music, contemporary Gothic seeks to evoke particular affective spaces informed by reflection on a world of sadness, pain and dis-ease. 'This world is a cruel place/ And we're here only to lose/ So before life tears us apart let/ Death bless me.... This life ain't worth living.... Baby join me in death/ Won't you die' (H.I.M., 'Join Me In Death', *Razorblade Romance*, 1999).[69] Its discourses are fundamentally transgressive, in that they can be understood as an attempt to prise open fissures that run through the modern world by refusing to respect the socially constructed boundaries that distinguish death and life, sickness and health, past and present, profane and sacred. 'I am so tired, please just take me away/ Just let me lay down here for awhile .... Come to me, be with me, sink with me, die with me ... I'm so alone, please won't you come and be with me ... I breathe in this air, so humid and dark ... Loneliness adds to our beauty and our decay/ Sorrow is her name and she's mine' (Lycia, 'Sorrow is Her Name', *A Day in the Stark Corner*, 1993). 'I'm a doomed drug addict/And I always will be .... Don't want to live atrial fib, from neurosis, cirrhosis .... The pickup's easy, but the put down's rough/ Up the nose or tap a vein ... I can't believe I died last night, Oh God I'm dead again .... Recently buried deep in Greenwood Cemetery ... ' (Type O Negative, 'Dead Again', *Dead Again*, 2007). 'I see the children, I see all their scars/ I fear the monsters that don't know who they are .... When did this all start? When did I fall apart? ... I am too frightened to open my door/ I can't stop shaking as I drop to the floor .... Can you help me? Can you hear me? ... My hands, unfaithful, did not protect me .... What really happened during those nights?/ My voice, transparent, when I need it to scream/ I could not move so I just turned off inside .... Hear me now ...' (Switchblade Symphony, 'Fear', *The Three Calamities*, 1999). As these lyrics indicate, Gothic functions as a useful lens through which to examine some of the most unsettling themes relating to mortality, such as depression, morbidity, abuse and suicide. This is typical of the deeply affecting depression and suicide-oriented music by bands such as Nocturnal Depression (*Soundtrack for a Suicide: Opus II*, 2007), Uaral (*Sounds of Pain ...*, 2005) and ColdWorld (*The Stars Are Dead Now*, 2006), all of which explicitly focus on teenage angst and misery: 'I wear black on the outside/ Because black is how I feel on the inside' (The Smiths, 'Unloveable', *The World Won't Listen*, 1987). (We will return to these themes in Chapter 4.)

What became the 'Goth subculture' – a term now frequently contested[70] – initially coalesced around the confluence of a particular music, sartorial style and sensibility.[71] Emerging in the early 1980s, it can be traced back to a number of bands such as Siouxsie and the Banshees, Bauhaus, The Cure, Sex Gang Children, Theatre of Hate, The Sisters of Mercy, Southern Death Cult, Flesh for Lulu, Danse Society, The March Violets, Play Dead, Gene Loves Jezebel, The Birthday Party, Christian Death and 45 Grave, and to clubs such as particularly London's Batcave. From the outset, central to this culture has been the expression of key Gothic themes, informed by ideas drawn from earlier boundary-crossing artists and movements, such as the glam-androgyny of Marc Bolan and David Bowie.[72] Musically, it was a development of the dark, urban, post-punk bands such as Joy Division and Throbbing Gristle. As Dean Lockwood discusses, to a large extent, the principal features of this embryonic British influence has its roots in a 'claustrophobic Northern Gothic … foregrounding a diabolical, vertical inheritance of corrupting, intoxicating and maddening forces'. As such, it is, he suggests, 'an important tributary of twenty-first-century Gothic, flowing into what is an increasingly pervasive and commodified current of "extreme" culture. Both post-punk and Gothic exult in extremes, in ruination, in dislocation and disquietude.'[73] Distorted, down-tuned guitars, foregrounded basslines and earnest vocal delivery conspired to produce 'an aural melancholia that has since become central to Goth style.'[74] However, rather than trawling through the short history of goth rock, its antecedents, its associated cultural tributaries and the contested boundaries between the increasingly refined and esoteric sub-genres, we are interested here simply in the social significance of goth morbidity in popular music.

There are few better musical moments to begin a discussion of the core themes in Gothic popular music than *Closer* (1980), Joy Division's most ethereal and claustrophobic work. It was described by its producer, Martin Hannett, as being 'kabbalistic', because he felt that it appeared to be 'locked in its own mysterious world'.[75] The listener does not have to spend much time with the album to understand what he means. There is something troubling and uneasy about *Closer* – uncanny. From the moment of its release, it was embedded within a Gothic field of discourse. Ian Curtis, the band's troubled lyricist and lead singer, hung himself on 18 May 1980, shortly after the album was recorded and two months prior to its release on 18 July. As soon as the band's grieving and shocked fans sat down with the album, it was clear to them that they were essentially listening to a suicide note, a document detailing the thoughts of an unhappy and conflicted man. Having said that, Joy Division fans were not unused to Curtis's morbidity. Reading through his lyrics since the band's planned debut album, *Warsaw* (eventually released in 1994) – which have been helpfully reprinted by his widow, Deborah Curtis, in her book *Touching From a Distance*[76] – it is clear that he rarely shied away from reflection on mortality. For example, 'She's Lost Control', a popular single from Joy Division's actual debut album, *Unknown Pleasures* (1979), draws directly on his friendship with a young epileptic girl at a rehabilitation centre in which he worked and who later died during a fit: 'And she screamed out kicking on her side and said/ I've lost control again/ And seized up on the floor, I thought she'd die/ She said I've lost control.'[77] A couple of points are worth noting here. First, Curtis was himself an epileptic who clearly identified with her suffering. Second, it is interesting that Freud described the condition as an 'uncanny disease'. It can, he reports, take the form of 'brief periods of *absence*, or rapidly passing fits of vertigo or … short spaces of time during which the patient does something out of the character, as though he were under the control of his unconscious'.[78] Curtis was haunted by this condition, which denied him control over everyday life and which threatened to deny him of life altogether. It is also important to understand that epileptics were, in the early 1980s, burdened further with a level of social stigma that is not common today. Hence, it is perhaps not surprising that he decided to flaunt the imperfection as a way of kicking against the pricks, so to speak. Not only did he sing about epilepsy, but his remarkable stage performance, his fit-like movements, his stare into the distance, evoked precisely this sense of the uncanny. It was as though he was performing epilepsy, providing a controlled reenactment of what, sadly, he could not control.

For *Closer*, however, his focus seems to have narrowed, and looking for inspiration, he increasingly immersed himself in literature that encouraged his morbidity. As Deborah Curtis recalls, 'it struck me that all Ian's spare time was spent reading and thinking about human suffering. I knew he was looking for inspiration for his songs, yet the whole thing was culminating in an unhealthy obsession with mental and physical pain.'[79] His morbidity on *Closer* is distilled into a particularly dark and melancholic example of 'northern Gothic': 'I fear every day, every evening…. Isolation, isolation, isolation/ Mother I tried, please believe me/ I'm doing the best that I can … ' ('Isolation'); 'This is the crisis I knew had to come/ Destroying the balance I'd kept/ Turning around to the next set of lives/ Wondering what will come next' ('Passover'); 'A cry for help, a hint of anesthesia/ The sound of broken homes/ We always used to meet here' ('Colony'); 'Existence, well, does it matter?/ I exist on the best terms I can/ The past is now part of my future/

The present is well out of hand' ('Heart and Soul'). 'A cloud hangs over me, marks every move .... Destiny unfolded, I watched it slip away .... A valueless collection of hopes and past desires .... Now that I've realized how it's all gone wrong/ Got to find some therapy, this treatment takes too long/ Deep in the heart of where sympathy held sway/ Gotta find my destiny, before it gets too late' ('Twenty-four Hours'). Although the evocative cover artwork for *Closer* by Peter Saville and Martyn Atkins was produced before his death, it was central to the Gothic aesthetic of the album, being organized around a photograph by Bernard Pierre Wolff of the Appiani family tomb in the Staglieno Monumental Cemetery in Genoa. The tomb, which includes Demetrio Paernio's sculpture of the body of Christ surrounded by mourners (*c.* 1910), the classical monument typeface used for the title and the tragedy behind the voice on the record all served to fetishize the album, to transform it into a powerful *memento mori*, an important text that encouraged earnest reflection on mortality. Dave Simpson's comments on why *Closer* became so important to him are worth noting here: 'My dad had died when I was young, and I'd always been susceptible to songs with references to mortality such as Terry Jacks's "Seasons in the Sun." ' However, he says, 'there was something more real and troubling about Joy Division's "New Dawn Fades" [*Unknown Pleasures*]. What kind of 22-year old writes lyrics such as "a loaded gun, won't set you free"? By the time their second album, *Closer*, was released only a few months later, Curtis had taken his own life. The clues were on the record in Colony's "The sound of broken homes/ We always used to meet here" and 24 Hours' "Destiny unfolded, I watched it slip away." '[80] Although devotees may quibble over whether Joy Division are musically 'Goth' or 'proto-Goth' or nothing of the sort, the argument is that the affective space into which that album cover, that music, those lyrics and that tragic life take us is one that is fundamentally Gothic, bringing us face to face with mortality and the Camusian struggle for meaning.

Even now, Mark Fisher argues, the music of Joy Division seems to capture 'the depressed spirit of *our* times .... From the start, their work was overshadowed by a deep foreboding, a sense of a future foreclosed, all certainties dissolved, only growing gloom ahead'.[81] Likewise, shaped by the dark urban spaces of Manchester during the late 1970s and 1980s, other northern musicians, such as, most enigmatically and idiosyncratically, Mark E. Smith of The Fall, have articulated a Gothic sensibility through their explorations of the disturbed minds that populated its streets, from the murdering physician Harold Shipman ('What About Us', *Fall*

Heads Roll, 2005) to tragic existences of the suicidal, the lonely and the misunderstood: 'I'm tired of walking/ Up and down the street all by myself/ No love left for me to give/ I try and try/ But no one wants me the way I am …. Maybe I'll just kill myself/I just don't care no more …. Who would care if I was gone?' ('I'm Not Satisfied', *Cerebral Caustic*, 1995). Again, in the 1990s, similar ideas were also reflected in post-rave culture. For example, the Future Sound of London's darkly Gothic (almost) instrumental album, *Dead Cities* (1996), transports the listener to a hopeless, post-apocalyptic, dystopian wasteland. More recently, these themes have been articulated in the work of artists such as the British dubstep producer Burial, whose debut album (*Burial*, 2006) is overcast with dark, brooding rhythms and rumbling bass.[82] Darker still, Matt Elliot's distinctive oeuvre (e.g. *The Mess We Made*, 2003; *Drinking Songs*, 2005; *Failing Songs*, 2006; *Howling Songs*, 2008), including his work as Third Eye Foundation (e.g. *The Dark*, 2010; *Ghost*, 2006), is exquisitely and playfully morbid, yet coloured by a deeply melancholic and jaundiced view of the world: 'When you can't stand the light when you wake/ You're reliving the same old mistake/ Just to escape the fear, you get fucked on your choice of gear/ It's the only choice round here/ If you'll top yourself anyway/ Why not bomb the stock exchange' ('Bomb the Stock Exchange', *Howling Songs*, 2008). Popular music consistently reflects the dominant discourses and everyday feelings of the masses. And, there are few of their experiences that engender reflection on mortality and the meaning of life than the experience of being disenfranchised, abandoned at the bottom of the social food chain, patronized by successive governments, terrorized by their systems of control and treated less as a person and more as an object, a problem requiring a solution.

Released the same year as *Closer*, and quoting Charles Manson, the Gothic sensibility was memorably summed on the cover of Throbbing Gristle's *Heathen Earth* (1980): '… can the world be as sad as it seems?' These words, originally uttered by a disturbed and profane figure who, perhaps more than anyone else, signified the end of the hippie dream of love and peace at the end of the 1960s, take us to the heart of the Gothic exploration of melancholia and mortality in the late 1970s. Again, they reflect – as I remember well – the significant social despondency that characterized northern Britain at the turn of the 1980s: urban decay, economic recession, grinding unemployment, industrial antagonism and debilitating pessimism. Gothic was ideal for exploring social ruin and hopelessness. Although the emphasis on surface, spectacle and performance can detach goths from the brutal realities of everyday life, nevertheless, the roots of the music lie in the experiences of disenfranchised youth living through a depressing period of British history. As Fisher reminds us, bands such as Joy Division and Throbbing Gristle 'connected not just because of what they were, but when they were. Mrs Thatcher just arrived, the long grey winter of Reagonomics on the way, the Cold War still feeding our unconscious with a lifetime's worth of retina-melting nightmares.' They were 'the sound of British culture's speed comedown, a long slow screaming neural shutdown'.[83]

Emerging out of this dark culture, as Gothic rock began to take shape during the 1980s, it increasingly indicated a boundary-crossing fascination with the dark corners of modernity, with ruin, with atrocity, with taboo and with depression. While a funereal corner of the foppish 'new romantic' dressing-up box was regularly raided in an effort to embody these ideas sartorially,[84] as it progressed into the 1990s, and as its discourse became increasingly influenced by themes articulated within Industrial music (such as those developed by Throbbing Gristle), there was a heightened sense that, as Nick Cave put it, we are 'entwined together in this culture of death' ('Abattoir Blues', *Abattoir Blues/The Lyre Of Orpheus*, 2004),[85] a culture of hopelessness, addiction, exploitation and depression. While the playfulness of horror increasingly shaped identities and contributed to the commercial potential of goth culture, the original substratum of morbidity has remained enormously important. Society was viewed in stark terms as – to quote Joy Division (following J.G. Ballard) – an 'Atrocity Exhibition' (*Closer*, 1980): 'Asylums with doors open wide ... the horrors of a faraway place ... mass murder on a scale you've never seen ....' These ideas have become memetic, spreading throughout popular music culture, combining most recently with the dark undercurrents of folk music in neo- or psych-folk.

Overall, while much Gothic rock makes good use of goth occulture (vampires, Victoriana, decadent aristocracy, profane religion, etc.), it is rooted in discourses about meaninglessness, death and decay. Other bands may have discussed these themes earlier in popular music history, but it was Joy Division and Ian Curtis who articulated these ideas to a new generation of disenfranchised youth. The preoccupation with melancholia and morbidity that formed Joy Division's discursive and sonic substratum quickly became central to the music of subsequent bands. For example, The Cult – a band that quickly evolved into a mainstream rock outfit following a brief 'Goth' period as the Southern Death Cult and then Death Cult – produced something of a goth anthem with 'She Sells Sanctuary' (*Love*, 1985). On the one hand, the song uses standard Gothic themes and tropes. On the other hand, the profane force from which Ian Astbury was seeking female sanctuary was the pressure of the sad, dark world that haunted Ian Curtis: 'And the world, the world turns around/ And the world, and the world, the world drags me down.' Very similar Gothic ideas were articulated two years earlier by Andrew Eldritch of The Sisters of Mercy. For example, their popular song 'Temple of Love' (1983) presents Curtis's melancholia in classic Gothic garb: 'And the tears he cried will rain on walls .... And the devil in black dress watches over/ My guardian angel walks away.' The song concludes with a reflection on mortality and meaninglessness: 'Life is short and love is always over in the morning/ Black wind come carry me far away.' Again, a similar emphasis on the impermanence of life and happiness was expressed in Bauhaus's 'Exquisite Corpse' (an archetypical Gothic title): 'Life is but a dream .... Now as the petals are no more/ A corroding, shrinking stalk remains/ Bereft of his blooms .... Now browning, sinking, dying' (*The Sky's Gone Out*, 1982). Although there is a fascination with horror imagery, with the imagined funereal laciness of Gothic aristocracy, with the sartorial elegance of foppish Victorian villainy and with the transgressive supernaturalism distilled in the various constructions of the vampire,[86] running through goth culture, from post-punk onwards, has been an interest in affective spaces evoked by melancholia and morbidity. Goth culture provides, as Catherine Spooner says, 'a language and a lexicon through which anxieties both personal and collective can be discussed'.[87]

This, of course, is not to say that goths are somehow, by nature, biased towards melancholia, morbidity and transgression. That would be ridiculous. They are not a separate species with distinct genetic traits – although some might imagine themselves to be so. They are people who choose to construct their identities around a particular set of interests. While, of course, some goths may be pathologically morbid (just as any person might be), most are only culturally attracted to 'the dark side' – although some may accrue subcultural capital by claiming a more pathological attraction. They have a penchant for the gloomy, which is expressed through material culture and taste, from coffin-shaped earrings to stuffed toys of the undead and from songs about vampires and faux occult rituals to music reflecting depression and suicide. This conflation of morbidity and playfulness is indicative of goth culture: 'Sex horror, sex bat, sex horror, sex vampire' (The Birthday Party, 'Release the Bats', 1981). As van Elferen notes (although perhaps a little too sweepingly), 'Goth, like Gothic, involves dwelling in the twilight zone enabled by the transgression of binaries, and making one-sided choices would un-Goth the process. Therefore Goths are not suicidal, Satanist, or nihilist – if these widely circulating prejudices regarding Goth reveal anything, it is the fact that the anxieties and desires surrounding such extremes signal social forms of the uncanny, an *Unheimlichkeit* that Gothic addresses.'[88] Nevertheless, while their interests might be more or less cosmetic, they are exposing themselves to affective spaces within which issues relating to mortality can be reflected upon.

However, again, although some goth music explores mortality close up, so to speak, typically it tends to observe death and decay from a safe distance. As Allan Lloyd Smith has noted of Gothic, it parallels postmodernism in that both are examples of 'an aesthetics of the surface, dominated by depthless image, divorced from attendant complications of reference.'[89] Focused on affect, it sanitizes mortality with intimations of the supernatural, with fashionable identities formed around bereavement, with poetic articulations of the grave as an aspirational bijou residence, and with the conflation of life and death: 'Death, death, death.... This is light.... Black is color/ Dark is this world/ Death is life ... I was born to mourn/ The grave is my home/ Who is the death giver?/ Life is a circle/ Death plays his role again' (Shadow Project, 'Death Plays His Role', *Shadow Project*, 1991). Mortality is deconstructed. The dead friend rests 'cold in his arms' and is laid 'on clammy ground'; death – 'Lying deep, six feet down' – is 'a dark paradise' (Shadow Project, 'Lying Deep', *Shadow Project*, 1991). Death is, in other words, *experienced* as pleasure. There is a sense in which the finality of death is subtly evaded, in that death is acknowledged, but as the *continuing experience* of the self.

Grotesque bodies

Visual art has been central to the construction of affective space throughout much of the history of recorded popular music. Before a record is placed on a turntable or a CD inserted into a player, a particular mood is created by the cover artwork. Indeed, much disappointing music has been bought on the strength of evocative cover art. 'Our aesthetic', says the artist Walter Velez, 'forces you to deal with being simultaneously enlightened and offended. It displays a keen sensitivity to universal fears, fantasies, frustrations, and stupidities.'[90] While this is a comment on Latin cover art, not only is it equally applicable to a broad range of album artwork, but it reveals the intention and the significance of much (not all) album design and marketing.[91] Of course, things have changed somewhat over the last couple of decades. Although video art is still central to the reception of individual tracks, the affective space evoked by digital albums is shaped far less by the accompanying artwork than it once was. Nevertheless, it is probably true to say that, because style and visual media are so central within Gothic occulture, popular music artwork has retained something of its initial significance.

The principal theme informing much goth visual art is mortality. Skulls, moonlit graveyards, cemetery sculptures, ravens, revenants, dying flora and fauna and so on are all prominent. However, while death and some suggestion of 'undeath' are important, also significant in goth culture is a fascination with that core experience of mortals, decay and putrefaction. There is a transgressive fascination with what modern society hides, with what Bonvesin de la Riva understood to be the grotesque and vile nature of the human condition. As we saw in Chapter 1, faced with the blood, bile and waste that naturally surrounds human existence, he became preoccupied with the repulsive processes of decay and decomposition. He was fascinated by the power of 'abjection', the power of that which disturbs the self by provoking fear, disgust and repulsion, yet which also intrigues and attracts.[92] In goth culture, while there is, typically, less of Bonvesin's focus on putrefaction – which, of course, was difficult to avoid in the thirteenth century – there is nevertheless a fascination with the processes of mortality and with the impermanence of the material world. Often, of course, this impermanence is explored in terms of the collapse of civilized, urban environments: the derelict house, the mouldering sanatorium, the ecclesiastical ruin and the overgrown garden. Here, where there was once colour, vibrancy, healing and life, there is now only gloom, silence, decomposition and death.[93] This of course reflects the same processes that bodies are subject to. Like buildings, they are formed, deformed, augmented, remade, possessed, neglected and decayed. Indeed, as Spooner comments, 'part of the capacity of Gothic texts to disturb derives from their presentation of the body as lacking wholeness and integrity, as a surface which can be modified and transformed'.[94] This constellation of Gothic ideas around transformation and impermanence has been central to constructions of the body in popular music, from the perennial interest in vampirism to a macabre fascination with the grotesque. Particularly evident in its visual art, there is an interest in romanticized images of decayed, violated, distorted and dead bodies.

The illustrator for some of the covers of Matt Elliot/Third Eye Foundation, the Russian-born, UK-based artist, Vania (Vania Zouravliov), focuses very closely on mortality, melancholia and religion. Sex and death, decay and beauty, violence and innocence, and sacred and profane are delicately mingled in beguiling illustrations that seem rooted in a Russian Orthodox morbidity. They are, in effect, a melancholic response to Manson's question, 'Can the world be as sad as it seems?' Like recorded memories from the dark spaces of modernity, they perfectly complement Elliot's music. Indeed, there are few artists and musicians whose work is so beautifully complementary. Hence, listeners who spend a few minutes with Vania's affecting illustrations for Elliot's albums on the Ici D'ailleurs label – *Drinking Songs* (2005), *Failing Songs* (2006), *Howling Songs* (2008) and *Failed Songs* (2010) – find themselves emotionally prepared for Elliot's hauntingly dark mortality music.

Perhaps the most arresting contemporary artist to focus on mortality is the photographer Joel-Peter Witkin, whose explorations of decay, deformity and death have found their way into popular music culture. Although the work of Vania and Witkin is distinctive in many respects, both are informed by a similar concern with human mortality and a desire to portray the beauty in death and decay. From Mark Romanek's video for 'Closer' by Nine Inch Nails (*Downward Spiral*, 1994), to the cover artwork for *Been Caught Buttering* (1991) by the Austrian death metal band Pungent Stench, and from the cover of *Grand Guignol* (1992) by John Zorn's Naked City to the back cover of *Failing Songs* (2006) by Matt Elliot (an illustration by Vania clearly inspired by Witkin's work), his photography and influence is conspicuous in transgressive milieux. Frequently photographing posed corpses and body parts, he claims to have been moved at a young age by witnessing a macabre accident, which fixed in his mind the relationship between religion and mortality. Indeed, much of his work is informed by a conspicuous Catholic piety:

> It happened on a Sunday when my mother was escorting my twin brother and me down the steps of the tenement where we lived. We were going to church. While walking down the hallway to the entrance of the building, we heard an incredible crash mixed with screaming and cries for help. The accident involved three cars, all with families in them. Somehow, in the confusion, I was no longer holding my mother's hand. At the place where I stood at the curb, I could see something rolling from one of the overturned cars. It stopped at the curb where I stood. It was the head of a little girl. I bent down to touch the face, to speak to it – but before I could touch it someone carried me away.[95]

This attempt to communicate with the dead is continued in his photography. The grotesque is conceptually distanced from putrefaction, but the viewer is brought face to face with the grotesque underbelly of mortality – so much so that Zorn's record company, Nonesuch, refused to release the album with Witken's artwork. (Zorn withdrew the album and released it on his own label, along with a number of other albums with equally confrontational covers.)[96]

People with distorted bodies inhabit a world in which they define beauty. The cadaver is arranged in such a way that it still appears to want to engage us. There is a sense in which the biological constraints of mortality are transcended. This sense of transcendence is further encouraged by his subtle and playful use of Christian signification.

While Witkin would probably resist his work being identified as 'Gothic', nevertheless, Spooner's comments on his significance in this respect are perceptive: 'Witkin's work, while perhaps the most thoroughly and consistently Gothic of any contemporary artist, ultimately signals a change in Gothic sensibilities. While the performativity of the images, their claustrophobia, their pastiched historical context, their uncanniness and sheer horror, are long-established Gothic properties, their restoration of the spirit to the suffering flesh seems to point to a new kind of Gothic revival, a spirituality for our times.'[97] Similarly, Charles Hagen notes that, while his 'gruesome images are shocking, exerting a primal, voyeuristic appeal', nevertheless, 'they allude to deep mysteries of death and physical existence. Contemplating them in the antiseptic confines of a gallery or museum can take on a quasi-metaphysical tinge.'[98] Something of this is revealed on the cover of Pungent Stench's *Been Caught Buttering*, which uses Witkin's 'The Kiss' (1982), a photograph of an amorous encounter between two severed, decomposing heads. Although it is actually a photograph of two halves of the same head, which Witkin had separated and arranged, nevertheless, there is a sense in which wills and urges of the self remain. That is to say, while the photograph – and, indeed, the macabre and violent songs on the album – functions as a *memento mori*, reminding us that we too will soon become putrefying still life objects, there is something pointing us beyond that fact, something that transcends the grotesque processes of mortality.

More evocative still is Romanek's use of Witkin's work in his video for 'Closer' (Nine Inch Nails, *The Downward Spiral*, 1994), a song by Trent Reznor inspired by the title of the Joy Division album.[99] Although the song is typically interpreted as a celebration of sadomasochism – its most memorable lyric being, 'I want to fuck you like an animal' – it is, in fact, much like Ian Curtis's reflections on *Closer*, a deeply disturbing articulation of self-loathing. A tormented man, in search of meaning, abandons himself to the intense experiences found in sex: 'Help me/ I broke apart my insides/ Help me/ I've got no soul to sell/ Help me/ The only thing that works for me/ Help me get away from myself.... My whole existence is flawed.... You can have my isolation/ You can have the hate that it brings/ You can have my absence of faith/ You can have my everything.' The video draws on the painful experience of mortality through its use of Witkin's ideas and images. Sepia-tinted references to decay, impermanence and ageing remind one of the brevity of human life. Dust, cobwebs, a soiled toilet, a beating heart on a chair, a pig's head on a spike, a crucified monkey, hung sides of meat that appear as profane angelic wings, a human head on a plate surrounded by fruit, a child's skeleton and cockroaches all narrow the viewer's focus on the processes and consequences of mortality. The artificially beating heart, the mechanical references and the anatomical drawings all suggest 'a soft machine' (to use William Burroughs term for the human body), destined to become obsolete at some point. We are little more than a mechanism. Having said that, again, while the video is a reminder of corporeal fragility and impermanence, Reznor and Romanek also articulate the Camusian quest for meaning in an apparently meaningless universe: 'Help me become somebody else .... You get me closer to God .... You are the reason I stay alive!' Reznor's attempt to find meaning in the extreme, liminal experiences of sex comes very close to Bataille's quest for 'inner experience' through 'states of ecstasy, of rapture ... of mediated emotion ...'.[100] Through immersion in 'an experience laid bare, free of ties,'[101] there is an attempt to transcend the constraints of embodied existence. Indeed, following Witkin, Romanek's use of religious signifiers suggests that such experiences might be conceived of in terms of mystical moments, in which there is a going beyond or outside of oneself. In other words, there is an expressed hope that intense experience will provide moments of temporary release from the pressure of being mortal. These are moments when Reznor feels 'closer to God', moments which inject his life with meaning. In Bauman's terms, this is immortality deconstructed, a life sliced up into brief experiences of transcendence, which serve to distract the experiencer from the wider implications of mortality.

The mise-en-scène of Romanek's film is organized around the idea of grotesque mortality. Although we have noted the hints of transcendence, which reflect those in Witkin's photography, the human is primarily portrayed as tortured flesh, emotionally disturbed meat, a vulnerable soft machine. Typical of contemporary Gothic, which is, as Spooner observes, 'more obsessed with bodies than in any of its previous phases', human flesh becomes 'spectacle, provoking disgust, being modified, reconstructed and artificially augmented'.[102] This concern, which is abundantly evident in popular music's fascination with the grotesque, can be understood in terms of Mikhail Bakhtin's theory of the body, which he formulated on the basis of his observation of 'the compelling difference between the human body as represented in popular festivity and the body as represented in classical statuary in the Renaissance'.[103] Usually elevated on a pedestal, viewed from below, closed, 'with no openings or orifices', affectively detached from its viewer, static and disengaged, the classical body can be understood as distant and, in this sense, 'disembodied'.[104] It is a body, in other words, that is not subject to the normal processes of mortality. Statuary immortalizes corporeality, separating it from decay, waste, decrepitude and death. Its approach to mortality could not be more different than that taken by Witkin, Romanek, Reznor, Elliot and Vania. In closing bodily orifices, it restricts the body's engagement with the external world, hiding all signs of inner life processes and bodily functions. Farting, urination, defecation, menstruation and even breast feeding in public all become taboo. Statuary ignores all evidence of fecundation and pregnancy, eliminating bodily protrusions and obscuring signs of mortality. The aim is to present an image of a completed, rational, individual body.

It is this approach to the human form which became reified in the West as a 'bodily canon', shaped and maintained by a culture uneasy with the facts of the human condition. Its sanitized, polished interpretation of corporeality is, of course, conspicuous in the body-perfect, 'I'm gonna live forever' (Michael Gore, *Fame*, 1980) culture evident throughout much of the world of popular music. Indeed, we have seen that much popular music is typical of what Bauman identifies as a postmodern life strategy, in that the self focuses on 'the eternal now', 'the majestic moment',[105] in order to capture a sense of symbolic immortality. Within these moments, during which the ghosts of death and decay are exorcized, there is an immersion in the experience of the perfect, classical, unchanging, 'immortal' body.

While this is undoubtedly the case, and while one cannot understand much popular music culture apart from the postmodern deconstruction of immortality, nevertheless, there is, in some genres, an attempt to embrace the 'grotesque body'. As Bakhtin argued, it still persists in the modern world, particularly in the folkloric imagination and in humour. Images of the grotesque body

> predominate in extra-official life of the people. For example, the theme of mockery and abuse is almost entirely bodily and grotesque. The body that figures in all the expressions of the unofficial speech of the people is the body that fecundates and is fecundated, that gives birth and is born, devours and is devoured, drinks, defecates, is sick and dying. In all languages there is a great number of expressions related to genital organs, the anus and buttocks, the belly, the mouth and nose.[106]

Popular music, of course, is central to 'the extra-official life of the people'. Even if compromised by the contemporary fetishization of statuary corporeality and diluted by cultural strategies to evade mortality, nevertheless, large areas of popular music – particularly those organized around a Gothic sensibility – embrace the grotesque. Through their transgression of taboos, their carnivalesque disregard of the politics of politeness and respectability, and their creative and enthusiastic engagement with carnality, they challenge the official bodily canon in the West. This is evident in John Landis's groundbreaking video for Michael Jackson's 'Thriller' – which includes stylized, sexually provocative portrayals of the living dead – and playfully grotesque album covers such as Carcass's *Reek of Putrefaction* (1988), as well as in the explicit and disturbing performances of artists such as Genesis P-Orridge and Kevin Michael 'GG' Allin. The latter, for example, embraced the grotesque during his notorious live performances, including defecation, coprophagia and self-mutilation. A troubled man, he even planned to commit suicide on stage, the execution of which was preempted by an accidental heroin overdose on 28 June 1993. Having anticipated his death, he had indicated his wishes for his funeral in his song, 'When I Die' (*The Troubled Troubadour*, 1990). Indeed, few human activities and bodily fluids have not found there way into performances of popular music over the years.

The argument is that, on the one hand, in cultures that distance us from the processes of mortality, the popular music industry typically reflects this obfuscation of mortality by trading in myths of the eternal body beautiful, insisting on white-toothed happiness as normative and promoting the received bodily canon of rational, statuary perfection. On the other hand, popular music also offers reflection upon human corporeality *in extremis*, forcing us to engage with the unappealing reality of the human condition. We are transported – at a safe distance – to an affective space within which defilement, decrepitude and destruction can be thought about.

Concluding comments

'Infidel to all creeds. Breaker of all vows. Enemy of happy ends. Confidant to the dead.' These words printed on the booklet accompanying Moonspell's *Moon in Mercury* (2008) identify not only the penchant for transgression typical of the liminal cultures of popular music, but also an orientation towards melancholia and morbidity. In *Goth Chic*, Gavin Baddeley's popular emic text for the 'darkly inclined', he describes 'a passion for a life draped in the symbolism of death'.[107] Popular music Gothic, in its struggle to pull away from the mainstream, to hide from its light, to create a culture that is Other, a culture that feeds on the forbidden, bends the gaze of its listeners towards death, decay and excess. In so doing, it challenges the hegemonic fetishization of health and happiness in Western societies. The Cure's *Pornography* (1982), a claustrophobic study in self-loathing fuelled by Robert Smith's depression, is a good example of this, as is, from a quite different perspective, the Appalachian Gothic articulated in the music of The Handsome Family: 'There are birds in the darkness that nest in wooden crutches/Eyepatches and bandages, broken spinal columns/Pots of withered plants/Birds you cannot see, filling every tree, falling out of closets and perched on the hands of dying men' ('Birds You Can Not See', *Twilight*, 2001).

We have noted, however, that much of this interest in mortality is often focused on surface, affect and nostalgia for an imagined past. Death and decay are viewed at a safe distance. Although some compositions are the result of an artist's actual melancholia and morbidity, as in the case of Joy Division's Ian Curtis, and although some artists, such as Nick Cave, do seek to grapple with the brutality of existence, generally speaking, we have seen that the treatment of mortality in popular music is what Ernest Becker refers to as an 'immortality project'.[108] That is to say, in a similar way to the immortality projects of religion, it tends to function as a denial of death. Popular music Gothic provides another way of making us feel better about mortality and of dealing with our worries about the impermanence of the self. Death and decay are sanitized and alluring. 'We find beauty in the macabre',[109] says Rebecca Schraffenberger. Gothic encourages, as Moonspell put it, attitudes that resist happy ends and embrace the dead. Mortality is dressed up, made attractive, sexy and, in the final analysis, impotent: the welcome death, the exquisite corpse and the beautiful undead. Pain, disease, decrepitude, putrefaction and bereavement are invested with new meaning in the affective spaces evoked by popular music Gothic.

Through its intertextual and musical evocation of the uncanny and its playful references to the undead, mortality is explored at arm's length. This, however, does not detract from its social significance. Such discourses, articulated through the powerful affective medium of popular music, not only provide a challenge to a society troubled by the impermanence of the self and distracted by an obsession with 'immortality projects' (both secular and religious), but they also inoculate listeners against the denial of death. That is to say, popular music Gothic injects into the lives of listeners a resemblance of mortality. As such, it introduces young people in particular to that which society would deny them. It is this that is important about popular music Gothic as *memento mori*. 'Death looms large', says Nick Cave, 'because it should'.[110] Just as medieval and early modern epitaphic *memento mori* formulas were designed to encourage self-reflection, so the discourses of popular music are likely to have a similar effect.

Finally, the world of Gothic is, of course, a modern world, in that it is only in an ostensibly secular modernity that death, the undead and the demonic can be exhumed from profane ground and cannibalized in order to draw energy into the construction of affective spaces with little risk of genuine angst. In premodern cultures, ideas that now furnish the Gothic imagination were too real, too close. The consequences of sin and the downward progress of the unsanctified soul were too awful to contemplate. Gothic can only really be a modern discourse if it is also to be popular. Hence, while, on the one hand, it can be interpreted as a reaction to the erosion of the supernatural in modern societies, which struggle with mortality, on the other hand, it is a product of that erosion. In its subversion of the brutal rationalism of modernity, the Gothic imagination ventures into the enchanted shadowlands of Western culture to summon the spirits, demons, revenants and forces of darkness, precisely because it is not itself vulnerable to the menace and angst such boundary crossing would have occasioned in premodern cultures. Had Schraffenberger or Moonspell, for example, been living in the twelfth century, they would not have found 'beauty' in 'what is dreadful and forbidding'; they would not have embraced the 'sinister' as a way of dealing with the 'brutality' of life; they would not have flaunted their 'deep-rooted attraction to anything mysterious and supernatural'[111]; and nor would they have claimed to be confidants of the dead. It is only because they are modern individuals shaped by a broadly secular culture that they can seek enchantment in the shadows and delight in the frisson of fear evoked by the cultivation of cosmetic morbidity.

Morbidity, Violence and Suicide

A morbid fascination with watching acts of violence seems endemic in contemporary culture: 'I was just a boy when I sat down/ To watch the news on TV/ I saw some ordinary slaughter/ I saw some routine atrocity' (Nick Cave, 'Nature Boy', 2004). While it is true that 'torture, blood, guts, despair, and destruction' are, as Victoria Nelson observes, 'the thirteen-year-old boy's Gothick rule of horror',[1] not only has the liminal interest in violence and gore been extended beyond adolescence into adulthood and interpreted in increasingly extreme ways in popular culture, but there is now, as she discusses, a growing fascination with what David Edelstein has referred to as 'torture porn' – the voyeuristic and sadistic obsession with increasingly violent and sadistic images. And, although there has been much discussion of this disturbing trend in modern cinema and the media,[2] the same themes are evident in popular music culture. Of course, having said that, the history of human culture is replete with discourses of cruelty and violence. Certainly, throughout the history of popular music, there has been a steady stream of songs about the dark corners of human life. From early folk songs such as the fertility ballad 'John Barleycorn', which describes the harvest metaphorically as a human slaying, and murder songs, such as 'Tom Dooley', a North Carolina song about the killing of Laura Foster in 1866 in Wilkes County (a version of which was recorded by The Kingston Trio in 1958), to Jimi Hendrix's 1966 hit, 'Hey Joe' – 'I said where you goin' with that gun in your hand?/ I'm goin' down to shoot my old lady' – it is difficult to avoid abjection and aggression in popular music. However, over the last few decades, there has been a particular concentration on extreme violence and gore. For example, one only has to think of the recent disturbing compositions within death metal and grindcore, the band names of which provide some indication of the popular themes explored: Autopsy, Cannibal Corpse, Carcass, Cephalic Carnage, Circle of Dead Children, Dying Fetus, Gore Beyond Necropsy, Impaled, Macabre, Mortician, Napalm Death, Prostitute Disfigurement, Suffocation, Trigger the Bloodshed and so on.

A vortex of summons and repulsion

While we will see that the articulation of violence in popular music is not always an example of 'the thirteen-year-old boy's Gothick rule of horror', much of it is. That is to say, it betrays the excitement of the profane, the playful revelling in the humour of offense, the sense of being Other than 'the mainstream', and the liminal accumulation of subcultural capital through an identification with the abject[3]– the transgressive Other.[4] As Audrey Sylvain of the French post-punk/black metal band Amesoeurs comments, 'to spit and shit on society … is a teenage reflex'.[5] Nevertheless, understandably, popular music's identification with abjection has led to expressions of moral concern and to claims that it has been implicated in acts of violence, suicide and murder.[6] Campaign groups, such as particularly the Parents' Music Resource Center (PMRC),[7] worried that it glorified, promoted and, as the court cases against Ozzy Osbourne and Judas Priest failed to establish,[8] explicitly incited aggression. Moreover, the very fact that popular music is directly related to the profanation of childhood and adolescence has always tended to magnify its perceived threat. That is to say, it explicitly confronts fundamental sacred forms relating to the family unit and is therefore perceived as striking at the heart of society. Good children from good homes are being defiled and parental authority is being undermined. Consequently, there is an emotional reaction/'moral panic' relating to the perception that society – 'civilized society' – is itself being threatened by popular music. This concern becomes particularly vocal when the perception appears to have been validated by extreme acts of violence, such as the Columbine shootings and other atrocities committed by youths with an interest in popular music.[9]

The response to such accusations from within, for example, heavy metal studies has typically been one of emic incredulity.[10] Part of the reason for this is perhaps, as Michelle Phillipov discusses, because the study of heavy metal emerged shortly after the height of the moral panic surrounding it in the 1980s.[11] Hence, academics, who are often fans as well, tended to focus on 'debunking such claims of connections between metal, violence and other problematic behaviours. Controversies in which metal music is implicated as a contributor to violence are typically understood by scholars as being fabricated by conservative groups seeking to impose their own moral agendas on those with different values, tastes, and cultural practices.'[12] Certainly, as I have myself argued,[13] there is more than a grain of truth to such claims. However, as Phillipov comments, while extreme metal may 'not "cause" violence in any straightforward way', and while it 'is rarely as extreme as its critics suggest', nevertheless, 'not all claims of a link between music and violence are entirely fabricated'.[14] Although it is, as Matthew Sampar says, 'foolish to disregard outside societal forces and suggest that one single song or artist is responsible for the violent actions of a heavy metal fan',[15] nevertheless, if music is, as we have argued, a prosthetic technology, a technology of the self, in that it has become one of the central ways in which many of us organize memory and identity, then it is unsurprising that it guides thought and action to some extent.[16] That is to say, while it would be naïve to blame a song, a band or a genre for an act of violence committed by a fan, nevertheless, we should not then disregard, as a contributory factor, the music an individual listens to.

It is worth noting at this point that this chapter is not interested in discussing the supposed culpability of the music industry and the arguments for and against censorship. Nor is it concerned to provide a catalogue of abjection, which trawls over the details of music-related murders and suicides. Rather, it is interested in abjection per se, in the relationship between popular music, anomie and aggression. While humans are anxious about the impermanence of the self – which is increased by the awareness that their lives might be cut short at any moment by some unforeseen act of violence – nevertheless, they are intrigued by fictional and non-fictional narratives of sadistic aggression that highlight that impermanence. There seems to be, as Julia Kristeva put it, 'a vortex of summons and repulsion'. The abject 'beseeches, worries, and fascinates desire.'[17] Hence, while Steven Pinker may very well be right that we are all becoming more civilized, less prone to the direction of our inner demons, and more influenced by 'the better angels of our nature',[18] nevertheless, we are fascinated by discourses of violence in the media and in popular culture. This contributes to the cultivation of a culture of fear, within which even those of us who have never experienced violence feel threatened. Again, popular music reflects and articulates this 'culture of fear'. As the Thievery Corporation put it, 'Maybe we're just so used to it at this point that it's just a part of us/ Part of our culture …. Culture of fear … I've never seen the threat/ Yet I feel threatened …' ('Culture of Fear', *Culture of Fear*, 2011). I feel threatened because the discourses of extreme violence, putrefaction and death on which the media and popular culture feed bring me to what Kristeva has called 'the border of my condition as a living being'.[19]

The fascination with gore is particularly interesting in this respect, in that the corpse and dismembered body parts are perceived as polluting. Death infects life.[20] In fact, as Kristeva says, all forms of bodily waste signify 'the other side of the border, the place where I am not' – the Other which threatens the self. Excrement, which is much referenced in liminal cultures, as it is in school playgrounds, is, in the final analysis, a putrid *memento mori*, a reminder of our impermanence and the fragility of our existence. Hence, the articulation of violence, decay and death is always perceived as 'a border that has encroached upon everything. It is no longer I who expel', as in the case of excrement, but rather ' "I" is expelled.'[21] Our fate is to become the waste, the excrement of life, the risk of infection that requires disposal. As such, reflection on violence, waste and death highlights our anxiety concerning the vulnerability of the self. 'The abject confronts us … with those fragile states where man strays on the territories of *animal*. Thus, by way of abjection, primitive societies have marked out a precise area of their culture in order to remove it from the threatening world of animals or animalism, which were imagined as representatives of sex and murder.'[22] The problem is that, regardless of our cultural strategies to imagine ourselves differently, we humans are in fact animals, vulnerable to aggression and decay. It is the articulation of this sense of vulnerability in popular music that concerns us in this chapter.

Thanatos, survival and *schadenfreude*

In *Beyond the Pleasure Principle*,[23] Freud sought to explain why those patients of his who had experienced 'traumatic neuroses'[24] during the First World War seemed not to be able to achieve psychic stability. Although the 'pleasure principle' – that instinctual human drive to seek pleasure and to avoid pain, which he believed necessary to satisfy basic biological and psychological needs – might be thought of in terms of a regulating mechanism, which would return the damaged psyche back to health, it seemed to be inhibited in some way. He concluded that it had been interrupted by a more powerful drive. The 'tendency towards stability'[25] was in fact pulling in a different direction, to that which he had anticipated. There seemed to be a 'death drive' (*Todestrieb*). The reason for this, he concluded, is that we carry an inherent awareness that, in death, the struggles and tensions of life are resolved, and prenatal homeostasis is ultimately retrieved. Indeed, there is a bias in all forms of organic life to return to an inorganic state. We emerge from nothingness and travel to nothingness and in that nothingness of non-life there is perfect stability and 'rest'. Consequently, counterintuitive though it may seem, the goal of life is death – perceived as the end of the strife, flux and mutability that defines organic life. Hence, we might expect (as discussed in Chapter 1) this return to inorganic rest to manifest in religion and culture. For example, in Nick Cave's 'Knockin' on Joe' (*The Firstborn Is Dead*, 1985), the protagonist, who awaits execution on death row, is torn between protest at his fate and relief that a troubled life is nearing its end: 'You can lay your burdens down here.... You can't hurt me anymore.' Again, on the same album, he sings of a 'Wanted Man' who 'won't lay down', who keeps running, yet 'who's lost his will to live' and simply wants to return 'home', to return to where he is 'not wanted', not pursued anymore: 'there's one place I'm not wanted Lord/ It's the place that I call home'. It would be a contradiction to the conservative nature of the instincts, says Freud,

> if the goal of life were a state of things that had never yet been attained. On the contrary, it must be an *old* state of things, an initial state from which the living entity has at one time or other departed and to which it is striving to return.... If we are to take it as a truth that everything living dies for *internal* reasons – becomes inorganic once again – then we shall be compelled to say that *'the aim of all life is death'* and, looking backwards, that *'inanimate things existed before living ones'*.[26]

Hence, there is a tension between the 'death drive' (what Freud's follower, Wilhelm Stekel, referred to as 'Thanatos') and Eros – the life-drive/sexual drive, which is linked to the need for self-preservation and survival. While Eros is a restless force, the death drive is its opposite, the pull towards equilibrium.[27]

It is also worth noting that, while the death drive is typically directed inwardly towards the dissolution of the self, the energy generated can also be turned outwardly towards violence and the destruction of others. This, in part, is an attempt to establish the release of tension that only the dissolution of the self can deliver. The point, however, is that 'beyond the pleasure principle' there is a basic drive towards the homeostasis of non-life, which accounts for both melancholia and, when turned outward, aggression. Again, much of the rest of the chapter will focus on these states.

While this concept has been a popular one, having been developed by thinkers such as Kristeva, Jacques Lacan and Slavoj Žižek, it is contested in psychoanalysis.[28] That said, it usefully identifies a number of points central to our discussion of mortality. For example, following Lacan, Žižek understands the death drive to refer to dark compulsions to repeat anxiety-inducing, yet fascinating behaviours from the sublime to the obscene. It is the loop of obsessively returning to that which eludes capture that identifies it as a drive, rather than simply an instinct. This is the troubled vortex of human existence.

Hence, as understood here, it is closely linked to abjection. As discussed in studies of horror films,[29] the appeal of that which repels seems insatiable. We are both attracted and repelled by depictions of the dissolution of other selves. As such, we are, like moths perilously circling a flame, fixated on the subject of mortality, on our condition of impermanence – 'condemned to circle around it.'[30] We are bewitched by the 'drive' itself because the need to come to terms with the dissolution of the self is never met. Indeed, for Žižek, we should 'not confuse the death drive with the so-called "*nirvana* principle", the thrust toward destruction or self-obliteration'. Hence, departing from the standard Freudian interpretation of the death drive, he argues that it 'has nothing whatsoever to do with the craving for self-annihilation, for the return to the inorganic absence of any life-tension; it is, on the contrary, the very opposite of dying – a name for the "undead" eternal life itself, for the horrible fate of being caught in the endless repetitive cycle of wandering around in guilt and pain.'[31] My point here is simply that, in our own analysis of the problem of mortality, we need not abandon the principle thrust of Freud's thesis to accept aspects of Žižek's. There is, within popular music, an articulation of the Freudian desire to be free of life-tension, which, we will see, is explicit in songs about melancholia and suicide. There is also the exposition of abjection and the constant returning to that which disturbs, which, we will see, is evident in songs about violence, gore and death. Indeed, it is this abjection, this 'vortex of summons and repulsion,'[32] that typically drives the discourses of mortality in popular music. As the French musician Neige (Stéphane Paut) noted regarding 'the dehumanization, the anxiety, the stress, and the sadness that stem from modern life', which are abundantly evident in cities, 'it fascinates me as much as it disgusts me.'[33]

With this in mind, I want to return to Bauman's analysis of mortality. 'We are not just alive; at every moment we are *still* alive. Success is always an "until further notice" success; it is never final. It must be repeated over and over again. The effort can never grind to a halt. Survival is a lifelong task.'[34] Again, we are in a vortex of forever returning to reflection both on our mortality and also on the fact that we are *still* alive. As Styx put it in their song 'Not Dead Yet', from their 1990 album *Edge of the Century*, which became popular with Gulf War troops,[35] 'Go out, get drunk, get wild, have fun … I'm not dead yet … I'm a mad dog fighting with the wall against my back … I've been machine-gunned, handgunned, hijacked, left for dead/ Dive-bombed, napalmed, nuclear warheaded/ Dropped from a jet plane with no parachute .... And I can still crawl and I'm not dead yet.' However, and this is significant, survival needs to be distinguished from the notion of 'self-preservation'. The idea of self-preservation, Bauman argues (again, drawing heavily on thought of Canetti), 'hides or beautifies the gruesome truth of survival. Survival is targeted on others, not on the self. Though we never live through our own death, we do live through the deaths of others, and their death gives meaning to our success: we have not died, *we* are *still* alive.'[36] And, as the economist Richard Layard has discussed, social comparison is central to the production of happiness. How our lives compare to those of others us fundamentally important to most humans. For example, 'people care greatly about their relative income, and they would be willing to accept a significant fall in living standards if they could move up compared to other people.'[37] Hence, to some extent, people thrive on *schadenfreude*. As Bauman puts it, 'I would not conceive of my own performance as a success if it were not for the fact that performances of others proved unsuccessful; I can only measure my own performances against those other performances. I want to know what I should do to escape or to postpone the other's lot – to *outlive* others. Others died of smoking; perhaps if I don't smoke, I'd survive them?'[38] The knowledge that we are alive while others are dead is at the heart of our experience of mortality and central, I suggest, to the death drive and to our experience of abjection. On the one hand, another's death reminds me of my own mortality and diminishes me to some extent.

> No man is an island, entire of itself; every man is a piece of the continent, a part of the main. If a clod be washed away by the sea, Europe is the less, as well as if a promontory were, as well as if a manor of thy friend's or of thine own were: any man's death diminishes me, because I am involved in mankind, and therefore never send to know for whom the bells tolls; it tolls for thee (John Donne, 'Meditation XVII', *Devotions upon Emergent Occasions*, 1624).[39]

Donne's point is, of course, an important one. As Alison Stone argues, there are two principal reasons why humans fear death: 'Firstly, we each have grounds to fear our own deaths because these will mark the end to the unique webs of relations of which we are constituted, and to which we are necessarily attached because these relations constitute us. Secondly,' she says, 'we have grounds to fear death on behalf of the related others who will also be caught up in the death, because my death is also the death of a part of those others.'[40] That said, while these relationally positive points are true, on the other hand, at some brute level, the death of another inevitably highlights my current success as a mortal: 'I'm not dead yet.'

While this innate *schadenfreude* need not be brutal, of course, it often is – and is frequently portrayed as such in popular culture. 'This is a dramatic, tragic vision of the inner tendency of *survival*', says Bauman.

> One wonders to what extent this tendency is truly *inner* (or innate); one is entitled to suspect that the destructive edge of survival is sharpened (and even more probably directed) by the socially organized setting in which the activity of survival takes place. It is this setting that may (or may not) arrange the survival as a zero-sum game, and then split the habitat into a part that is threatening and has to be subdued or better still annihilated, and another part whose well-being enhances the chance of my own survival; this is what most societies have been doing all along, and continue to do.[41]

In other words, murder can be understood as being located at the radical extreme of survival, in that murderers survive their victims. The killer, says Canetti, 'wants to kill so that he can survive others; he wants to stay alive so as not to have others surviving him.'[42] Of course, there are numerous social and psychological factors that lead a person to kill, but here Bauman and Canetti are identifying a 'drive' relating to the human awareness of mortality. There is a constellation of reasons for our complex relationship to violence and death, which can be understood in terms of the tension between, on the one hand, the desire to survive others, to bolster our futile quest for immortality, and, on the other hand, the innate awareness that, in death, the struggles and tensions of life are resolved. As such, we can appreciate Žižek's comments regarding the repetitive cycle of being drawn to that which repels and to Kristeva's thoughts on abjection. In other words, first, our innate *schadenfreude*, our quest for immortality, which is engendered by the feeling that we have survived others, is encouraged by discourses of violence and death. Others die; we survive. Although disturbing, at some primal level this probably applies to many of us – although, of course, we can interpret it positively as an entirely legitimate celebration of life. Second, discourses of violence and death – which we will see are common in popular music – not only highlight our survival, but they also identify our own vulnerability and impermanence as mortals. This repels us.

For some people, of course, this drive to survive is fatally eroded by the longing for rest.

Suicidal tendencies

'Wine is fine/ But whiskey's quicker/ Suicide is slow with liquor/ Take a bottle drown your sorrows/ Then it floods away tomorrow' (Ozzy Osbourne, 'Suicide Solution', *Blizzard of Oz*, 1980). On 26 October 1984, a 19-year-old, John Daniel McCollum, shot and killed himself while he was lying on his bed, wearing his headphones, and listening to, so it was claimed, this song at his home in Indio, California. His parents unsuccessfully sued Osbourne on the grounds that the song was a 'proximate cause' for their son's death. Sadly, they are not the only bereaved parents to have wondered whether music might have played a part in their loss. While music-related suicides are rare, suicide *per se* is not. Worldwide, around 100 people an hour commit suicide. In France, for example, in 2000, 'after an almost continual increase since 1975, the number of suicides reached 11,000 per year, i.e. more than one every hour.'[43]

Popular music is no stranger to discourses of self-destruction. Musicians write about suicide and, sadly, some embrace it. For example, on 8 April 1991, Dead (Per Yngve Ohlin) of the band Mayhem, took a knife, slit his wrists and then his throat before shooting himself in the head with a shotgun. On finding the body, fellow band member, Euronymous (Øystein Aarseth), took a photograph prior to calling the police. This photograph was then used as the cover for an infamous early live bootleg album, *Dawn of the Black Hearts* (1995). While such events can, of course, be examined from a Freudian perspective,[44] I want to begin with one of the most influential sociological analyses of suicide, that of Durkheim. This will help to widen our understanding of the significance of popular music in relation to suicide, self-harm and depression.

For Durkheim and much subsequent sociological thought, suicide can be accounted for largely in terms of coercion by social forces.[45] That is to say, he sought to demonstrate that even our most subjective actions are part of a constellation of sociostructural reflexes. While those who commit suicide will have personal reasons for so doing, in the final analysis, fatal self-aggression is structural, a 'social fact', a product of a particular relationship between the individual and society. Hence, for Durkheim, a suicide reveals something about the state of the community to which the individual belonged. While his work in this area has, of course, been contested and superseded,[46] nevertheless, it was instrumental in moving the discussion of suicide away from a focus on perceived personal and moral failings and towards a more scientific analysis

of the statistics. And, even if, as Christian Baudelot and Roger Establet have
shown, aspects of his thesis, such as the relationship between poverty, wealth
and suicide, need revising,[47] it does provide a useful framework for our
discussion. Of course, in the final analysis, it has to be acknowledged that,
while sociology can provide some indication of how the risk of self-harm
varies between societies and cultures, the very act of suicide is an individual
and exceptional act, the causes of which are difficult to ascertain simply from
sociological analysis.

Rooting his ideas in a statistical study of suicide rates, he found that suicides
were typically associated with the degree of social integration an individual
experiences. This led to the identification of four types of suicide: altruistic
suicide, egoistic suicide, anomic suicide and, discussed only in a footnote,
fatalistic suicide. Altruistic suicides, for example, are committed by people
who wholeheartedly identify with the group, its identity and its goals. The
cohesion of the group is such that it erodes autonomy and individual identity,
encouraging members, if necessary, to sacrifice themselves in the service of
the group. A good example of this is the suicide of Captain Lawrence Oates
in 1912. According to Captain Scott's journal, in order to save the lives of
his companions, rather than allow him to carry his frostbitten body over the
Antarctic wastes, he left his tent on the Ross Ice Shelf, uttered the words 'I am
just going outside and may be some time', disappeared into a blizzard and was
never seen again. As the theologian H.H. Farmer commented several years
later, 'this was calm, unadulterated self-immolation, with no hot emotion, no
public applause, no ecstatic vision to urge him on: there was just something
within the Captain's soul which pointed the way to death, and there was the
quiet bowing of his spirit to it.'[48] Perhaps needless to say, this type of heroic,
largely non-transgressive, non-liminal self-sacrifice is of little interest to
many within popular music. When altruistic suicide is indicated – which it
rarely is – it is not with socially responsible, unadulterated self-immolation
in mind. Rather, the focus is typically the far more brutal and selfish urging
of another person to commit altruistic suicide: ' ... please kill yourself/ And
save my world....The world's better/Without you' (X-Fusion, 'Please Kill
Yourself', *Rotten to the Core/Bloody Pictures*, 2007).

The focus on suicide in popular music is, however, predominantly
introspective, an articulation of the disenfranchised self: 'Travels through
my veins, poisoning my soul/ Makes me hate myself, makes my anger blow/
Suffocates the hope, eats away my will/ Traps in all the hate, depression/ And
I don't wanna feel this way, but I can't stop it at all/ And I don't wanna hurt

no more, but I can't stop it at all/ And I don't wanna lie here numb, but I can't stop it at all/ And I don't wanna have to give in, but I can't stop it at all/ Depression, it's got me … ' (Suicidal Tendencies, 'Depression and Anguish', *Suicidal for Life*, 1994). Drawing on Durkheim's analysis, such expressions of suicidal thoughts can be understood as fatalistic, anomic, egoistic or a confluence of two or more types.

Fatalistic suicide is the result of 'excessive regulation' and is typical of 'persons with futures pitilessly blocked and passions violently choked by oppressive discipline'.[49] Such individuals suffer from the perception of a lack of agency and, consequently, feel trapped. For example, Donna Gaines's study of 'suburbia's dead-end kids' found that, as part of an interest in transgressive music and discourses, many expressed a sense of helplessness and despair, which led to morbidity and, particularly, to a fascination with violence and self-harm. This, Gaines argues, can be partially explained in terms of Durkheim's fatalistic suicide, in that the young people she spent time with had 'lost their ability to dream' and, as such, felt 'fated, doomed'.[50] There was a feeling, according to one young person she spoke to, that 'they were beaten down as far as they could go'. Hence, she says, 'lacking confidence in themselves and the world "out there", they felt trapped. Without a sense of meaningful choices, the only way out *was suicide*.'[51] This is supported by a recent study for the Prince's Trust in the UK: 9 per cent of all respondents (which equates to around 751,230 young people) agreed with the statement: 'I have nothing to live for'. Consequently, 'one in three unemployed young people (32 per cent) had contemplated suicide, while one in four (24 per cent) had self-harmed.'[52] Again, this disaffected perspective accounts to a large extent for the misanthropic and transgressive themes developed within the popular music cultures. For example, hardcore punk and industrial bands, such as Bad Brains, Black Flag, Circle Jerks, The Dead Kennedys, D.O.A., Minor Threat, The Misfits, Nine Inch Nails, Skinny Puppy and State of Alert, all responded to urban decay and a perception of hopelessness, systemic disenfranchisement, the loss of personal agency and a stolen future.[53] The violence and despair that this loss of agency can lead to is a common theme in their songs: 'I'm a fucking bum, can't you understand that man/ I live on welfare, that's where I'm at/ I don't work … I'm a fucking creep, people don't pick up on that/They don't understand me, they don't know where I'm at' (D.O.A., 'I Don't Give A Shit', *Hardcore '81*, 1981); 'You're fucked up baby/ Your eyes are like glass/ Your mind's like a beer bottle filled with butts … I'm lying in a pool of blood, won't you leave me alone' (D.O.A., 'Fucked Up

Baby', *Hardcore '81*, 1981); 'Society is burning me up/ Take a bit then spit it out/ Take their rules/ Rip 'em up, Tear 'em down' (Circle Jerks 'World Up My Ass', *Group Sex*, 1980). This sense of self-loathing and powerlessness engendered by overwhelming emotional distress is evoked in Trent Reznor's song about self-harm and addiction, 'Hurt' (Nine Inch Nails, *The Downward Spiral*, 1994) – movingly covered by Johnny Cash at the end of his life (*American IV: The Man Comes Around*, 2002): 'I hurt myself today/ To see if I still feel/ I focus on the pain/ The only thing that's real/ The needle tears a hole/ The old familiar sting/ Try to kill it all away/But I remember everything.'

Having said that, while, in extreme cases, such disaffection can lead both to self-harm and to outward aggression, despite Gaines's study, Durkheim actually did not consider fatalistic suicide to be a particularly significant contributor to suicide rates. He was far more interested in egoistic and anomic suicides. Indeed, while Gaines is correct to identify the lack of agency and hope as central to adolescent self-harm, it is difficult to avoid the fact that egoistic and anomic suicides are more common within youth cultures.

Egoistic suicide occurs when individuals become disenfranchised and not adequately integrated into a society – and, of course, there may be broadly 'fatalistic' reasons for this. As such, with no significant ties to the community, individuals feel alone and misunderstood – like fish out of water. This leads to increasing introspection and an unwillingness 'to emerge from' oneself. That is to say, as Durkheim puts it, 'what is lost in activity is made up for in thought and inner life. In revulsion from its surroundings consciousness becomes self-preoccupied, takes itself as its proper and unique study, and undertakes as its main task self-observation and self-analysis. But by this extreme concentration it merely deepens the chasm separating it from the rest of the universe.'[54] Again, this orientation towards society is not unusual in youth subcultures. For example, to return to the findings of study for the Prince's Trust, one young person, Chris Newell, describes his feelings as follows:

> I just got into a cycle of staying in bed because I had nothing to wake up for. Then I began noticing my mental health getting worse and worse. I became depressed and anxious. When I went out in public it got to the point where I felt paranoid and edgy around people. And I think that's all because I didn't have a routine and structure, because I think that's important in a lot of people's lives, to have something to wake up for in the morning, to have something to live for. I just felt horrible about myself. I were suicidal at times 'cause I felt worthless and it just went on and on and I weren't getting anywhere. I took a load of tablets and thankfully I'm still here.[55]

These sorts of feelings, which are relatively common, are explicitly articulated and even normalized within some popular music subcultures. Goth and Emo music and subcultures, for example, encourage identities constructed around introspection and melancholia. The term 'Emo' is an abbreviation for 'emotional', indicating its focus on affective states. In particular, its music seeks to evoke dispositions that often reflect an exaggerated sense of vulnerability, nostalgia, despair and social dislocation. The problem is, as Durkheim says, 'self-absorption is not a good method of attaching oneself to others'.[56] Hence, subcultural discourses can, in some cases, lead to introspection and detachment. In other words, a vulnerable adolescent with a melancholic disposition can be drawn into pathological states of mind that are maintained by the liminal pursuit of subcultural capital: 'You gotta go down, deep down into the pain/ Let it purge your soul like flesh to a razor blade/ Dig down deep into the pain/ Surrender, surrender, dig into euphoria' (Steve Vai, 'Down Deep Into the Pain', *Sex & Religion*, 1993). 'She's upset/ Bad day .... Mom and dad had no right she screams/ As the anger runs down both of her cheeks/ Then she closed her eyes/ Found relief in a knife/ The blood flows as she cries/ All alone the way she feels/ Left alone to deal with all the pain-drenched sorrow relief/ Bite the lip, just forget the bleeding' (Between the Trees, 'The Way She Feels', *The Story and the Song*, 2006).

It should be noted, of course, that some musicians recognize the susceptibility of young people to destructive affective states and seek directly to address issues relating to adolescent morbidity. The above song by Between the Trees, for example, reflects the band's involvement with the non-profit organization To Write Love on Her Arms – a charity which exists to provide help to those who struggle with depression, addiction, self-harm and suicide.[57]

If a person belongs to a subculture in which articulations of melancholia and self-harm elicit subcultural capital and are, as such, encouraged to model themselves accordingly, this can exacerbate a susceptibility to destructive behaviours. This, in turn, can lead to further isolation from those who might be able to help them, yet who are perceived to be uncool and Other. For example, a recent longitudinal cohort study of the prevalence of deliberate self-harm and attempted suicide within contemporary goth subcultures (which were fairly broadly defined) found that 'identification by youth aged 19 as belonging to the Goth subculture was the best predictor of self-harm and suicide attempt .... Self-harm could be a normative component of Goth subculture including emulation of subcultural icons and peers who self-harm (modelling mechanisms). Alternatively', and this is important, 'it could be explained by selection, with young people with a particular propensity to self-harm being attracted to the subculture.'[58] That is to say, some young people with a melancholic disposition are attracted to music and subcultures that express what they feel. While aspects of the study might be questioned,[59] nevertheless, the evidence does suggest that there is a connection between cultures oriented around self-harm and melancholia and behaviours oriented around self-harm and melancholia.[60] This will not, of course, apply to those interested in cultural melancholia, particularly those who are older, but, as we have seen, music and culture do have a strong relationship with identity and emotion.[61]

Hence, while such dispositions are sometimes unsympathetically parodied or otherwise trivialized by musicians, as in Elton John's 'I Think I'm Going to Kill Myself' (*Honky Château*, 1972), The Police's 'Can't Stand Losing You' (1978) and Queen's 'Don't Try Suicide' (*The Game*, 1980), as current research demonstrates, society cannot afford to ignore adolescent morbidity as faddish, juvenile attention seeking. That said, while music might be seen as a contributory factor to cycles of self-harm in young people, it is also, perhaps, able to communicate their feelings in ways that they feel unable to themselves. That is to say, while popular music may become part of the problem, its positive role also needs to be acknowledged and understood. Indeed, music is often enormously significant for those who feel isolated and misunderstood. Few readers will not, at some point in their lives, have been helped by popular music to organize their thoughts and to make sense of their feelings. As we have seen, music, as a prosthetic technology, is able to manipulate emotion and thus to articulate deeply held feelings.[62] For example, the sense of becoming disengaged from family and friends is movingly described in Peter Gabriel's 'Don't Give Up' (1985), sung with Kate Bush. In the duet, Gabriel is urged not to give up by Bush: 'Don't give up...you have friends....You're not beaten yet....You still have us....Rest your head/ You worry too much/ It's going to be alright.' Unfortunately, Gabriel has 'No fight left'. He feels himself to be 'a man whose dreams have all deserted' and is convinced that 'no one wants you when you lose'. A similar sense of disenfranchisement, hopelessness and self-loathing is expressed in 'Loser' by 3 Doors Down (*The Better Life*, 1999): 'You're getting closer to pushing me off of life's little edge/ because I'm a loser/ And sooner or later you know I'll be dead....You're holding the rope and I'm taking the fall'. Again, from a slightly different perspective, these feelings are explored in Dashboard Confessional's thoughtful anti-war song, 'Slow Decay' (*Dusk and Summer*, 2006), which describes the struggle of a young soldier trying to adjust to life at home following military service. Although his father tries to support him, he gradually becomes more isolated from his family and begins to identify with those friends who have been killed in action: 'Stand down, son/ And start resting easy .... But you look scared now/ Hollow eyed .... Come on back/ Where you belong/ The pressure releases/ If you just let down your guard.' The soldier responds: 'I'm not hurt, I'm not dead/ I just should be/ Where my friends are lying/ And I didn't hate/ Those that I killed/ But they're all dead now.' Songs frequently articulate the complex emotions of those listeners who feel isolated and suicidal, in that they are uniquely able to create affective spaces within which individuals can make some sense of mortality, can come to terms with longing and loss, and can find some meaning in situations which are overshadowed by the threat of meaninglessness. Music allows us to explore feelings of rejection and self-loathing by coming alongside us and reflecting what we feel: 'I want a perfect body/ I want a perfect soul/ I want you to notice when I'm not around ... I wish I was special/But I'm a creep/ I'm a weirdo/ What the hell I'm doing here?/ I don't belong here' (Radiohead, 'Creep', 1992).

The musical construction of affective spaces within which such reflection can take place is important. As Lawrence Grossberg comments, 'by making certain things matter, people "authorize" them to speak for them, not only as a spokesperson, but also as a surrogate voice (e.g. when we sing along to popular songs). People give authority to that which they invest in; they let the objects of such investments speak for and in their stead. They let them organize their emotional and narrative life and identity.'[63] The Norwegian musician Jenny Hval makes a good point when she asks, 'What is music if not a series of mothers?' Music, she continues, 'is about longing and belonging.'[64] It creates affective spaces within which the self can be understood, nurtured and accepted.

It is hardly surprising, therefore, that concerned musicians with religious convictions have sought to exploit this sonic access to the subjective life as a pastoral – even evangelistic – opportunity to meet the perceived needs of disturbed young people. Take, for example, 'All Alone' by the Christian band Kutless (*Sea of Faces*, 2004). The song, written from God's perspective, quickly moves from empathy with the listener to evangelical spiritual advice: 'It seems like life is out to get you/ To destroy what you want/ I know that that you blame me/ For all that you go through.' However, dear listener, 'there is a better way .... If you would change your perspective/ You'd see that it is true/ Life is not always what you want/ Sometimes it's hard to bear.' But, worry not, for 'I'd be with you, and help you/ In all that you go through/ I love you, let me change your heart/ By coming in.' Whether such songs are able to prevent suicide and convert unbelieving listeners is difficult to ascertain, but what they do indicate is the widely acknowledged significance of popular music in managing emotion.

Turning now to anomic suicides, these are typically the result of sudden and unexpected changes in social circumstances that individuals find themselves ill-equipped to adjust to. They feel themselves to be detached from regulatory frameworks in society. For example, 'it is a well-known fact', says Durkheim, 'that economic crises have an aggravating effect on the suicidal tendency'.[65] This is supported by recent research into suicide rates during the recession, which show, for example, that austerity in Greece has led to a significant rise in male suicides. And, of course, Greece is not alone. The correlation between spending cuts and self-harm is replicated in the official statistics of other countries.[66] This brings us to Durkheim's central argument, namely that 'no living being can be happy or even exist unless his needs are sufficiently proportioned to his means'.[67] If an individual's needs surpass the capacity to satisfy them, the result is frustration, suffering and an overall weakening of the impulse to live – *ergo* suicide. To drive home this point, he compared humans to animals. 'In the animal, at least in a normal condition, this equilibrium is established with automatic spontaneity because the animal depends on pure material conditions. All the organism needs is that the supplies of substance and energy constantly employed in the vital process should be periodically renewed by equivalent quantities....Its power of reflection is not sufficiently developed to imagine other ends than those implicit in its physical nature.'[68] The problem for humans is that our needs are not limited to the body alone: 'beyond the indispensable minimum which satisfies nature...a more awakened reflection suggests better conditions, seemingly desirable ends craving fulfillment.'[69] Such aspirations, such 'desirable ends craving fulfillment', of course, are inherently unlimited, constrained only by the imagination. There is nothing in human psychology or physiology that would inhibit them. This is a problem because unfettered desire is insatiable, and if unrealized, it becomes a source of human misery: 'unlimited desires are insatiable by definition and insatiability is rightly considered a sign of morbidity. Inextinguishable thirst is constantly renewed torture....To pursue a goal which is by definition unattainable, is to condemn oneself to a state of perpetual unhappiness.'[70] If societies do not regulate these aspirations in some way – as religious communities typically used to do – individuals strive for that which is unattainable. Their experience of life will, therefore, be typically one of dissatisfaction and disillusionment. For Durkheim, modern capitalist economies are chronically anomic, driven by, as he puts it elsewhere, 'a crass commercialism which reduces society to nothing more than a vast apparatus of production and exchange'.[71] Again, part of the problem in the modern period is that traditional sources of social regulation, such as religion, have failed to exercise moral constraint on an increasingly unregulated capitalist economy. More particularly, central to capitalist and consumer economies has been the emergence of modern commercial advertising, the aim of which is to create perpetual desire.[72] It aims to produce wants that were not there before. When desires and aspirations are frustrated in modern societies, as they are most obviously during periods of rapid social change, individuals experience a loss of happiness and meaning.[73]

These life experiences are frequently reflected popular culture. Most ubiquitously, they are articulated in popular music, which serves to provide affective spaces within which listeners can reflect on their dissatisfaction and unhappiness. For example, Tori Amos's 'Maybe California' (*Abnormally Attracted to Sin*, 2009) invites the listener to eavesdrop on a conversation between two mothers, one of whom is contemplating suicide as a result of her perceived inability to meet her family's needs: ' ... please don't jump/ Why not? Nothing is making sense anymore to me/ I don't know when I stopped making him smile/ Now the kids see me cry all the time ... '. The song, says Amos,

> is about the mother's role in our new world, where so many men are losing their jobs and the women are not, because they're cheaper. What is that doing to a home? If the mothers start breaking down then everything starts breaking down. It's one thing to have young college girls cutting themselves, and that's tragic .... The idea that the mothers could really be contemplating jumping off a bridge or a cliff – that's coming out of a reality where a man is defined by being successful because he's a provider, and that's being taken away from so many homes. He's left there being stripped of this. And she can't give him that back. Wives and mothers live to make it better, and wives can't make this better.[74]

The same point is made by Alan Vega of the band Suicide in his powerful song 'Frankie Teardrop' (Suicide, *Suicide*, 1977), which tells the tragic story of a poor factory-worker who 'can't make enough money ... can't buy enough food' and who is 'getting evicted' from his home. Eventually, he takes a gun and shoots his family before committing suicide. The visceral nature of the song is enhanced by dissonant electronica and Vega's distraught and anguished screams. While some might question whether Amos and Vega have actually provided insightful social analysis, they unarguably do reflect some people's experience of a 'disturbance of equilibrium', which, as Durkheim puts it, 'is an impulse to voluntary death. Whenever serious readjustments take place in the social order ... [people] are more inclined to self-destruction'.[75] Because Vega's and Amos's protagonists are unable to provide for their families in the ways they had been socially conditioned to, they experience a loss of meaning in life and, finally, choose death.

We have seen that, for Durkheim, in modern societies there are two major forms of suicide: increasing detachment from others leads to egoistic suicide; dissatisfaction in relation to expectations leads to anomic suicide. However, these types of suicide often overlap. They are not discrete categories. Hence, as we have seen, adolescents often experience weak or absent social bonds, which then lead to a sense of alienation, inferiority and dissatisfaction: 'Life it seems, will fade away/ Drifting further every day/ Getting lost within myself/ Nothing matters, no one else/ I have lost the will to live/ Simply nothing more to give/ There is nothing more for me/ Need the end to set me free ... . Death greets me warm/ Now I will just say goodbye' (Metallica, 'Fade to Black', *Ride the Lightening*, 1984). This sense of a loss of meaning and belonging is reflected in Gaines's research in the 'teenage wasteland'. It feels, said one young person, as though 'you don't fit in anywhere, there is no place for you: in your family, your school, your town – in the social order'.[76] Hence, the breakdown of a significant relationship, such as that between a girlfriend and a boyfriend, can become unbearable. 'You've been killing me softly/ And finally the pain is too much/ And I'm all out of whisky/ To soak up the damage you've done ... . It was suicide/ Don't sugarcoat it/ Just let them know' (James Arthur, 'Suicide', *James Arthur*, 2013).

Again, Layard has also shown that habituation has an impact on levels of happiness. That is to say, those things we strive for, when realized, do not deliver the satisfaction we had anticipated. 'When I get a new home or a new car, I am excited at first. But then I get used to it, and my mood tends to revert to where it was before.'[77] As indicated in the initial chapter, this fetishization of material goods, which can be understood as a life strategy for dealing with the awareness of mortality, ultimately fails to satisfy. This is central to what Bauman refers to as the deconstruction of immortality, the celebration of the evanescent and the focus on immediate gratification. In an attempt to avert our gaze from our inevitable demise, we slice life up into a series of goals that, we anticipate, will bring some level of happiness and fulfilment. Unfortunately, this is typically fleeting and we are left disappointed and desiring something else, something better. Again, this is reflected in popular music. For example, as we have seen, David Byrne reflects on this process in the Talking Heads' song 'Once in a Lifetime' (*Remain in Light*, 1981): 'You may ask yourself, where is that large automobile?/ You may tell yourself, this is not my beautiful house/ You may tell yourself, this is not my beautiful wife...'. Throughout the song, there is a growing sense of anxiety and unease, as, one after another, goals that were once important, giving temporary meaning to mortality, fail to satisfy. As Layard comments, 'living standards are to some extent like alcohol or drugs. Once you have a certain new experience, you need to keep on having more of it if you want to sustain your happiness. You are in fact on a kind of treadmill, a "hedonic" treadmill, where you have to keep running in order that your happiness stand still.'[78]

Perhaps unsurprisingly, therefore, this can significantly affect those that one might otherwise expect to be happy, such as popular and influential musicians. For example, while much myth surrounds their biographies, both Peter Green of Fleetwood Mac and Syd Barrett of Pink Floyd struggled with success. Their personal needs were not met by wealth and adulation, which quickly became more a source of suffering than a source of happiness. As David Gilmour says of Barrett, while psychedelic drugs probably contributed to his breakdown, 'it would have happened anyway. It was a deep-rooted thing ... I just don't think he could deal with the vision of success and all the things that went with it.'[79] Likewise, Martin Celmins notes that, between 1970 and 1977, Peter Green sought 'to go back and regain that simple inner peace that he had once taken for granted'. Unfortunately, he 'gradually became more desperate. More than anything else it was the trauma of fame that had hived him off from everything and everybody.' As he says, like David Bowie's 'Space Oddity', Fleetwood Mac's 'Green Manalishi' articulates 'rock star alienation'.[80] Similarly, James Arthur struggled with depression and anxiety as a direct result of winning *The X Factor* in 2012. Having been made homeless at the age of 16, like Green, he found that his musical success did not bring him the happiness he had imagined:

> I wasn't sure how to cope with the transition from being nobody, a person that didn't contribute to society, to someone who had a purpose. I had come from nothing, living rough or staying in awful bedsits. Then suddenly everyone had an opinion about me and I was staying in nice hotels ... I was so tired and I was trying to get to grips with my reality .... It's quite clear that money doesn't do anything for me, it's quite clear that fame doesn't do anything for me ... I just didn't know why I was feeling so unhappy ... I wanted to fall flat on my face and never wake up.[81]

Again, following Durkheim, the experience of increasing detachment from others and the disappointment in relation to expectations or the inability to deal with the change in circumstances that success can bring has serious psychological consequences.

While Barrett, Green and Arthur suffered psychologically, but did not commit suicide, other musicians have found the force of the Freudian death drive too difficult to resist. Most famously, on 5 April 1994, Kurt Cobain, the lead singer of Nirvana, put a shotgun to his head and ended his life.[82] Near to his body lay a letter to his wife, Courtney Love, which articulated many of the characteristics of egoistic-anomic suicide. Describing himself disparagingly as 'an experienced simpleton', he outlines how he had become disengaged from society, from his family and from the music business. Consequently, he felt worthless: 'I haven't felt the excitement of listening to, as well as creating, music along with reading and writing for too many years now. I feel guilty beyond words about these things.' He continues,

> I can't fool you, any one of you. It simply isn't fair to you or me. The worst crime I can think of would be to rip people off by faking it and pretending as if I'm having 100% fun ... I've tried everything within my power to appreciate it (and I do, God, believe me I do, but it's not enough) ... I have a goddess of a wife who sweats ambition and empathy and a daughter who reminds me too much of what I used to be, full of love and joy, kissing every person she meets because everyone is good and will do her no harm. And that terrifies me to the point to where I can barely function. I can't stand the thought of Frances [his daughter] becoming the miserable, self-destructive, death rocker that I've become .... Please keep going Courtney, for Frances. For her life, which will be so much happier without me.[83]

One of the most famous popular reflections on self-destruction, which distils feelings such as those of Cobain, is 'Suicide Is Painless' by Johnny Mandel and Mike Altman (written as the theme song for the popular TV series *M*A*S*H*): 'The game of life is hard to play/ I'm gonna lose it anyway/ The losing card I'll someday lay/ So this is all I have to say ... suicide is painless.'[84] Although these lyrics were hastily written by a perfectly happy 14-year-old as an assignment for his father, Robert Altman, the director of *M*A*S*H*, nevertheless, they unwittingly articulate the rationale for egoistic and anomic suicides. It is not surprising, therefore, that the song has been covered numerous times, perhaps most poignantly by the Manic Street Preachers in 1992, along with a bonus track, on which the staff of the *New Musical Express* are recorded discussing whether to publish an image of the band's self-harming guitarist, Richey

Edwards, with '4 Real' carved into his forearm[85] and wearing a shirt across which were sprayed the words 'Spectators of Suicide'. A sufferer of depression, Edwards went missing on 1 February 1995 and, finally, on 23 November 2008, having not been found, was legally recorded as deceased.

The wider problem, of course, is that, as indicated above, those poor souls who have formed a significant relationship with the music of struggling artists, music which has, as Jenny Hval indicated, functioned parentally and expressed their deepest longings and fears, suffer when that musician finally commits suicide. The possibility of suicide is brought into the subjective affective space of the listener, which has been shaped by the music and identity of dead artist. While music is particularly potent in this respect, the widely documented negative effect of reporting celebrity suicides is also significant. Hence, as a recent study concluded, 'there is a need to remain vigilant about how suicide news is reported. Mental health professionals and suicide experts should collaborate with media professionals to try to balance "public interest" against the risk of harm.'[86] As will be discussed in Chapter 5, this is particularly the case regarding the suicide of an icon of popular music.

Disaffection, violence and death

We have seen that, in the modern Western world, public discourse pertaining to mortality has become disengaged from the subjective experiences of the dying and the bereaved. Death and decay are typically screened out of everyday life. They are tabooed, muted by euphemisms, reimagined through glamorized portrayals of sanitized deaths or simply avoided by means of other life strategies, such as focusing on the promises and pleasures of a consumer society. However, the very fact that human culture is organized around obscuring the brutal reality of mortality testifies to the fact that, while death can be kept in the background, in the final analysis, intelligent mortals cannot ignore it. Hence, humans need to develop cultural strategies (religious or otherwise) in order to make life less lugubrious than it otherwise might be. A corollary of this, as we have seen in Chapter 3, is that mortality becomes 'pornographic'.[87] Because death and dying are perceived as unseemly taboos, they tend to be voyeuristically viewed at a distance – often through the lens of popular culture. Again, we are both repulsed and fascinated by reminders of our mortality.

In order to understand such pornographies of death and gore in popular music, there needs to be some discussion of the disaffected music-oriented subcultures within which violence became de rigueur. Those that have been most influential in the development of the transgressive potential of extreme violence and gore within popular music have their roots in punk and heavy metal. Such discourses, while often playfully transgressive, are typically driven by juvenile disaffection. Punk in particular has consistently provided spaces within which to articulate the feelings of disenfranchised youths in Western societies.[88] For example, certainly in its early period, American hardcore punk was, as Mick Farren commented in the *New Musical Express* in 1981, a violent reaction to Ronald Reagan's America: 'Something nasty is lurking on the fringes of Reagan-land. The children of this polluted capitalist utopia are being dragged by a grim, black anger into the nihilist world of Darby Crash' – the lead singer of the punk band The Germs who committed suicide on 7 December 1980.[89] They are, Farren observed, 'being infected with an inarticulate rage against everything that has been sold to them as good and desirable since the time they could crawl.'[90] More particularly, these are the children that have benefitted from 'the best that capitalism can offer. They come from the solid upper middle class suburbs of L.A., Mirada, Anaheim, Newport Beach, Huntington Beach and Fullerton . . . . Somewhere along the way, though, something went wrong . . . . They want nothing more than to throw it all away, to trash and burn it.'[91] Of course, the iconoclasm of youth was not limited to the middle classes. The anger expressed was also often an anger nurtured by poverty, oppression and disenfranchisement. As the British musician Justin Broadrick (of Napalm Death and Godflesh) recently commented, 'I came from a really horrible area, a revolting place, a council estate in central Birmingham . . . . People often say to me, "Your music is filled with negative emotions. Is that down to your immediate environment as a kid?" And I say, yep! . . . I was very isolated . . . I always felt like a permanent outsider.'[92]

There is, however, more to hardcore and grindcore than a visceral response to conservatism, capitalism and consumerism. Along with disillusionment, there was an introspective self-loathing, which was often the result of emotional, physical or sexual abuse. Typical and influential in this respect was Henry Rollins (of State of Alert and Black Flag) who, despite a childhood in Glover Park, a relatively affluent suburb of Washington, D.C., suffered from depression and low self-esteem. This led to his immersion in discourses of morbidity and violence: 'I accumulated a lot of rage by the time I was seventeen or eighteen.'[93] 'Depression' from Black Flag's debut studio album, *Damaged* (1981) – 'perhaps *the* key hardcore document'[94] – clearly articulates these feelings: 'Right here, all by myself/ I ain't got no one else/ The situation is bleeding me/ There's no relief for a person like me .... Depression's got a hold of me ... I ain't got no friends to call my own/ I just sit here all alone/ There's no girls that want to touch me/ I don't need your goddamn sympathy .... Everybody just get away/ I'm gonna boil over inside today/ They say things are gonna get better/ All I know is they fuckin' better .... Depression's gonna kill me.' Again, Black Flag's 'Rat's Eyes' (*Slip It In*, 1984) is a good example of this type of self-loathing introspection and one which exposes a state of mind with which many adolescents could empathize: 'I want you to touch my filth/ I want you to feel my filth/ I want you to look into my eyes/ I want you to look through my eyes.' Indeed, it is this liminal need to articulate an emotional response to life, to share despair, to scream at society, that led hardcore to increasingly transgressive discourses and behaviours.

American hardcore punk, particularly in early years, bristled with anger and embraced the aesthetics of violence and excess.[95] Although, as Tobi Vail of the pioneering riot grrrl band, Bikini Kill comments, 'punk isn't genre-based ... [it's] is an attitude',[96] nevertheless, the music was typically brutal, fast and loud, and the lyrics expressed a level of aggression that reflected the anomie experienced by many adolescents. As Michael Azerrod comments of Black Flag's *Damaged*, 'it boiled over with rage on several fronts: police harassment, materialism, alcohol abuse, the stultifying effects of consumer culture, and, on just about every track on the album, a particularly virulent strain of self-lacerating angst – all against a savage, brutal backdrop that welded apoplectic punk rock to the anomie of dark seventies metal like Black Sabbath.'[97] The violence of the music, the visceral anger articulated in the lyrics, the fanzines and the visual culture,[98] again, often betrayed a troubled upbringing, abuse and alienation: 'street punks and runaways found their home in the hardcore scene', recalls Steve Blush. 'At shows, you'd see plenty of damaged and abused kids with anger, rage, and pain. For them the scene offered hope.'[99] Rollins himself told *Rolling Stone* in 1992 that he 'had been sexually molested several times as a child' and has, in his monologues, referred to his father as 'mentally abusive'.[100] All I wanted, he says, was 'life to be like the shows I saw on television', in which 'the children were happy'.[101] Such feelings of unhappiness, disenfranchisement, pain and anger permeate hardcore, influencing both the lyrics and the style of music, as well as the subcultures that formed around them.[102] 'Broken home, broken heart/ Now you know just how it feels/ To have to cry yourself to sleep at night', sang Bob Mould of Hüsker Dü ('Broken Home, Broken Heart', *Zen Arcade*, 1984).[103] Indeed, as a gay man, Mould himself has written movingly of his own anger, sexual frustration and self-loathing.[104] For example, in the song 'Whatever' (*Zen Arcade*), he explores the struggle he had with his parents: 'Mom and Dad, I'm sorry/ Mom and Dad, don't worry/ I'm not the son you wanted, but what did you expect?/ I've made my world of happiness to combat your neglect.'[105] Again, many bands, such as Steve Albini's Big Black and, later, Rapeman (a name taken from the title character of an infamous and offensive Japanese comic) openly explored explicitly transgressive themes such as murder, torture, mutilation, rape, child abuse, racism and misogyny. This needs to be understood, not simply as juvenile transgression, but also as a refusal to ignore the underbelly of Western culture. Again, while, of course, many fans simply enjoy the transgressive nature of the music, which articulates their liminal adolescent identities, for other fans and artists it reflects, not only what they observe in society, but, sadly, also what they experience.

As Albini comments of punk and hardcore generally, these were 'records made by anti-social people under bad conditions where nothing was working properly'. Hence, 'they sound fucked up. If everything was tightened up and tidied up and in tune and in time and had impressive lush production, they wouldn't have anything like the sort of urgency that they do.'[106] The focus on violence and death simply reflected meaninglessness evoked by the experience of being treated as an object, a problem, rather than a person: 'I am a product, I am a symbol of endless... I'm the dirt that everyone walks on/ I am the orphan nobody wants... I am the leper nobody wants to touch much/ I am a sample/ I am a scapegoat... I'm a number on the paper you file away....Wouldn't you love to see me dead?' (Crass, 'End Result', *The Feeding of the Five Thousand*, 1978). 'You're paying for prisons, you're paying for war/ Paying for lobotomies, you're paying for law/ Paying for their order, paying for their murder' (Crass, 'You Pay', *The Feeding of the Five Thousand*, 1978). For many within the punk and hardcore subcultures, popular music was an expression, not only of mindless violence – although the enjoyment of that for many should not be underestimated – but also of a genuine revolt against an apparently sadistic social system and the subsequent perception of Sisyphean meaninglessness.

From punk to hardcore and from industrial to extreme metal, the liminal cultures of popular music – which, again, are typically populated by those who stand at some distance from death – have often established identities through engagement with mortality. In the song 'Kerosene' (Big Black, *Atomizer*, 1986), for example, Albini expresses the anomic sense of disconnect and meaninglessness that many of his listeners experience: 'I was born in this town/ Lived here my whole life/ Probably come to die in this town....Never anything to do in this town .... Nothing to do/ Sit around at home .... Stare at the walls/ Stare at each other/ Wait until we die ...'. His solution is brutal and typical of hardcore: 'There's Kerosene around/ There's something to do .... Set me on fire.' This orientation towards aggression and self-harm is prominent within subcultures defined by anomie, anger and angst. 'Kill my dad/ He is weak/ Tried to shut me up ... I can be killed ... Go ahead, come on, do me in/ Come on, face the dark' (Big Black, 'I Can Be Killed', *The Hammer Party*, 1986). The listener is almost able to feel the aggression, the oppressive atmosphere and the misunderstanding experienced by other young people.

This aggression was (and still is) typically manifested at gigs in the form of ritualized violence – 'moshing' or 'slam-dancing'.[107] Essentially, this activity emerged out of the hardcore scene in the early 1980s and consists of violent and frenzied dancing in a space, usually in front of the stage, often referred to as the 'mosh pit'.[108] To help us to make sense of this apparently bizarre behaviour, with the above comments in mind, I want to briefly turn to Durkheim's discussion of 'collective effervescence'.[109] Immersed in the power of the social group, such ritualized violence,[110] while, at one level, (a) it is, again, simply testosterone fuelled fun, and at a deeper level, it also serves as both (b) a release valve for pent-up aggression and (c) arouses a passionate intensity through which an individual experiences something greater than the solitary self. All three of these outcomes can, I suggest, be constructive and positive. The necessary and enjoyable venting of frustration and anger[111] leads to what we can think of in terms of *communitas* (as discussed in Chapter 2).

In a relatively safe liminal space, individuals respond to social anomie and to their sense of disaffection by expressing aggression and exposing themselves to the aggression of others in a ritualized performance. In this atmosphere, there is a contained, safe reaction to the frustration, to the sense of futility, to the lack of purpose, and to angst. Hence, in some respects such events can be understood as socially significant safety valves, along the lines suggested by Roger Caillois. That is to say, moments of misrule, understood as managed, bounded eruptions of popular energies, have the effect of reducing the likelihood of more serious, unregulated outbreaks of transgression, thereby limiting the threat of the profane.[112] In such ritualized moments of misrule, a sense of liminal *communitas* is engendered. Hence, while anomie indicates the erosion of social ties and the consequent sense of personal insignificance, moshing rituals can serve to establish new, meaningful bonds with other disenfranchised youths both through the shared venting of aggression and frustration and through complicity in discourses and behaviours that society profanes. While moshing is, of course, at one level simply enjoyable, I want to suggest that it can, for some participants, be more than this. As noted above, it can be understood in terms of 'collective effervescence' as discussed by Durkheim. As Rina Arya notes of football violence in the United Kingdom, 'What happens is that the individuals within the group experience a heightening of sensations'. As she says, quoting Durkheim, 'they experience themselves as grander than at ordinary times; they do things they would not do at other times; they feel, and at that moment really are, joined with each other and with the totemic being. They come to experience themselves as sharing one and the same essence – with the totemic animal, with representation, and with each other.'[113] The heightening of sensations, 'which occurs throughout the ritual and transforms the group from being individuated and apart from one another to partaking of a fervour which binds them communally, conveys the switch from the profane to the sacred.'[114] Helpfully comparing this process to the shift from *Gesellschaft* to *Gemeinschaft*, as developed by Ferdinand Tönnies, she notes that there emerges a collective sense of identity, 'which imparts a feeling of totality, where the whole is greater than the sum of its parts'.[115] Within this affective space, the individual experiences a profound moment of belonging and meaning in a way not dissimilar to feelings evoked within the context of religious worship. Needless to say, this is enormously significant for disenfranchised youths, who experience isolation and emotional detachment from family and society. They are bound together by a shared sense of outrage enacted in ritual violence. As it becomes more frenzied, more transgressive, so individuals enter into that 'inner experience' that Georges Bataille describes in terms of the mystical state.[116] It is hardly surprising, therefore, that moshing quickly became definitive of punk culture. As Azerrad notes of Black Flag concerts, they 'became more and more a focal point for violence .... All the media hype was now attracting a crowd that was actually *looking* for violence.'[117] It became 'a genre that was feared by the mainstream (often for good reason)'.[118] The mosh pit, a liminal space 'outside' mainstream society, within which cultural norms are temporarily suspended, galvanized the sense of *communitas*, evoking intense feelings of belonging. The sense of meaninglessness and isolation evaporates in communal moments of intensive violence. And, again, the subcultural focus on violence and death in the music, lyrics and visual culture, which is tabooed in mainstream society, contributes to a subversive discourse that binds liminal beings together.

Turning now to the important release of aggression that moshing affords, René Girard's widely read work on violence, death and the sacred sheds a little more light on the significance of these evanescent moments of *communitas*. Central to his analysis is the premise that violence is a universal feature of human life. Because of this, when the object of violence is not available, a surrogate needs to be found in order to release the build up of aggression. Hence, his thinking in this respect is not dissimilar to that of Caillois, in that, for Girard, sacrificial rituals have an important social function. The sacrificial victim is a necessary surrogate: 'society is seeking to deflect upon a relatively indifferent victim, a "sacrificable" victim, the violence that would otherwise be vented on its own members, the people it most desires to protect.'[119] The key point here is that 'violence is not to be denied.'[120] Although key musicians within the hardcore scene, such as Henry Rollins (State of Alert, Black Flag, Rollins Band), Ian MacKaye (Minor Threat, Fugazi) and Bob Mould (Hüsker Dü, Sugar) became understandably weary of the excessive violence as they got older,[121] we have seen that during the 1980s hardcore was driven by a raw anger. Moments of ritualized violence, during which numerous small secular sacrifices were made, acted as an important release. Again, such apparently meaningless juvenile excess reinforces social bonds within the community and, consequently, can alleviate those pressures that might otherwise lead to destructive morbidity.

Real expression of actual violence is, therefore, important, in that, for many young people, listening to punk, hardcore or extreme metal on an iPod, worshipping as a solitary metal/hardcore hermit on a bedroom, is not enough. There has to be a crossing of the threshold between mimetic violence and what Arya has referred to as the 'real presence' of violence. Launching into the mosh pit, physically engaging with others and drawing blood in small sacrifices is psychologically and socially significant. 'From the first stage of mimetic violence to the second phase of the "real presence" of violence we experience something which is different not simply in degree but also in kind.'[122] There is a shift, in other words, from the individual to the collective. This shift has, insists Girard, a cathartic effect that benefits both the individual and the community: 'If the sacrificial catharsis actually succeeds in preventing the unlimited propagation of violence, a sort of *infection* is in fact being checked.'[123]

Finally, concerning the performance of physical violence, it is also important to remind ourselves that it brings us back to Bauman's discussion of immortality and the focus on the significance of immediate experiences: 'a happy life is one perceived as the perpetuity of new beginnings'.[124] Juvenile morbidity is checked. Concern regarding the extinction of the self and the loss of meaning in life is alleviated by the focus on intensive experiences and moments of 'collective effervescence'. Sonic and physical experiences in the mosh pit are engagements in the eternal now. The experience of mortality is reduced to a series of moments of communal, life-enhancing violence. Postmodernity, Bauman suggests, 'instead of trying (in vain) to colonize the future ... dissolves the future in the present. It does not allow the finality of time to worry the living; and it attempts to do it, mainly, by slicing time (all of it, every shred of it, without residue) into short-lived, evanescent episodes.'[125] In other words, the horizon of the self's mortality is dissolved in the intensity of the moment.[126] The sense of meaninglessness engendered by feelings of isolation and disaffection is alleviated by a succession of 'immortal experiences'.[127]

The pornography of gore, violence and death

Drawing on the above discussion, I want briefly to reflect on the fascination with gore, violence and death that has emerged in extreme metal since the 1980s. As discussed in the previous two chapters, subjects relating to mortality are significant in popular music, in that they function as *memento mori*, forcing listeners to engage with the brutal realities of life, transporting them to an affective space within which defilement, decrepitude and destruction can be thought about and experienced at a distance. However, we have also seen that such discourses function as part of a wider liminal strategy for challenging mainstream taboos, creating *communitas* and generating evanescent moments of immortality, during which the awareness of anomie recedes into the background. There is a shared, almost competitive immersion in abjection, in profane discourses that bond the disenfranchised in an experience of *communitas* over against the dominant values of mainstream society.

More than this, immersing oneself in pornographies of gore, violence and death, which are, *particularly at live events*, accompanied by the impact of loud, aggressive music – the 'death growl' vocals, 'blast beats', heavy riffs, driving bass and so on – opens up the possibility of what Bataille has referred to as 'inner experience', within which listeners 'lose themselves', momentarily transcending the quotidian awareness of mortality.[128] In these intense moments, immortality is experienced, during which the angst of anomie is alleviated.

Purposefully offensive though their subjects often are, genres such as goregrind and deathgrind can, moreover, be understood as the working out of a liminal identity. Disenfranchised youths situated beyond 'their mundane structural context' are – to quote Victor Turner's anthropological work on

African tribal rituals and rites of passage – 'in a sense "dead" to the world'. This is why, separated from normative cultural structures, liminal culture 'has many symbols of death – novices may be classed with spirits or painted black ... . They are also "polluting" ... because they transgress classificatory boundaries. Sometimes they are identified with feces; usually they are allowed to revert to nature by letting their hair and nails grow and their bodies get covered with dust'.[129] Because certain physical substances and objects, notably those linked with disease, excrement and death, signify impurity – and are therefore associated with taboos – liminality explicitly inverts this signification. As such, *communitas* is created around the inverted, transgressive interpretation. Consequently, in subcultures, as I have argued elsewhere,[130] death, decay, gore and disease accrue subcultural capital. They're cool!

Moreover, as Michelle Phillipov has argued, with reference to research into the reception of horror cinema, depictions of extreme violence, gore and death 'can promote experiences of viewing largely unrelated to the particularities of plotting and narrative, as well as a lack of emotional investment in the action witnessed on screen'. This, she notes, 'provides audiences with forms of "distanced" or "technical" appreciation, in which texts are enjoyed for their constituent parts and not as narratively coherent wholes'.[131] In other words, 'horror texts are divided into their individual components and assessed at an emotional remove, rather than offering intense and immersive experiences'.[132] Typically, popular music offers snapshots of death and gore with little of the narrative context that would allow the listener to make sense of what they are presented with. In other words, we are treated to an unlikely parade of dismembered limbs, pools of blood and mutilated corpses. Mortician's 'Brutally Mutilated' (*Mortal Massacre*, 1993) is typical: 'Dismembered limbs/ Severed spine/ On your flesh/ Maggots dine/ Cut off head/ Ripped out eyes/ A bloody corpse/ Unrecognized/ Torn apart/ Mangled flesh/ You are left/ A bloody mess'. Similarly, Carcass's 'Oxidised Razor Masticator' (*Reek of Putrefaction*, 1988) simply provides a collection of verbs and body parts: 'Chomping and splicing, your gums sliced to shreds/ Tattered bloody ribbons, incisored skin is shred/ Scraping on sore teeth, cracking and chipping/ Shredding and mincing raw nerve endings'. Although some bands, such as Colonize the Rotting, focus on subjects such as psychopathy and, therefore, provide some narrative to the slaughter, the focus tends to be on the act of killing and its aftermath. Again, this discourages affective investment: 'Beyond the horizon lies my collection of bodies heaped high/ Relics of lives taken, piles of the savagely hacked and disfigured ... . Entangled limbs hanging by threads/ Screams echo in my mind' (Colonize the Rotting, 'Formation of Worms', *Composting The Masticated*, 2010). The effect of this is to distance the self from the portrayals of death and violence. Hence, while, on the one hand, the listener is presented with a *memento mori*, on the other hand, there is little here that invites identification with the dead, empathy with the bereaved, or, indeed, moving reflection on personal mortality. Gore is simply used as profane subject matter to evoke transgressive experiences, which, in the final analysis, detract from reflection anomie or the dissolution of the self. That is to say, as well as a weak *memento mori*, it can also be seen as a strategy for mitigating the awareness of mortality. It's transgressive fun!

Having said all that, these are clearly morally problematic discourses. For example, while it takes us too far beyond the focus of this book, something does need to be said about the confluence of gore and misogyny within extreme metal. Simon Frith and Angela McRobbie famously discussed heavy metal as a conspicuous example of 'cock rock'. Implicit within other rock styles, heavy metal is conceived quite literally as male sexual performance, 'an explicit, crude, and often aggressive expression of male sexuality'.[133] While such rock masculinism has been widely discussed, there has been little analysis of cultures within which misogyny is articulated in discourses of gore. That is to say, sexual pornography and the pornography of gore and violence are conflated. Much of the artwork and lyrical content typically involves females as victims of extreme violence. It is not simply a case of 'bodies' being disassembled at an emotional remove, but a very particular case of female bodies being tortured, raped and dismembered in an explicitly masculine culture. Clearly, it is difficult to insulate such representations of violence against women from wider gender politics. Regardless of the musicians' intentions, misogynistic pornographies of gore fundamentally reinforce the worst extremes of hegemonic masculinism. Take, for example, *Slut Decapitator* (2008) by Unburied or Cannibal Corpse's *The Bleeding* (1994), which includes the tracks 'Fucked With a Knife' and 'Stripped, Raped, and Strangled'. These include graphic descriptions of extreme violence against women with no sense that such discourses and behaviours are ethically problematic. Again, the cover artwork of Unburied's *Murder 101* (2012) is an explicit illustration of a woman having her throat slit with a knife. While such texts and discourses can be understood in the ways discussed above, and while few fans will actually consider these musicians to be life coaches and relationship counsellors, it is difficult to understand in what ways they are counter-hegemonic. Again, these are worrying discourses in masculine cultures supported by patriarchal societies. Hence, while it has been argued that gore can be understood in terms of 'play',[134] this interpretation becomes explicitly problematic when it is gendered.[135]

More generally, it has been shown that, not only are 'degrading sexual references more prevalent than non-degrading references' in popular music, but that listeners 'exposed to more degrading sexual references ... are more likely to initiate intercourse at a younger age'.[136] There is, again, some evidence of a link between popular music discourses and behaviour. Indeed, there is some evidence to suggest that popular culture generally contributes 'to coerciveness and sexual assault toward women .... Along with being victims of violence in society, women are victims of violence in the media and most violent acts in the media are carried out by men.'[137] In popular music, at one end of the spectrum, there are songs such as 'Kiss With a Fist' (2008) by Florence and the Machine, which details the violence that can happen within apparently loving relationships: 'Broke your jaw once before/ I spilt your blood upon the floor/ You broke my leg in return/ So let's sit back and watch the bed burn/ Blood sticks sweat drips/ Break the lock if it don't fit/ A kick in the teeth is good for some/ A kiss with a fist is better than none ... '. In the same vein, but more explicit, is The Prodigy's 'Smack My Bitch Up' (1997), which, understandably, attracted feminist protest. At the other end of the spectrum, along with extreme metal, rap and hip hop music has provoked much criticism as a result of songs which explicitly advocate rape and murder,[138] such as Eminem's 'Kim' (*The Marshall Mathers LP*, 2000), a disturbing fantasy about murdering his wife: 'Sit down bitch/ If you move again I'll beat the shit out of you .... Bleed bitch, bleed'. Again, MC Ren's 'You Wanna Fuck Her' (*Shock Of The Hour*, 1993) is brutally misogynistic: '... she might start to bitch 'cause she's nothin' but a bitch/ Shoot the bitch, a dead bitch, then bury the bitch, a gone bitch/ What else can I say to take the place of that?/ I saw my nigga, DJ Trane, shoot a bitch in the back'. Again, it is difficult to insulate such discourses from criticism. While some might argue that they are merely satirical or parodic, this fails to appreciate their power within masculinist cultures.

Living on death row

'Death Row/ That's where motherfuckers is endin' up ... I turned to a life of crime, 'cause I came from a broken family/ My uncle used to touch me, I never told you that .... Bye bye, I was never meant to live/ Can't be positive, when the ghetto's where you live . . . . Bye bye, and I got no place to go/ Where you find me? 16 on Death Row/ Dear mama, they sentenced me to death/ Today's my final day, I'm countin' every breath' (2Pac, '16 On Death Row', *RU Still Down? (Remember Me)*, 1997). There are conspicuous parallels between the cultures of hardcore and hip hop. Indeed, to some extent, this accounts for the fusion of the two in innovative genres such as rapcore. As Adam Horowitz of the Beastie Boys put it, 'when you think about it, hardcore and hip hop aren't that different. The attitude is the same.'[139] Similarly, Chuck D (Public Enemy) has recommended that his fans read the work of Henry Rollins: 'He's an inspiration.'[140] As in some hardcore, hip hop's culture of death emerged from the experience of oppression, marginalization and disenfranchisement.[141] That said, there are some significant differences between the two cultures, the principal of which is that the roots of hip hop need to be traced back into the history of Black America. That is to say, hip hop is, to a large extent, the product of a particular historical experience of exploitation and suffering. This is, for example, powerfully and very explicitly articulated in Lauryn Hill's song 'Black Rage'. As a thoughtful subversion of the Rodgers and Hammerstein song (now a popular Christmas song), 'My Favourite Things' from *The Sound of Music*, it challenges hegemonic readings of Western culture. Instead of remembering 'raindrops on roses and whiskers on kittens/ Bright copper kettles and warm woolen mittens', as some people do in order to not '*feel* so bad', she recalls her forebears and the African American history of oppression in order to not '*fear* so bad'. 'BLACK RAGE is founded on two-thirds a person/ Rapings and beatings and suffering that worsens/ Black human packages tied up in strings/ BLACK RAGE can come from all these kinds of things/ Black Rage is founded on blatant denial/ Squeezing economics, subsistence survival/ Deafening silence and social control/ BLACK RAGE is founded on wounds in the soul!'[142]

Hip hop became, as Tricia Rose says, a source of 'alternative identity formation and social status in a community whose older local support institutions had been all but demolished along with large sectors of its built environment'.[143] Understanding this context is enormously important. For many artists and fans, everyday was like living on death row.

While hip hop has occasioned moments of moral panic, particularly surrounding gangsta rap from the mid-1980s, as John Hagedorn comments in his international study of gang cultures, 'it should come as no surprise that desperate conditions in ghettos, barrios, and favelas produce angry alienated groups of armed young men and women'.[144] Hip hop is largely (although not solely) the musical articulation of death row culture, a culture within which life expectancy is low and, consequently, within which mortality has a medieval proximity. 'When your heart turns cold/ A baby's cry means nothing/ A dead corpse is trivial....Loneliness becomes your routine friend/ Death seems like tranquility'.[145] These lines from a poem by Tupac Shakur/2Pac reflect the reality of a life with which he was very familiar. That is to say, these are not the words of transgressive adolescence, the words of youths seeking to establish an identity over against what they perceive to be mainstream Western culture. This is not Carcass's playful celebration of gore, 'Exhume to Consume' (*Symphonies of Sickness*, 1989). This is simply reportage. Death is a fact of daily life. A dead corpse is trivial and death does seem to him like tranquility.[146] This is, in other words, an articulation of 'black rage'. It is a Camusian response to mortality. It is 'a legitimate and necessary' enquiry, as Camus puts it, into 'whether life has meaning'.[147]

Moreover, while violence is frequently and graphically expressed as a manifestation of the drive for self-preservation and survival, in hip hop culture this is often explicitly in tension with articulations of the 'death drive', that pull towards equilibrium and rest. To quote Shakur again, 'death seems like tranquility'.[148] This is perhaps hard for many readers to understand – certainly for those readers who, like me, come from middle-class, loving homes. Although I have enjoyed hip hop for many years and although I am fascinated by the culture it reflects and shapes, I cannot pretend that the social context to which much of it introduces me is anything other than alien. Consequently, I find emic discussions of hip hop, such as Shawn Taylor's superb little book on A Tribe Called Quest's album *People's Instinctive Travels and the Paths of Rhythm*, both revealing and disturbing:

> As I sit here embarking on my own journey to illuminate ... *People's Instinctive Travels and the Paths of Rhythm*, I find myself reliving the situations under which I was first exposed to the group....My mother was queen of the replacement fathers. Every five or six weeks, she would allow some dude into our apartment and, for some odd reason, allow them to practice their hooks and jabs on us. I had no idea there were so many boxers in Brooklyn, let alone that my mother knew them all and allowed us to become an essential component of their training regime.

Before the album is discussed, Taylor takes us to a place where hip hop matters, a place where hip hop is more than pop music, a place where hip hop is more important than entertainment. It reflects a political, social, emotional and historical context. As such, it liberates the listener from that context.

It was 1989 ... and my home life wasn't the best. I was junior in high school and many other young black men at the time, I was having male identity issues .... For young black dudes, we were only allowed one projection: stone-cold hardness .... Young black boys were supposed to be tough and unflappable – but we were also supposed to know our place. So, as mom was getting the hell beat out of her, I was not supposed to do or say anything about it. It was a strict noninterference policy .... So, this one night, as I huddled in a corner of my cave, I heard a particularly loud cracking sound coming from my mother's room. I waited a couple of minutes and heard the front door open and then slam. I crept into my mother's room and she was laid out on her bed, blood and other fluids leaking from her face and ears. I called the ambulance and they took her on a three-day vacation in the hospital. I feel guilty for saying this now, but those three days when my mother was hospitalized, that was the most peaceful time I had.

On the second day of this new existence, my friend Stirling came over ... carrying one of those ancient Sony Walkmans draped over his shoulder. It was that huge silver brick of a tape player with buttons so big they could be seen from outer space .... He rewound the tape and pressed that enormous play button. And it was over. Hearing 'Description of a Fool' for the first time was like pulling Excalibur from the stone. I knew, from that moment forward, that hip hop and I would be inextricably linked.[149]

These were not unusual experiences for many young rappers. Hip hop was a language they understood about a life they lived. Shakur, for example, was brought up in poverty in a series of apartments by a single mother with an addiction to crack cocaine.[150] Male role models were frequently violent and not infrequently dead before they reached old age. As is evident in hardcore culture, these experiences were not, of course, limited to young black people. Hence, the discourses of hip hop soon began to appeal to many youths beyond the black community. Although there are differences in their experiences of society, many also felt as though they were living on death row. Eminem, for example, experienced a very similar upbringing to that of Shakur and has articulated similar concerns in equally visceral ways.

Sadly, of course, gun and gang culture often leads to the early extinction of hip hop artists themselves. Tupac Shakur, the Notorious B.I.G., Scott La Rock, The Almighty RSO, D-Boy, Charizma, Stretch, Yaki Kadafi, Fat Pat, Big L, Freaky Tah, Bugz (D12), Jam Master Jay (Run DMC) and Yella Boy (U.N.L.V. – Uptown Niggas Living Violent) are just a few names from a long list of young, murdered hip hop artists. Shakur, for example, having become embroiled in a feud between East Coast and West Coast rappers – focused on the labels Bad Boy (East Coast) and Death Row Records (West Coast) – was the victim of a drive-by shooting by an unknown assailant in Las Vegas on 6 September 1996. He died in hospital at the age of 25. East Coast rapper, the Notorious B.I.G/ Biggie Smalls, who was involved in the same feud, met almost exactly the same end in Los Angeles six months later. In the early hours of Sunday morning, on 9 March 1997, his car stopped at the traffic lights. Another car pulled up alongside, an unknown man wound down the window and opened fire. By 1.15 a.m. he was dead at the age of 24.[151]

The point here is not, of course, to rehearse arguments I am ill-equipped to assess, arguments central to hip hop studies that have been very ably posited and analysed by other scholars.[152] Rather, as noted above, following on from the discussion of hardcore, the aim is simply to focus attention on the distinctive culture of death reflected in hip hop. Drawing on a tradition of black oration and storytelling, hip hop artists provide musically compelling reportage about social and individual anomie.[153] They describe contexts closely related to those which Durkheim argued tend to produce psychological states characterized by a sense of futility, a lack of meaning, emotional disengagement and, ultimately, despair. One only need have a cursory grasp of hip hop culture to appreciate the depth of disaffection and angst produced by the social contexts within which many rappers grew up. As Michael Dyson commented in 1996,

> during the last decade, blacks have tried to shatter a chain of challenges to our communal flourishing from within and outside black life. The chain is composed of many links that are both familiar and frightening. It includes the conservative assault on affirmative action. The fateful lapse in black political and civil rights leadership. The resurgence of racism and xenophobia. The development of underground drug economies and gang violence in the inner city. The painful collapse of a liberal consensus on race. The increase in sexual violence among teens. The chilling rise in rates of black imprisonment. The expanding material misery of the working-poor and ghetto-poor. And much, much more.[154]

Life has not changed very much since that time. Hence, as Monica Miller discussed in 2013, 'the culture of death continually lurks and no "real" protective shields are formed, only a will to survive'.[155]

Sat next to Tupac Shakur, driving the car in which he was shot, was Suge Knight, the co-founder of one of the most well-known and perhaps the most lucrative of early hip hop record labels, Death Row Records.[156] Established in 1991, there was little about the record label that was subtle regarding mortality. Its logo depicted a hooded man about to die in an electric chair. Again, this logo, along with the name of the record label, referenced the sense of futility and despair that many artists and fans experienced. Some would die as a result of gang aggression, some as a result of state aggression and some as a result of self-aggression. Reflection on mortality and a Sisyphean existence permeated and shaped hip hop culture in a particularly disturbing way. This is perhaps nowhere more powerfully communicated than in the title of The Notorious B.I.G song, 'You're Nobody (til Somebody Kills you)', which was, poignantly, released on the album *Life After Death* (1997) shortly after someone killed him. Indeed, the title of his previous album was also a distillation of core ideas that emerged within a gang-oriented hip hop culture, *Ready to Die* (1994).

With such contexts in mind, scholars such as Rose have helped us to make sense of death row culture and the aggression articulated in hip hop. For example, with reference to the police brutality and racism that many young blacks experience, which serve only to exacerbate anomie, in *Black Noise* (1994) she analyses 'cop killing' lyrics. These reflect fissures in American society that need to be taken seriously by policy makers. Unfortunately, as she has subsequently discussed in *The Hip Hop Wars* (2008), since the 1990s, an unfettered and irresponsible version of this discourse has emerged as dominant in the media and, as such, has come to define hip hop culture. Consequently, although there is of course much irenic, spiritually constructive and politically engaged 'conscious hip hop', the primary reading of it is informed by discourses of sexual violence, drug abuse, murder and aggressive, gang-oriented black masculinity: 'hip hop is in a terrible crisis', Rose bemoans. 'Although its overall fortunes have risen sharply, the most commercially promoted and financially successful hip hop – what has dominated mass-media outlets such as television, film, radio, and recording industries for a dozen years or so – has increasingly become a playground for caricatures of black gangstas, pimps, and hoes.'[157] Hence, although there is much within hip hop that seeks to respond positively to death row culture, conspicuous currents within it seem to have shifted away from grim, social realist reportage to a cosmetic and ultimately destructive celebration of aggression. Again, there was always this potential within hip hop, because rappers lived and died in anomic social contexts. Hip hop provided a mirror to this existence,[158] and in so doing, aspirational young artists found it difficult also not to promote what they saw and experienced in increasingly transgressive terms. This proved to be a lucrative strategy, in that it appealed to liminal, disaffected youth. As such, it was socially problematic.

On the one hand, therefore, hip hop and particularly gangsta rap can be understood, not simply as reportage about and, indeed, resistance to death row culture, but also as a *memento mori*. It forcefully reminds listeners of the fragility of human life. However, on the other hand, there is also the question raised by Rose as to whether the 'hip hop industry' has become part of the problem. Unlike politically engaged and socially aware outfits such as Public Enemy, which arguably exposed and resisted death row culture, much contemporary hip hop is simply the capitalist exploitation of it. As such, it has become a culture in which money and mortality are fatally entwined. For any who might not quite grasp this point, 50 Cent makes it crystal clear: *Get Rich or Die Tryin'* (2003). This is what Shawn Taylor refers to as 'the gangsta universe of "get money at any cost", fuck-the-world nihilism'.[159] Such discourses cultivate a culture within which mortality is both obscured and trivialized.

In the nihilistic focus on wealth and death, there is a sense in which immortality is deconstructed. The bliss of immortality (however that was understood) was once a future prospect in anticipation of which individuals were encouraged to organize their lives. As Bauman puts it, 'everything in the present weighed heavily on everything still to come: the future fate of the project hung heavily on the things of today'.[160] Immortality, the anticipated bliss, which transcends mortality, has now been collapsed into the present moment. The focus has shifted from life as a preparation for death to experiencing life now – the eternal now! Hence, 50 Cent encourages his listeners to die – a word almost emptied of its original content and force – in an effort to fill the present with meaning. 'Each moment, or no moment is immortal.... Immortality is as transient and evanescent as the rest of things.'[161] There are two important points to be drawn from this vision: first, 'each moment is important; there is, after all, nothing to expect in the future which will not be another "moment", fluid, bound to self-destruct'; and, second, all moments are equal and, therefore, 'in a life composed of equal moments, speaking of directions, projects and fulfillments makes no sense. Every present counts as much, or as little, as any other'.[162] So, get rich or die tryin'! The death of the self is, by definition, a future concept. As such, it can be evaded by immersion in the experience of present moment. Consequently, much popular hip hop has, in recent years, become less about 'speaking truth to power', about creating a better future, and more about making large amounts of money through the articulation of destructive discourses that sell to disenfranchised and angry youth cultures.[163] Actual mortality, the extinction of the self, is evaded. Discourses of death simply become part of a lifestyle in the service of the eternal now. Consequently, the 'black rage' articulated in much early hip hop has been eroded.

Concluding comments

Music, insisted Deryck Cooke, 'is a language of the emotions, through which we directly experience the fundamental urges that move mankind.'[164] It is hardly surprising, therefore, that it is one of the primary ways in which humans communicate meaning. Indeed, for some, such as Nietzsche, it is able to do this in a way that words cannot: 'Compared with music all communication by words is shameless; words dilute and brutalize; words depersonalize; words make the uncommon common.'[165] While we might want to be a little more circumspect than Nietzsche in our assessment of the value of words, nevertheless, he makes an important point about the power of music. In particular, we have seen that music is potent in its ability to create affective spaces within which anxieties can be expressed, vulnerabilities explored and the awareness of death, dying and bereavement contemplated. Moreover, because all these subjects are explicitly dealt with in popular music in ways that society, friends and family often find difficult to address, we have seen that it can serve important psychosocial functions. Again, this is the case because listeners have a particularly close relationship to the music they appreciate. It is able to articulate *their* emotions in profound and important ways, which would be lacking if we were simply to read the lyrics of a song without the musical accompaniment. As the anthropologist Thomas Turino discusses, 'musical sounds are a powerful human resource, often at the heart of our most profound social occasions and experiences.'[166] Hence, typically, not only does it enrich the lives of listeners – becoming associated with significant moments in their history – but it contributes to the construction of personal and group/tribal identities.[167] Despite the nature of the lyrics, which may or may not be profound – and may not even make any discernible sense – and despite the nature of the music, which may or may not be sophisticated – and may even be little more than a sonic miasma of white noise – because of its particular relationship to the private self, popular music often has a meaning beyond that which can be expressed verbally. Moreover, we have seen that, because music is uniquely bound up with the subjective lives of individuals, it also has a relational and, indeed, public dimension. At one level, individuals can be quickly drawn together by a shared love of the same music – which indicates, at least superficially, shared values; people can be united in a cause by singing the same song; lovers can reignite their passion for each other by listening to a piece of music associated with a significant moment in their shared history. At another level, subcultures coalesce around the affective impact of music and the countercultural meanings evoked, which, in turn, manifests significant moments of *communitas*.[168] Hence, the argument here is that music is peculiarly effective when it comes to reflection on mortality, in that it feels intimately connected with the deepest levels of who we are as human beings and social animals.

Consequently, we have seen that popular music makes an enormously important contribution to our ability to deal with the core experiences of mortality. Again, it is able to have an emotionally powerful *momento mori* impact, reminding us, however, fleetingly, transgressively, sordidly and ludically, of our own mortality and impermanence. While this is typically done at a distance, through the discourses of death, violence and gore, it is also able to create affective spaces shaped by brooding melancholia and morbidity that encourage listeners to reflect far more closely on their feelings of disaffection and vulnerability. As such, on the one hand, popular music culture counters the thanatological timidity of Western societies, and, on the other hand, it articulates the anxieties that many young people find hard to express.

While a significant profit can be made out of selling discourses of abjection to liminal personae and, as a result, legitimate ethical concerns need to be raised, nevertheless, popular music's willingness to expose/exploit mortality has value. Saturnine elegies, songs of self-harm, morbid music and discourses of death all articulate a level of reflection on mortality that is largely absent in the modern West. That is to say, there is a difference between viewing mortality in films, reading about it in books and reflecting on within the affective spaces evoked by music.

Finally, we can think of much mortality music as constructive protest against the fading of the light. That is to say, in morbidity, there is both an acceptance of and a resistance to mortality. Such songs are, to use Douglas Davies's term again, but thinking of Camus, 'words against death'.

Transfiguration, Devotion and Immortality

'Do you know who Elvis Presley was?' Charles Wolfe, Professor of English at Middle Tennessee State University, asked a group of children. 'He was an old guy who was a king somewhere ... a great big man .... He lives in a big house in Memphis and he only comes out at night.'[1] While the children clearly had little understanding of who Elvis actually was, not only had they all heard of him, but they clearly recognized him to be a person of peculiar significance. He was 'a great big man' and, as with many mythic characters, he had peculiar habits: 'he only comes out at night.' When I read these words, they not only made me smile, but struck me as important, because they indicated something of the cultural impact a dead celebrity can achieve. 'Dead Elvis' was quickly superimposed onto a number of cultural signifiers, some of which have been folkloric and religious. As Nik Turner put it in the Inner City Unit song 'Bones of Elvis' (*Maximum Effect*, 1981), 'TV Flash – announcers say/ Elvis the First has passed away/ Millions of tears in '77/ They laid him down in hamburger heaven .... We're going to raise the bones of Elvis ... E – everlasting/ L – life/ V – via/ I – induced/ S – suspended animation .... From Graceland to the Promised Land .... They say he didn't die/ Just sitting in an icebox/ Like grandma's apple pie.' In other words, dead Elvis is a different being than the historical Elvis, just as in Christology the kerygmatic Christ (the proclaimed Christ of faith) can be distinguished from the Jesus of history.[2] Mythic narratives, typically shaped by Christian discourse, were constructed to make sense of Elvis's passing and his continued significance in the lives of believers: Had he actually died? Has he been resurrected in some sense? Is he in 'suspended animation ... sitting in an icebox/ Like grandma's apple pie', awaiting some future purveyor of immortality to defrost him? Perhaps, he is now in heaven interceding on behalf of the faithful, much like the saints of Christian history?[3] Through a process of popular canonization, or even deification, dead Elvis has, in the imaginations of some of the faithful, been 'transfigured'. And, he is not alone. He rubs shoulders in celestial society with several other notable dead celebrities.

While such idiosyncrasies may strike us as quirky, perhaps rather silly, and moderately interesting, we have already seen that, for some people, they can have far-reaching implications. As Chris Rojek comments of living celebrities, such 'narcissistic idealization and hero worship have their roots in the human need for elevated, transcendent forms of meaning. The desire for larger-than-life versions of ourselves, or superhuman gods, leads to the birth of stars'.[4] Consequently, an individual's identity becomes enmeshed in the imagined life of the living celebrity. This has serious implications, in that, on the one hand, the ascendancy of the celebrity, the release of a new album or the announcement of a tour has a direct impact on the emotional well-being of the fan. On the other hand, however, the decline or suffering of a celebrity is also replicated in the life of the fan.[5] For many people, of course, this leads to little more than mood swings. For others, however, as indicated in Chapter 4, the consequences are more serious. Media reports of the suicide of celebrities, for example, can lead to copycat incidents of self-destruction – known as 'the Werther effect' after Goethe's novel *The Sorrows of Young Werther* (1774).[6] While the Werther effect concerns the media coverage of all suicides, recent studies have found that there is a particular need to remain vigilant about how the news of celebrity suicides is reported.[7] There is, for example, evidence to suggest that visits to hospital emergency departments 'for suicide attempts or self-injury increased following the announcements of celebrity suicides'.[8] This is supported by the research of King-wa Fu and Paul Yip, who analysed the impact of the suicide in 2003 of the Hong Kong Cantopop star, Leslie Cheung. They found that 38 per cent of their respondents had been adversely affected by Cheung's death.[9] There was, for example, a significant increase in the suicides of men using the same method as Cheung. While this applies to the suicides of all celebrities, the death of a musician might be considered a particular concern. That is to say, as we have seen, largely because of the affective power of music and, therefore, its significance for the subjective lives of individuals, musicians have a very particular importance. Indeed, I want to suggest that, for some fans, dead musicians become 'transfigured'.

A note on myth

Central to the transfiguration of dead musicians is the construction of a mythic narrative – a mythic interpretative framework. While we need not discuss the various theories of myth, of which there are several,[10] the term, as it is used here, refers quite simply to a 'story' (*mythos*), a sacred narrative that makes sense of existence for an individual or group of people.

In seeking to understand a myth, generally speaking, scholars have attended to its origins, its function and its subject matter, including its cast of characters – its heroes, deities and near-deities. For most scholars, however, it is the *function* of a myth that is crucial, which, of course, is closely related to its *origin* (i.e. why it was constructed in the first place). Myths arise to meet a need. What that need is varies, but these peculiar stories emerge because they do something important for humans; they help us to explain our world, our place in it and our relationships with others; they make sense of our existence. In short, the purpose of myth is, as Rudolf Bultmann argued many years ago, 'to express man's understanding of himself in the world in which he lives. Myth should be interpreted not cosmologically, but anthropologically, or better still, existentially.'[11] In the final analysis, as Camus put it, 'myths are made for the imagination to breathe life into them'.[12] Stories about transfigured celebrities can be understood in such terms.

Having said that, a commitment to a dead musician need not, and often does not, lead to transfiguration and the construction of mythic narratives. As studies of fandom as popular devotion indicate, a person can still organize his or her life around a commitment to a celebrity without that commitment becoming, in some sense, '*religious* devotion' – which is how the term 'devotion' is used in the following discussion. Such commitments may have similarities to those in religion, in that they can be understood as 'intensive concerns with extensive effects',[13] but do not progress much beyond fandom. Understanding this distinction is important, because not to do so can lead to a common confusion between fandom and religious conviction, supported by a mythic narrative. While, of course, such issues – which have, for example, been central to the debates surrounding 'implicit religion' or 'secular religion'[14] – are not easy to resolve, an accurate understanding of the phenomenon does require some clarity of thought about the differences.

Transcendence and transfiguration

For many people in advanced capitalist societies, popular culture is increasingly the only space where existentially meaningful commitments can take shape. Consequently, we should not be surprised that fandom and devotion have emerged as overlapping 'fields of discourse'.[15] Are not religious devotees or worshippers simply *fans* of some deity or other? While this is true, nevertheless, distinguishing between fans and devotees is important.[16] On the one hand, there is a continuity between the two, in that, typically, fan culture provides the context for devotion, but, on other hand, there is discontinuity, in that, there is a process of conversion separating the fan from the devotee. As with most experiences of conversion, as Diane Austin-Broos argues, it can be understood as 'a form of passage, a "turning from and to" that is neither syncretism nor absolute breach'.[17] For example, the death of Diana, Princess of Wales on 31 August 1997 led very quickly to her popular canonization in the minds of some people.[18] While many simply found her an inspirational figure and mourned her passing, others converted to a sanitized and sanctified idea of her. A few even began to receive messages from her ascended spirit. Books such as *The Celestial Voice of Diana: Her Spiritual Guidance to Finding Love* by the Norwegian Rita Eide, *Princess Diana's Message of Peace: An Extraordinary Message of Peace for Our Current World* by Marcia McMahon and *In Her Own Words: The After Death Journal of Princess Diana* by Christine Tooney all channelled the wisdom of a newly transfigured Diana.[19] Such individuals who had been fans of Diana during her life had, at her death, converted and claimed to have been visited by her 'presence' in some significant sense. The myth of dead Diana and the experiences supported by that myth go well beyond the fan's celebration of her significance. As one devotee related, 'I have just spent a few hours chatting with Diana, Queen of Hearts, and am enjoying that wonderful internal glow fuelled by the spark of stimulating conversation with a good friend. My soul feels satisfied and nourished…'.[20] Again, Marcia McMahon has also recently communicated messages from John Lennon, who now spends time with Diana, George Harrison and Mother Teresa composing, playing music and planning world peace: 'Darling, it's great to hear your vibration', says John to Marcia. 'I have to adjust my earphones as we're rehearsing for a special show… George and I came up with it, of course… Lady Diana… sends her love…. The show is all about what you can do for peace… Mother Teresa is assisting Diana in the project. Well, anyway, George and I got roped in, so to speak.'[21] While such claims are rare and while it is, of course, very difficult for the vast majority of us to take such ideas seriously, nevertheless, they are idiosyncratic manifestations of the refusal to believe in the extinction of significant individuals and, of course, examples of the ubiquitous denial of death. That is to say, the postmortem continuity of a celebrity's life entails the postmortem continuity of one's own life.

Such sacralized experiences within popular culture – experiences 'packed with cosmological and theological meaning', as Victor Turner described them[22] – involve what I have theorized as 'the transfiguration of celebrity'.[23] In doing so, I am drawing on Arthur Danto's understanding of the transfiguration of the commonplace.[24] Although, of course, Danto, an art critic, was not interested in the sacralization of popular culture, nevertheless, his understanding of 'art' – shaped by a particular cultural context or 'artworld' – evoking and embodying meaning, provides a useful starting point. Informed by a particular mythic narrative, within certain contexts – 'worlds' or 'fields of discourse' – a celebrity is transfigured. The story oriented around that elevated being provides a framework within which meaning and significance can be constructed, the celebrity becoming a living ally of the believer. Testimonies within groups of believers – disseminated on pilgrimages, in books, at meetings, on the Internet and so on – provide a 'fiduciary framework', a community of verifiers[25] and a discursive context within which further interpretation occurs.

The transfiguration of the deceased, rather than the living, is obviously far more common, in that, first, the dead no longer have the capacity for unfortunate manifestations of humanness. At death, the history of the celebrity is fixed and theological reconstruction can begin. Princess Diana will now always be, as Luciano Pavarotti declared, 'the most beautiful symbol of humanity and love for all the world'.[26] Flawed human individuals, such as Diana, Elvis and Jim Morrison, at their deaths, are quickly sanitized and elevated to sacralized icons. Second, death also requires a strategy of immortalization, in that it is important for some devotees that the celebrity's life is not completely extinguished in order for it to have continued significance in their own lives. This is often important for the devotee's continued well-being. Third, and relatedly, as noted above, if one accepts the extinction of the celebrity's self, then one is forced to accept the termination of one's own self. Finally, generally speaking, the death of *young* musicians, such as Brian Jones, Nick Drake, Jim Morrison, Kurt Cobain and Tupac Shakur, has a particular resonance with fans because not only is their youthful vitality fixed in the minds of fans, but they died at the height of their influence. This is largely why it is commonly understood that, as the British deejay and television presenter Lauren Laverne commented, 'self-destruction is part of rock and roll; it's part of the rock and roll mythology'.[27] As David Halberstam says of Elvis and Marilyn Monroe, 'they each became part of the ... cult of the hero/star who dies young, a victim, it would seem, of the very same adoring society that had turned them into cult figures. Their early deaths added to the power of their mystique, for they remained forever the gods of youth, and we were spared having to see them grow old.'[28]

As well as canonization, death can also lead to a significant fetishizing of associated material culture. Hence, in the case of Elvis, 'like all pilgrims, visitors to Graceland want to take away a piece of the holy land. It is possible to buy little glass bottles with a coin in "from Graceland" and grains of soil, encased in glass and reminiscent of the talismans bought by pilgrims at medieval European shrines.'[29] For worshippers of transfigured celebrities, unlike fans, items are not merely precious memorabilia, they are relics.[30] Whether taking a memento from the sacralized mise-en-scène, kissing the image of Elvis, touching the grave of Jim Morrison at Père Lachaise Cemetery in Paris or pinning a message to the bulletin board erected at the site of Marc Bolan's fatal car crash,[31] there is evidence of 'ultra-subjectivization'.[32] 'The individual is overcome with emotion to such a degree' that the symbolism of the material object, the fetish, 'seems to possess an inner force that compels its subject to act emotionally.'[33] The commonplace becomes impregnated with the solemn, the serious, the sublime and the sacred.[34] The relic is, in some sense, a material manifestation of what I will call 'the vertical axis' (see below).[35] It represents an empirical connection to the spiritual self of a dead and transfigured celebrity. As such, of course, a discourse of immortality is developed that erodes the impact of the awareness of personal extinction.

Metaphorical identification, typical within fan cultures – e.g. 'Elvis is king' – becomes, through the processes of transfiguration and conversion, religious identification – e.g. Elvis as saint: 'he prays for us in heaven'.[36] The conversion of the fan into a devotee entails the conversion of fan discourse into theological discourse. Again, this process of conversion is an important one, in that, not only does it shift the celebrity into a religious frame of reference, for which theological language is literally appropriate, but also in so doing it supports discourses of immortality that implicate the fan. It is, in other words, part of a more profound immortality strategy.

That said, *it is important not to confuse theological discourse with the metaphorical language common within fan cultures.* Just because fans declare 'Elvis is god' does not mean that they invest him with any soteriological significance, pray to him or build him into a prior theological system. Only the converts – of which there may only be a few – invest celebrities with that level of significance. Only they literally reconstruct the deceased as immortal. Only they actually worship. Only they develop popular theologies of celebrities. In the words of one Elvis devotee, 'there is a distance between human beings and God. That is why we are close to Elvis. He is like a bridge between God and us ... I believe in Jesus Christ and I believe in God ... but Elvis was special.

Elvis was … given to us to remind us to be good … .'[37] In other words, there are those for whom Elvis has been canonized and incorporated into a Christian theological system. Gregory Reece provides a good example of Elvis's spiritual significance. In the summer of 1991, he found himself, in the early hours of the morning, sitting in a hospital emergency room in Memphis, Tennessee. On the chair next to him was a woman who had been crying.

> Her mother had suffered a stroke and she was waiting to hear from the doctors. This was especially difficult, she said, because she had no family in Memphis. A few years before, she had divorced her husband, said goodbye to her children, packed up her mother, and moved from southern California to Memphis, Tennessee. She moved, she said, 'just to be with Elvis'. It was then that I noticed that the ring on her left hand, as well as her earrings and necklace, were adorned with images of Elvis. Elvis, she told me, was the most important thing in the world to her. He gave her inspiration and hope. The one good thing about the passing away of her mother was that her mother would then get to go to heaven to be with Elvis.[38]

Similarly, not only have numerous conspiracy theories emerged about the death of Jim Morrison,[39] but, as Peter Margry notes, some visitors to his grave clearly believed that, now dead, he possessed 'a special, effectual power',[40] an ability to help individuals through the difficult moments of their lives. The following letter left at his grave is a good example of devotion to a transfigured celebrity:

> Dear Jim,
>   Thank you for everything. Years ago I had a vision and in it you told me to keep the flame alive. I now promise you, I will. You have my word. Please give me any help you can, and watch over me. I will make you proud. Thank you.[41]

As James Riordan and Jerry Prochnicky indicate, such ideas have been encouraged by the growing occulture surrounding Morrison. Central to these discourses have been comments by, for example, his partner, Pamela Courson, regarding her belief that 'Jim's spirit often left his body and went off travelling by itself'[42] and also claims by another partner, Patricia Kennealy, who insisted that she had a postmortem encounter with him: 'I had a vision of Jim standing at the foot of my bed in the middle of the night. It was no dream … . In the vision Jim had no beard and at that time I didn't know that he had shaved it off in Paris.'[43] And, of course, as with other celebrities, Riordan and Prochnicky note that 'of all the myths concerning Morrison's death, the most popular one has been that he never died at all. Many have believed that Jim Morrison pulled off the ultimate ruse and faked his own death'.[44]

As I have discussed elsewhere,[45] central to the cultivation of such mythic narratives and subsequent experiences has been a vibrant celebrity 'occulture',[46] core to which is a thriving industry of films and visual art. For example, the interest in Morrison mythology increased significantly in the 1990s following the release of *The Doors* (1991), a film directed by Oliver Stone.[47] Essentially, a countercultural hagiography, in which Morrison is beatified by Stone, the film served to ignite fan devotion, which, for some fans, evoked an affective space within which he became transfigured. As Margry comments, 'the film opens significantly with a mystical representation, set to music, of how Morrison took on [shamanic] qualities as a small child by means of "spiritual transmission" from a dying Native American in the New Mexico desert. With references made in passing to the secularization … of American society, the film continues with the words "the ceremony is now to begin" …. His interest in the occult and his shamanistic trances and performances during concerts are shown at length.'[48] Margry's subsequent ethnographic research shows how this film became a key factor in the construction of Morrison as 'someone with supernatural or transcendent qualities'.[49] Similarly, Joel Brodsky's iconic 'Young Lion' series of photographs, the most evocative of which was used for the cover of *The Best of the Doors* (1985),[50] stimulated and informed the transfiguration of Morrison. 'Not only did fans see him as someone divine, but for many fans these photos functioned as images of the human ideal.'[51]

As indicated above, painting, of course, has been central to the sacralization of musicians in that artists have, wittingly or unwittingly, often functioned as iconographers, superimposing traditionally religious signifiers onto transfigured celebrities. One only has to think of, for example, Roger Law's painting of Jimi Hendrix as avatar, which was used for the cover of *Axis Bold as Love* (1967). Again, paintings of Elvis, such as Alexander Guy's *Crucifixion* (1992), Rena LaCaria's *Elvis the King* (1989), Carol Robinson's *Crying Icons* (1992), Joanne Stephens' *Homage to Elvis* (1991) and, of course, Bill Barminski's *Elvis Christ* (1988), are good examples of such iconography, which both reflect his cultural significance and also increase his potential as a component of a discourse of immortality.[52]

Finally, as Chris Rojek comments, dead celebrities,

> embody and reflect the spirit of the times. In their import about the glories, setbacks and achievements of human life, they stand square in the searchlight of eternity. In this generation, and for generations to come, they offer parables for the lives of others. The most prestigious celebrities have replaced the gods of ancient societies as the immortals …. As recorded people, their films, radio broadcasts and TV interviews have a timeless quality.[53]

This is an important point. Following death, that catalytic moment in a celebrity's history, transfiguration begins almost immediately. This process of immortalization and sacralization is further encouraged by material culture. Not only are artefacts fetishized as relics, as we have seen, but pop iconography serves the process of transfiguration. Their *recorded* lives (films, journalistic footage, photographs, records, websites and so on), which are so central to celebrity culture, also contribute to the construction of mythic narratives. They provide a fixed lens through which to interpret the significance of an individual's life, thereby granting them immortality and a continual presence. Moreover, the celebrity is frozen within a particular timeframe, a particular period of history. As such, for both the fan and the devotee – in different, but related ways – the celebrity becomes the lens through which to read the significance of that historical period and that culture. Consequently, the celebrity emerges as the embodiment of the zeitgeist of that period. This is significant for the fan/devotee, because it is this perception of the zeitgeist that contributed to the construction of his or her identity. As such, the transfigured celebrity tends to embody 'sacred forms',[54] core values around which a fan/devotee's life is oriented. Not only did those halcyon days constitute an idyllic 'good time', a time when core areas of my identity were formed, a time when I was 'happy', but the transfigured celebrity is perceived as the incarnation of that 'goodness', that idealized moment. As such, there is something vital and invigorating about reflecting on that celebrity and on that period of youth, which, again, mitigates the impact of ageing and the awareness of death.

Recorded immortality

With the above comments in mind, it is important to remind ourselves of the significance of recorded music. Rojek's point is an important one. As *recorded people*, musicians 'have a timeless quality'.[55] The cultural significance of recorded music is discussed in fascinating detail by Timothy Day in his *A Century of Recorded Music*, which has the intriguing subtitle, *Listening to Musical History*.[56] At one level, of course, this subtitle simply makes the point that we can now listen to the history of music. Archives, such as those at the Smithsonian Institution or Cecil Sharp House, give the researcher access to music of earlier cultures and traditions. But, of course, at another level, recorded sound per se is a way of listening to history now. It is a simple point, but it is one worth making. That is to say, when I hear Elvis sing 'That's All Right' on the radio, I am literally listening to that musician on 5 July 1954 in the Sun Studio. In this sense, as the band Scouting for Girls put it, 'Elvis isn't dead/ I heard him on the radio' ('Elvis Ain't Dead', 2007). Recorded people are immortalized. Not only has, as Day shows, a century of recording technology changed the way we listen to and perform music, but it has also introduced a discourse of immortality. It is able to evoke affective spaces within which we listen to timeless beings, who never die and who are always there for us. Like the saint and the deity, the recorded musician is always on hand to comfort us, to provide emotional succour.

Day makes the point that recordings allow a 'kind of intimacy to develop between listener and performer', which was not previously available.[57] My point here is simply that this has implications for our perception of dead musicians. They are never entirely dead to us. For example, one listener described to Day the 'sense of human contact' which was present to him when listening to records of Caruso and Lotte Lehmann: 'we feel we know these people ... '.[58] Hence, he says, 'recordings have been used as aural icons to which a listener may return time and time again over many years, like a poem or a biblical text or a picture, surrounding the unchanging sounds with personal and ever-developing associations and memories.'[59] Hence, as the theologian Karl Barth commented, in a discussion about his own devotion to Mozart, 'I confess that, thanks to the invention of the phonograph, which can never be praised enough, I have for years and years begun the day with Mozart .... And when I hear him, it gladdens, encourages, and comforts me ... '.[60]

Thinking in this way about recorded music takes us back to the earlier discussion in Chapter 3, namely that contemporary culture is sonically haunted by the past. I discussed this in relation to, for example, Bass Communion's *Ghosts on Magnetic Tape* (2004), which is a collection of ambient compositions directly inspired by the idea that dead people might be able to communicate from beyond the grave. The album creates eerie sonic environments through the use of samples of old recordings. Hence, as I argued earlier, the album is able to evoke an affective space within which the boundaries between the past and the present, and between the beyond and the mundane appear to have collapsed. The living and the dead seem occupy the same space. That which should be deceased and in the past now speaks and engages our emotions in the present. Not only does this have the effect of immortalizing musicians, who, while dead, still move us emotionally, but, through memory, it also shifts us back into our own past – back to a time, as discussed above, when we were immersed in the vitality of youth and when our identities were being formed. For example, while, on the one hand, George Harrison's record *All Things Must*

Pass (1970) reminds me of just that fact, on the other hand, it very powerfully transports my past into my present and, as such, is able, momentarily, to recreate for me feelings from my youth – some of which shaped the person I am now. As such, it interrupts my perception of mortality. Hence, on the one hand, it is a *memento mori*, reminding me (as I remember it doing very poignantly in my adolescence) that 'Sunrise doesn't last all morning/ A cloudburst doesn't last all day.... All things must pass/ All things must pass away' ('All Things Must Pass', *All Things Must Pass*, 1970). On the other hand, now later in life, it is able to deconstruct immortality through affectively evoking the past. Recorded music, which can be meditatively listened to over and over again, engages with perceptions of mortality in emotionally complex ways.

Pilgrims and dead rock stars

At 7:30 a.m. on a sweltering July day, I climbed the curving driveway of Graceland, Elvis Presley' mansion/museum in Memphis, Tennessee.... A dozen or so others made the trek with me, heading to the back of the house, its décor flash-frozen in 1977, when the King died at age forty-two. Near the swimming pool, Elvis, his parents, and his grandmother are buried in a semicircle under massive bronze slabs.... But the most galvanizing sight was a young woman in her early twenties sitting on the steps near the graves, weeping. It wasn't sniffles-and-a-tissue kind of crying. Her shoulders were heaving; the sobs came from the center of her being.... She was far too young to have seen Elvis when he was alive.... The music that moved her as a teen would have been R.E.M., Garth Brooks, or Madonna. But here she was, raw and wounded, pulled by some compulsion to the burial place of a man would have been almost seventy had he lived.[61]

The rest of this chapter is focused on trying to make sense of this type of response to deceased people not personally know to those who grieve. In particular, with reference to the notion of transfiguration, I want to examine the nature of pilgrimage to sites associated with popular musicians. Moreover, in examining this phenomenon, I also want to challenge the currently popular notion of 'secular pilgrimage'.

Popular devotion to saints, to relics and to shrines looks very similar to the activities of the committed fan.[62] Similar rituals are performed and there is a comparable level of emotional investment. It is hardly surprising, therefore, that particular places associated with celebrities, especially dead celebrities,[63] have become sacred *topoi* for pop pilgrims. However, again, it is important not to confuse fans with devotees. As indicated above, because there are overlapping fields of discourse, sites associated with dead musicians can be both places of cultural interest and shrines. How a site is experienced depends on a person's conception of a celebrity and of that celebrity's perceived relationship to the sacred. A devotee's sacralized encounter with a site is a very particular one, which, as noted above, might be understood in terms of 'ultra-subjectivization'. That is to say, the emotions that arise in response to the physical site of the pilgrimage and its related material culture, which have, as a result of the growing anticipation engendered by the pilgrim's preparation and subsequent journey, become 'so overwhelming that the individual is overcome with emotion to such a degree' that the symbolism of the site itself 'seems to be a powerful agent in its own right'; 'it seems to possess an inner force that compels its subject to act emotionally'.[64] Again, this is, I suggest, a rather different response to that of the tourist. It is so, because it is informed by the transfiguration of a celebrity and a mythic narrative. Hence, while locations such as Graceland are both popular tourist destinations and sites of pilgrimage, for the pilgrim, unlike the tourist, they are spaces in which, in a particularly focused way, an individual encounters that which is of 'ultimate concern' (to use Paul Tillich's helpful concept[65]), that which provides meaning and makes sense of existence. There is a feeling of standing in the presence of the central character of the mythic narrative around which one's life is oriented. As discussed above, having died, the transfigured celebrity can be omnipresent and, indeed, omniscient. In other words, the dead can be reimagined in spiritual and mythological terms. As John Eade and Michael Sallnow comment, 'a pilgrimage locale is typically a site associated either with the manifestation of the divine to human beings or with the human propensity to approach the divine'.[66] Hence, needless to say, the devotee's visit to such a site is an ultimately meaningful event, different in kind from fan/tourist interest. Indeed, the pilgrims, as liminal personae (see below), are now themselves located within the mythic mise-en-scène; they are a small part of the transfigured celebrity's mythic narrative.

Such experiences have always, since the Middle Ages, been central to the meaning of pilgrimage. While the original Latin term, *peregrinus*, bore little of this sacralized weight, being principally a general term used of strangers and migrants,[67] by the medieval period, it had become invested with a very particular meaning. The pilgrim journeyed to a shrine, 'an earthly traveller seeking a sacred destination and, through that journey, an experience of the divine'.[68]

Similarly, today, although the term 'pilgrimage' is used metaphorically in secular parlance to indicate a meaning-making journey to a place of significance, strictly speaking, it still refers to 'a journey based on religious and spiritual inspiration, undertaken by individuals or groups, to a place that is regarded as more sacred or salutary than the environment of everyday life, to seek a transcendental encounter with a specific cult object for the purpose of acquiring spiritual, emotional or physical healing or benefit'.[69] Even if, as Anna Davidsson Bemborg discusses in her study of contemporary Swedish pilgrimages, the destination 'has lost its significance as a holy place', nevertheless, the journey itself is interpreted spiritually, in that it 'creates a sacred space' during which 'experiences of spirituality as well as of self-transformation can take place'.[70] While we need not discuss the various strengths and weaknesses of competing definitions of 'pilgrimage', which have been helpfully unpacked elsewhere,[71] the important features that, *taken together*, distinguish 'pop pilgrimage' from, say, heritage tourism, are as follows: first, the journey is often just as important as the destination; second, destinations need not be traditionally 'religious';[72] and, most importantly, for it to be a 'pilgrimage', there needs to be some affective experience of spiritual significance, personal transformation and transcendence of the mundane. Hence, sites of particular importance in the personal histories of popular musicians or film stars are just as likely to receive pilgrims as those of the saints and deities of the world religions.

Conversely, of course, one must avoid the genetic fallacy of assuming that, simply because people travel to sites of special interest or use 'pilgrim-talk', they are pilgrims. Often they are not. Indeed, because boundaries between tourism and pilgrimage are notoriously fuzzy, there has been much scholarly debate, particularly in tourism literature, about where lines should be drawn. However, if the term 'pilgrimage' is to mean anything useful at all, that meaning must be related to the religious and cultural contexts and discourses in which the ritual emerged, rather than the discourses and contexts of contemporary tourism, where it seems to be frequently used in a colloquial sense as a metaphor for journeys and events of personal significance. Certainly, discussions of the history of travel have, as Simon Coleman and John Eade point out, 'tended to emphasize the need to understand pilgrimage in the context of other, roughly parallel activities, and this has sometimes blurred the boundaries between genres and mobility'.[73] Indeed, although some scholars have used the compound modifier 'pilgrim-tourist',[74] this too inhibits clarity: first, the very combination assumes an important distinction between 'pilgrimage' and 'tourism', which is not always acknowledged; and, second, intertextually, 'pilgrim' tends to be used as a modifier simply to add gravitas to the word 'tourist', rather than, again, acknowledging the distinctive nature of the pilgrim's experience. Similarly, while it is clear what the term 'secular pilgrimage' is attempting to articulate – namely ostensibly secular sites at which 'pop devotion' might take place – it is, in fact, an unhelpful oxymoron, in that the pilgrim's experience is *not* secular. Without wanting to deny that tourists might become pilgrims (or, indeed, *vice versa*), in the final analysis, if a celebrity's grave is a pilgrimage destination, it has been sacralized in the imagination of the pilgrim. It is *not* a 'secular shrine' and those journeying to it are *not* 'secular pilgrims'. Those who engage with a grave as a secular site, rather than as a 'shrine', are fans and tourists. Hence, again, such terminology encourages category confusion.

In using the term 'pilgrimage' of journeys to sites associated with dead musicians – usually graves – I have a particular set of experiences in mind, directly related to what we might term 'the vertical axis'. That is to say, in pilgrimage – whether it involves journeying to what many would identify as an ostensibly 'secular' site or a conspicuously 'religious' shrine – the horizontal and vertical axes are intimately related. There is a journey away from everyday, 'normal' life (horizontal axis) and towards that of ultimate concern to the pilgrim (vertical axis), rather than that which is merely of special interest (as in the case of the fan/tourist). Unlike the tourist's journey, the pilgrim's horizontal movement away from the loci of everyday life and towards the sacred *topos* anticipates an experience of transcendence, in the sense of a meaningful event interpreted according to a mythic narrative. Hence, while 'thin description' may not identify very much that distinguishes the pilgrim from the tourist, in that both can be situated within semantic and theoretical discourses relating to mobility, from an emic perspective or employing 'thick description', the difference is profound.[75] For pilgrims, the journey and the sacred *topos* evoke an affective space within which there is produced a particular feeling of transcendence, a peculiar sort of devotional mood informed by myth, that is meaning-making and that distinguishes it from the experience of the fan/tourist. Not to acknowledge this distinction in some sense is to ignore the emic experience of the pilgrim and to confuse worship with intellectual interest. Edith Turner's observations are worth repeating here: 'pilgrimage is not an intellectual activity but rather a religious one. Many middle-class people also undertake it, not because they are doing something "in" or touristy, but because they ... have felt the call to do so.'[76] This 'call to do so' has its genesis in myth and anticipates an experience of the vertical axis.

As indicated above, the immortalization of musicians not only has the effect of establishing their continued and increased significance in the life of believers, but also, perhaps most importantly, challenges the notion of the extinction of selves generally. As such, in a number of overlapping ways, meaning is established in an individual's life.

Kinetic rituals

Central to the study of pilgrimage over the last few decades has been the work of Victor and Edith Turner. Published in 1978 and building on Victor Turner's earlier work, *The Ritual Process*,[77] their groundbreaking study, *Image and Pilgrimage in Christian Culture*, presented these sacralized journeys as subversive movements from structure to antistructure. This movement, they observed, appeared to have significant similarities with rites-of-passage, with those events that mark (and create) transitions between places, stages of life, social states and so on. More specifically, they argued that the pilgrims' journeys, horizontally and vertically (geographically and spiritually/transcendentally), could be understood in terms of separation from their everyday existence into a liminal space beyond normal society. This movement constituted a departure from the structured social worlds to which they belonged to new spaces of antistructure, in which the rules of the normal world were partially suspended. Within this liminal space, self-discovery, liberation and transformation are encouraged. As Nancy Frey observed of pilgrims travelling to Santiago de Compostela, the journey provided 'opportunities to live, at least temporarily, another reality and to discover alternative ways of perceiving and acting in the world'.[78] Finally, the pilgrim experiences 'aggregation' through reintegration back into everyday life. 'The vast majority of pilgrims claim that the pilgrimage is a positive experience that they want, in some way, to integrate into their daily lives .... Going home ... can bring a joyous sense of well-being, renewal, and appreciation for what is.'[79]

This 'kinetic ritual', as Edith Turner referred to it,[80] has another significance, in that the close, shared liminal experiences of pilgrims generate a sense of *communitas*.[81] Although the actual subjective experience of *communitas* is difficult to articulate – Turner conceding that it is 'almost beyond strict definition'[82] – 'it has to do with the sense felt by a group of people when their life together takes on full meaning. It could be called collective *satori* or *unio mystica*, but the phenomenon is far more common than the mystical states.'[83] She even identifies in the experience of *communitas* moments of 'unconditional love'.[84] However, her interpretation of it in terms 'collective *satori* or *unio mystica*' is important, in that it places the encounter at the conjunction of both axes, horizontal (the community) and vertical (transcendent experience). During a pilgrimage away from home comforts and support structures, individuals form intimate, meaning-making associations with each other on the basis of their common spiritual goals and interests. Such *communitas* manifests an alternative social structure, a counterculture within which equality is primary and in which barriers that pertain to everyday society are removed. In summary, the pilgrim's experience of liminality includes 'release from mundane structure', 'reflection on the meaning of basic religious and cultural values', the 'ritualized enactment of correspondences between religious paradigms and shared human experiences' and so on.[85]

This transitory, in-between state, in which 'liminal personae' or 'threshold people'[86] move away from the ordinary and the everyday, through existentially meaningful moments of antistructure and back to normal life, is a form of 'acceptable disorder' when the conventional and the everyday is suspended and questioned. The pilgrim slips through 'a kind of crack between worlds, like the looking glass of Alice',[87] into a 'realm of pure possibility'.[88] This intriguing metaphor identifies the 'movement from a mundane center to a sacred periphery which suddenly, transiently, becomes central for the individual, an *axis mundi* of his faith'.[89] There is, for many pilgrims, an existentially significant communal experience, again, directly related to the vertical axis.

This, again, is quite distinct from the experience of the fan. Although there is a growing literature on 'fan pilgrimage', as indicated above, much of it involves a misreading of the term 'pilgrimage', in that it tends to be used as a synonym for any emotionally significant journey, whether actual or virtual. This confusion, in turn, has the effect of both overlooking the significance of the spiritual experiences of pilgrims, of liminality and of *communitas*. As such, it evacuates the term of much of its meaningful content. For example, in a discussion of the Lewis Carroll Society as a fan community, Will Brooker extends the notion of pilgrimage to 'the fan practice of visiting geographical sites associated with the author',[90] largely, it would seem, both because the fan has to travel away from a familiar home environment and also because there is some emotional investment in the journey. Although clearly 'an important part' of the society's activities, it is telling that he also refers to these 'pilgrimages' as 'outings' and 'trips'. Indeed, while one enthusiastic member of the society related to him that 'it is essential and imperative to visit places with a LC connection and particularly to see collections in libraries and universities the world over', this is hardly the language of a pilgrim. Rather, it suggests tourism around sites of particular interest to fans.[91] Another member suggested that the visits were 'quite important' (again, hardly pilgrim language), because, 'occasionally one gets a bit closer to the man and his time by being in places associated with him'.[92] There is little sense of Carroll being a transfigured being with mystical or soteriological significance. Indeed, in another discussion, Brooker supports the thesis that a fan viewing a favourite film might be considered a pilgrim. Fans undertake, so it is claimed, a 'symbolic pilgrimage', in that they are transported from the ordinary to the extraordinary while sitting in front of a screen.[93] One could think of similar home-based activities during which such transitions occur that would just as effectively empty 'pilgrimage' of any meaningful content. Again, there is little sense of transformative *communitas* or of a genuine experience of the vertical axis.

Pilgrimage is more than simply focused travel, virtual or otherwise, by fans. Many enthusiastic memorabilia collectors and scrapbook fillers never progress beyond fandom and tourism, in the sense that they would not situate their fandom in a sacralized context, such as that described by Turner: 'as one approaches the holy of holies the symbols become denser, richer, more involuted – the landscape itself is coded into symbolic units packed with cosmological and theological meaning.'[94] Hence, while not wanting to deny that a fan's preoccupations are emotionally important or socially significant, the difference between such commitments and those of the pilgrim is not one of degree, but of kind. Fans may, as Lisa Lewis comments in her study of fan cultures, 'wear the colours of their favourite team … record their favourite soap operas … tell you every detail about a movie star's life and work … [and] sit in line for hours for front row tickets to rock concerts',[95] but they are not pilgrims seeking experiences of transcendence according to a mythic narrative around which their lives are oriented. Fandom, of course, is important, in that it identifies a significant set of human behaviours relating to what Lawrence Grossberg has referred to as 'maps of mattering'.[96] Indeed, at some level, we are all fans of something or someone. To be a fan is to identify with that which 'matters' to us and has contributed in some sense to the construction of our identities: 'everyone is constantly a fan of various sorts of things, for one cannot exist in a world where nothing matters.'[97] But, again, this is somewhat different from arguing that everyone is committed to those ritualized, liminal behaviours focused on the vertical axis.

Concluding comments

We have seen that, in an attempt to come to terms with the death of a musician, some individuals convert from fandom to devotion. While, of course, it will always be unwise to attempt to identify which fans have actually converted and which have not, there is an important difference between the experiences of each. For the convert, there has been an epiphany that not only leads to an elevated estimation of the musician's importance, but also often to a denial of the extinction of the musician. Consequently, the horizontal, earthly plane of everyday life is intersected by a vertical, transcendent plane, around which quotidian existence has been reoriented, making life a little less ordinary and a little more bearable. 'To be converted is to reidentify, to relearn, reorder, and reorient.'[98] As dead musicians are transfigured, so everything associated with them is bathed in epiphanic light. They are purified and elevated. This sacralizing process transforms metaphorical language about artists into theological language, and, as such, objects and artefacts associated with them are treated 'not just symbolically, but as personal embodiments of the transcendent. In the right circumstances, they act as personal agents of communication and transformation'.[99] Once musicians die and slip away from the material world of human error, corruption and decay into the mythic world of the imagination, they are transfigured, becoming immortal, omnipresent beings. 'And now we rise/ And we are everywhere/ And now we rise from the ground' (Nick Drake, 'From the Morning', *Pink Moon*, 1972).[100] The dead musician rises from the ground and is relocated to the centre of the world of the fan/devotee, recreated according to the values and ideals of the fan/devotee. That is to say, while there is, of course, some link, culturally, between the historic musician and the sanctified dead musician, in effect, transfiguration is an ultimately creative process that breaks that link. A *fan* may elevate the musician but ultimately remains fascinated with the details of the historic person's life and work. A *devotee*, on the other hand, reimagines the dead icon according to a particular mythic/theological framework, which, in turn, has implications for their own awareness of mortality.

Such responses need not, of course, be limited to popular music. For example, to a large extent, this is how the theologian Karl Barth responded to Mozart:

> I am not a musician or a musicologist. But I can – indeed, I must – testify to my devotion to Mozart...I have sometimes been asked whether, if I were to have proceeded on the basis of my theology, I should not have discovered quite different masters in music. I must insist...no, it is Mozart and no one else...I

have for years and years begun each day with Mozart ... I even have to confess that if I ever get to heaven, I would first of all seek out Mozart and only then inquire after Augustine, St. Thomas, Luther, Calvin, and Schleiermacher.[101]

He even wrote a letter of thanks to the immortalized, sanctified Mozart: 'Well now, someone hit upon the curious idea of inviting me and a few others to write for his newspaper a "Letter of Thanks to Mozart." At first I shook my head, my eye already on the wastebasket. But since it is *you* who is to be the subject, I find it almost impossible to resist.'[102] He continues, 'there where you are now – free of space and time – you ... know more about us than it is possible here. And so I don't doubt, really, that you have known for a long time how grateful I have been to you, grateful for as long as I recall, and that this gratitude is being constantly renewed.'[103] Such sentiments, which are not dissimilar to those of Elvis devotees, are hardly those of a fan. While, of course, Barth does not imagine that he can channel messages from Mozart (thank goodness), the composer is much too important to him for his appreciation to be interpreted simply in terms of fandom. 'Whoever has discovered Mozart even to a small degree and then tries to speak about him falls quickly into what seems like rapturous stammering.'[104]

As Barth indicates, not only does music have the ability to articulate some of our deepest feelings and evoke some of our most important memories, around which we organize our identities and emotional well-being, but it also makes our short lives bearable. Typically, we have seen, the dead artist, particularly the artist who dies young, incarnates the idealism and vitality of our youth, which is so important to us as mortals seeking strategies to manage the awareness of personal dissolution. As Laurence Binyon's evocative First World War poem 'Ode of Remembrance' (1914) has it: 'They shall grow not old, as we that are left grow old/ Age shall not weary them, nor the years condemn.' While this interpretation of death as an escape from the ravages of ageing can be applied to all who die young, for the artist whose music still evokes affective spaces within which we are transported back to significant moments in our own past, it takes on a peculiar significance. Their music, their persona and the culture to which they contributed, which is entwined with our own histories and identities, have not been tainted by their vulnerability. They represent frozen moments in our own emotional history, idyllic snapshots within which we ourselves feature. It matters little whether the artist died before we were born or before we became familiar with their music. If my identity has been constructed within affective spaces evoked by their music and the culture they represented, that artist becomes to me something more than simply a popular musician. Nick Drake, for example, although not widely recognized during his life, has, for many people, become the distillation of a particular folk-hippie, Romantic idealism. He never released a bad album, he never embarrassed himself at a London nightclub, he never sold insurance, he never descended into haggard, drunken old age and he never embarked on a disappointing comeback tour. Consequently, the Romantic emotional charge he is able to evoke has only increased with the passing of time. Dead musicians such as Nick Drake, Jimi Hendrix, Jim Morrison, Kurt Cobain, Gram Parsons and, indeed, Tupac Shakur will always remain iconic because they epitomize a particular reading of youthful immortality. Any foibles and character deficiencies are simply obscured in the glow of what they represent to us.

In the final analysis, the death of a musician unleashes a complex web of emotional and cultural responses. Again, it functions as a *memento mori*, declaring that all of us, no matter how significant, are impermanent. As such, the death of a musician also requires a response to mortality, which lessens the impact of our awareness of impermanence. This brings us back to Bauman's argument. An artist's music, which links us to significant moments in our past, and our constructions of that artist as immortal in some sense – whether literally or figuratively – is part of 'the sediment of the ongoing attempt *to make living with the awareness of mortality liveable*'.[105]

Notes

Introduction

1   J. Macmurray, *Persons in Relation* (London: Faber & Faber, 1961).

2   J. Donne, *Devotions upon Emergent Occasions and Death's Duel*, available at: http://www.gutenberg.org/files/23772/23772-h/23772-h.htm (accessed 15 October 2010).

3   R. Wilkins, *The Fireside Book of Death* (London: Robert Hale, 1990), 13.

4   Z. Bauman, quoted in M.H. Jacobsen, 'Sociology, Mortality and Solidarity. An Interview with Zygmunt Bauman on Death, Dying and Immortality', *Mortality* 16:4 (2011), 382 (original emphasis).

5   A. Camus, *The Myth of Sisyphus*, trans. by J. O'Brien (Harmondsworth: Penguin Books, 1975).

6   See D. Hesmondhalgh, *Why Music Matters* (Chichester: John Wiley & Sons, 2013); C. Partridge, *The Lyre of Orpheus: Popular Music, the Sacred and the Profane* (New York: Oxford University Press, 2014). Also, simply to read through almost any of the books in the 33 1/3 series published by Continuum/Bloomsbury, each of which is essentially a paean of praise for a single album, reminds one of the significance of popular music in the everyday lives of individuals: http://333sound.com (accessed 15 October 2014).

7   A. de Botton & J. Armstrong, *Art as Therapy* (London: Phaidon Press, 2013), 64–65.

8   E. Burke, *A Philosophical Enquiry into the Origins of the Sublime and Beautiful: And Other Pre-Revolutionary Writings* (New York: Penguin Classics, 1998), 54.

9   Ibid., 86.

10 Ibid., 24.

11 See E. Parisot, *Graveyard Poetry: Religion, Aesthetics and the Mid-Eighteenth Century Poetic Condition* (Franham: Ashgate, 2013).

12 See Partridge, *Lyre of Orpheus*, 37–59; C. Partridge, 'Popular Music, Affective Space, and Meaning'. In G. Lynch, J. Mitchell & A. Strhan (eds), *Religion, Media and Culture: A Reader* (London: Routledge, 2012), 182–93.

13 See T. DeNora, 'Aesthetic Agency and Musical Practice: New Directions in the Sociology of Music'. In P. Juslin & J. Sloboda (eds), *Music and Emotion: Theory and Research* (Oxford: Oxford University Press, 2001), 165.

Chapter 1

1   R. Otto, *The Idea of the Holy: An Inquiry into the Non-rational Factor in the Idea of the Divine and Its Relation to the Rational*, trans. by J.W. Harvey (Oxford: Oxford University Press, 1958).

2   See Patricia Jalland's revealing discussion of death and bereavement between 1830 and 1920, *Death in the Victorian Family* (Oxford: Oxford University Press, 1996).

3   See, for example, Roy Porter's critical review of his work, 'The Hour of Philippe Ariès', *Mortality* 4:1 (1999), 83–90.

4   P. Ariès, *The Hour of Our Death*, trans. by H. Weaver (New York: Alfred A. Knopf, 1981), 19. See also P. Edwards, 'Existentialism and Death: A Survey of Some Confusions and Absurdities'. In J. Donnelly (ed.), *Language, Metaphysics, and Death* (New York: Fordham University Press, 1978), 53–56.

5   Ariès, *Hour of Our Death*, 19.

6   Ibid., 19.

7   For an interesting overview of changing attitudes towards death in the West, see L.A. DeSpelder & A.L. Strickland, *The Last Dance: Encountering Death and Dying* (Palo Alto: Mayfield Publishing Company, 1983), 5–33. See also Antje Kahl's discussion of attitudes to death in Germany: '"Our Dead are the Ultimate Teachers of Life": The Corpse as an Inter-mediator of Transcendence: Spirituality in the German Funeral Market', *Fieldwork in Religion* 8 (2013), 223–40.

8   See R. Turnock, 'Death, Liminality and Transformation in *Six Feet Under*'. In K. Akass & J. McCabe (eds), *Reading Six Feet Under: TV To Die For* (London: I.B. Tauris, 2005), 39–49; S. Smith, '"I felt a funeral in my brain": The Politics of Representation in HBO's *Six Feet Under*', *Psychoanalysis, Culture & Society* 14:2 (2009), 200–06. See also the Lyra Sihra's moving personal account in 'An Open Casket', *Journal of Palliative Medicine* 14:2 (2011), 245–45; K. Garces-Foley & J.S. Holcomb, 'Contemporary American Funerals: Personalizing Tradition'. In K. Garces-Foley (ed.), *Death and Religion in a Changing World* (Armonk: M.E. Sharpe, 2006), 207–27.

9   Ariès, *Hour of Our Death*, 600.

10   Garces-Foley & Holcomb, 'Contemporary American Funerals', 209.

11   Ibid.

12   J. Mitford, *The American Way of Death Revisited* (London: Virago, 1998), 17. This groundbreaking text was originally published in 1963.

13   See A. Gawande, *Being Mortal: Illness, Medicine and What Matters in the End* (London: Profile Books, 2014).

14   Bonvesin de la Riva, quoted in M. Gragnolati, 'From Decay to Splendor: Body and Pain in Bonvesin de la Riva's *Book of the Three Scriptures*'. In C.W. Bynum & P. Freedman (eds), *Last Things: Death and the Apocalypse in the Middle Ages* (Philadelphia: University of Pennsylvania Press, 2000), 84–85.

15 Ibid., 85.

16 Ariès, *Hour of Our Death*.

17 W.M. Spellman, *A Brief History of Death* (London: Reaktion Books, 2014), 7.

18 Ariès, *Hour of Our Death*, 557–601.

19 See, for example, A. Giddens, *Modernity and Self-Identity: Self and Society in a Late Modern Age* (Oxford: Polity Press, 1991); A. Giddens, *The Transformation of Intimacy* (Stanford: Stanford University Press, 1993); E. Hobsbawm, *Age of Extremes* (London: Abacus, 1995); C. Taylor, *Sources of the Self* (Cambridge: Harvard University Press, 1990); C. Taylor, *The Ethics of Authenticity* (Cambridge: Harvard University Press, 1991); C. Taylor, *A Secular Age* (Cambridge: Harvard University Press, 2007).

20 Taylor, *Secular Age*, 720.

21 Kansas, 'Dust in the Wind', *Point of Know Return* (1977). Kerry Livgren of Kansas recalls the following: 'One day ... my wife heard me doing this acoustic fingerpicking bit. She said, "That sounds really nice. You should make it into a song." I said, "Nah, it's just an exercise." I was reading a book of American Indian poetry at the time and happened to come across this line: "All we are is dust in the wind." It really struck me and stuck with me. I was humming that line along with this fingerpicking exercise, and 15 minutes later I had a song.' Acoustic Nation, 'Kansas's Kerry Livgren Shares the Story Behind "Dust In The Wind"'. Available at: http://www.guitarworld.com/acoustic-nation-kansas-ken-livgren-shares-story-behind-dust-wind (accessed 25 March 2014).

22 See Taylor, *Sources of the Self*, 34.

23 See Christina Welch's discussion of English carved cadaver monuments: 'For Prayers and Pedagogy: Contextualizing English Carved Cadaver Monuments of the Late-Medieval Social Religious Elite', *Fieldwork in Religion* 8 (2013), 133–55.

24 Dead Can Dance, 'Black Sun', *Aion* (1990).

25 Ambrose Bierce, quoted in J. Bowker, *The Meanings of Death* (Cambridge: Cambridge University Press, 1993), 6.

26 For a helpful discussion of some of the issues, see Taylor, *Secular Age*, 720–26.

27 F. Dastur, *How Are We to Confront Death: An Introduction to Philosophy*, trans. R. Vallier (New York: Fordham University Press, 2012), 1.

28 See M.R. Leming & G.E. Dickinson, *Understanding Dying, Death and Bereavement*, seventh edition (Belmont: Wadsworth, 2011), 513–15.

29 Z. Bauman, *Mortality, Immortality and Other Life Strategies* (Cambridge: Polity Press, 1992), 3.

30 H.H. Farmer, *Reconciliation and Religion*. Gifford Lectures, 1951. Ed. by C. Partridge (Lewiston: Edwin Mellen, 1998), 160.

31 Frank Sinatra, 'My Way', on *My Way* (1969). Lyrics by Paul Anka.

32 Richard H. Kirk and Stephen Mallinder, interviewed in M. Fish, *Industrial Evolution: Through the Eighties with Cabaret Voltaire* (London: SAF Publishing, 2002), 241.

33 S. Freud, 'Thoughts for the Times on War and Death'. In S. Freud, *The Standard Edition of the Complete Psychological Works of Sigmund Freud*, Vol. 14. Ed. by J. Strachey (London: Vintage, 2001), 289.

34 For an interesting discussion of just this issue, see Liran Razinsky's comparative analysis of Freud and Georges Bataille: 'How to Look Death in the Eyes: Freud and Bataille', *SubStance* 38 (2009), 63–88.

35 F. Dastur, *Death: An Essay on Finitude*, trans. J. Llewelyn (London: Athlone, 1996), 2.

36 Freud, 'Thoughts for the Times on War and Death', 294.

37 Marcus Aurelius, *Meditations* (Ware: Wordsworth, 1997), 50.

38 Ariès, *Hour of Our Death*, 23. See also P. Edwards, 'Existentialism and Death: A Survey of Some Confusions and Absurdities'. In J. Donnelly (ed.), *Language, Metaphysics, and Death* (New York: Fordham University Press, 1978), 32–34.

39 See Mitford, *American Way Of Death Revisited*, 17.

40 See ibid., 51.

41 B. Malinowski, *Magic, Science and Religion and Other Essays* (London: Souvenir Press, 1974), 47.

42 Ibid., 51.

43 Ibid., 50–51.

44 Ibid., 51–52.

45 Ibid., 52.

46 Camus, *Myth of Sisyphus*, 11.

47 D. Davies, *Death, Ritual and Belief: The Rhetoric of Funerary Rites*, second edition (London: Continuum, 2002), 44–45.

48 Ibid., 45.

49 Ibid., 45.

50 See Partridge, *Lyre of Orpheus*.

51 Michael Gira, quoted in A. Licht, 'Tunnel Vision: Michael Gira', *The Wire* 223 (2003), 34.

52 R. Christgau, *Grown Up All Wrong: 75 Great Rock and Roll Artists from Vaudeville to Techno* (Cambridge: Harvard University Press, 1998), 375.

53 See also Reed's reflections on death on his final solo album based on the poems of Edgar Allan Poe, *The Raven* (2003), the words of which have reproduced in an accompanying book, *The Raven* (New York: Grove Press, 2003).

54 D. Fricke, 'Lou Reed, *Magic and Loss*', *Rolling Stone* (23 January 1992). Available at: http://www.rollingstone.com/music/albumreviews/magic-and-loss-19920123 (accessed 23 August 2013).

55 'Seasons in the Sun' is a reworking of Jacques Brel's 'Le Moribond' (1961), which was translated into English by the American poet Rod McKuen. The American folk group The Kingston Trio first covered this English version in 1963.

56 C. Wiser & T. Jacks, 'Seasons in the Sun', *Songwriter Interviews*. Available at: http://www.songfacts.com/blog/interviews/terry_jacks_seasons_in_the_sun_/ (accessed 10 April 2014).

57 See Alison Stone's analysis of death and the significance of relationships: 'Natality and Mortality: Rethinking Death with Cavarero', *Continental Philosophy Review* 43 (2010), 353–72.

58 Gerard Way, quoted in T. Bryant, *The True Lives of My Chemical Romance* (London: Sidgwick & Jackson, 2014), 156.

59 Epicurus, quoted in Dastur, *How Are We to Confront Death*, 2–3.

60 Dastur, *Death*, 46–47.

61 Z. Bauman, quoted in M.H Jacobsen, 'Sociology, Mortality and Solidarity. An Interview with Zygmunt Bauman on Death, Dying and Immortality', *Mortality* 16:4 (2011), 382 (original emphasis).

62 Ibid.

63 Bauman, *Mortality, Immortality*, 5.

64 Bauman, quoted in Jacobsen, 'Sociology, Mortality and Solidarity', 383.

65 Ibid.

66 Bauman, *Mortality, Immortality*, 14 (original emphasis).

67 See C. Partridge, 'Haunted Culture: The Persistence of Belief in the Paranormal'. In O. Jenzen & S. Munt (eds), *Research Companion to Paranormal Cultures* (Farnham: Ashgate, 2013), 39–50.

68 Bauman, quoted in Jacobsen, 'Sociology, Mortality and Solidarity', 383.

69 Ibid., 389.

70 P. Kostenbaum, quoted in Bauman, *Mortality, Immortality*, 16.

71 E. Becker, quoted in ibid., 15.

72 Bauman, quoted in Jacobsen, 'Sociology, Mortality and Solidarity', 382 (original emphasis).

73 Bauman, *Mortality, Immortality*, 1.

74 Davies, *Death, Ritual and Belief*, 16–18; D.J. Davies, *A Brief History of Death* (Oxford: Blackwell, 2005), 116; J. Dollimore, *Death, Desire and Loss in Western Culture* (London: Allen Lane, 1998), 121–22.

75 Bauman, *Mortality, Immortality*, 2.

76 Ibid., 5.

77 Ibid., 5–6.

78 M. Foucault, *The Birth of the Clinic: An Archaeology of Medical Perception*, trans. A.M. Sheridan Smith (New York: Sheridan Books, 1972).

79 Bauman, *Mortality, Immortality*, 145.

80 Ibid., 143.

81 See J. Hick, *The Metaphor of God Incarnate*, second edition (London: SCM, 2005).

82 Taylor, *Secular Age*, 720.

83 Z. Bauman & K. Tester, *Conversations with Zygmunt Bauman* (Cambridge: Polits Press, 2001), 126.

84 Bauman, *Mortality, Immortality*, 187.

85 Ibid., 164.

86   Bauman & Tester, *Conversations*, 127.

87   Bauman, *Mortality, Immortality*, 170.

88   Ibid., 169–70.

89   David Byrne, quoted in S. Steenstra, *Song and Circumstance: The Work of David Byrne from Talking Heads to the Present* (New York: Continuum, 2010), 261.

90   V. Nobokov, *Speak, Memory* (London: Penguin, 2000), 5.

91   Spellman, *Brief History of Death*, 7.

92   P. Tillich, *Theology of Peace* (Louisville: Westminster/John Knox Press, 1990), 172.

93   Bauman, *Mortality, Immortality*, 163.

94   Ibid., 6.

95   Tillich, *Theology of Peace*, 172.

96   Spellman, *Brief History of Death*, 211.

97   See *Hull Daily Mail*, 'Yorkshire's Top Ten Funeral Songs', *Hull Daily Mail* (29 October 2012). Available at: http://www.hulldailymail.co.uk/Revealed-Yorkshire-s-funeral-songs/story-17194566-detail/story.html (accessed 09 May 2014); The Telegraph, 'Monty Python Classic Tops List of Best Funeral Songs', *The Telegraph* (27 January 2009). Available at: http://www.telegraph.co.uk/news/newstopics/howaboutthat/4352276/Monty-Python-classic-tops-list-of-best-funeral-songs.html (accessed 09 May 2014); Hans ten Cate, ' "Always Look on the Bright Side of Life" Among Funeral Favorites', *PythOnline's Daily Llama* (13 March 2005). Available at: http://www.dailyllama.com/news/2005/llama276.html (accessed 09 May 2014).

98   Bauman, quoted in Jacobsen, 'Sociology, Mortality and Solidarity', 386 (original emphasis).

99   Farmer, *Reconciliation and Religion*, 163.

Chapter 2

1   See, for example, Jeffrey Weinstock's discussion of the profanation of religion in goth subcultures: 'Profaning the Sacred: Goth Iconography, Iconoclasm, and Subcultural Resistance'. In A. Grønstad & Ø. Vågnes (eds), Cover Scaping Discovering Album Aesthetics (Copenhagen: Museum Tusculanum Press, 2010), 163–78.

2   See J.C. Bivins, *Religion of Fear: The Politics of Horror in Conservative Evangelicalism* (New York: Oxford University Press, 2008).

3   M. Dean, 'Christian Death Interview'. Available at: http://www.vamp.org/Gothic/Text/cd-interview.html (accessed 31 March 2014).

4   See R. Williams, *The Art of Rozz Williams: From Christian Death to Death*, ed. by Nico B. (San Franscisco: Last Gasp, 1999); S. Michaud, *Rozz Williams: Le théâtre des douleurs* (Rosières-en-Haye: Camion Blanc, 2010).

5   See B. Clack, *Sex and Death: A Reappraisal of Human Mortality* (Cambridge: Polity Press, 2002), 21–38.

6   C. Partridge, *The Lyre of Orpheus: Popular Music, the Sacred and the Profane* (New York: Oxford University Press, 2014).

7   Chris Jenks, *Transgression* (London: Routledge, 2003), 178–80.

8   See Christian Smith (ed.), *The Secular Revolution: Power Interests and Conflict in the Secularization of American Public Life* (Berkeley: University of California Press, 2003).

9   Émile Durkheim, *The Elementary Forms of Religious Life*, trans. by Carol Cosman (Oxford: Oxford University Press, 2001), 46.

10 Gordon Lynch, *The Sacred in the Modern World: A Cultural Sociological Approach* (Oxford: Oxford University Press, 2012), 29.

11 J.W. Green, *Beyond the Good Death: The Anthropology of Modern Dying* (Philadelphia: University of Pennsylvania Press, 2008), 31.

12 See Jeffrey Alexander's discussion of the historical contingency of sacred forms in his analysis of shifting perceptions of the holocaust: *The Meanings of Social Life: A Cultural Sociology* (New York: Oxford University Press, 2003), 27–84.

13 D. Eck, *Banaras: City of Light* (New York: Columbia University Press, 1999), 325.

14 Mary Douglas, *Purity and Danger: An Analysis of the Concept of Pollution and Taboo* (London: Routledge, 2002 [1966]), 9.

15 J.W. Green, *Beyond the Good Death: The Anthropology of Modern Dying* (Philadelphia: University of Pennsylvania Press, 2008), 31–61; D.J. Davies, *Death, Ritual and Belief: The Rhetoric of Funerary Rites*, second edition (London: Continuum, 2002), 83–84.

16 See, for example, D. Brill, 'Gender, Status and Subcultural Capital in the Goth Scene'. In P. Hodkinson & W. Deicke (eds), *Youth Cultures: Scenes, Subcultures and Tribes* (New York: Routledge, 2007), 111–26; S. Frith & A. McRobbie, 'Rock and Sexuality'. In S. Frith & A. Goodwin (eds), *On Record: Rock, Pop, and the Written Word* (New York: Pantheon Books, 1990), 371–89.

17 See Partridge, *Lyre of Orpheus*, 37–59. A. Gabrielsson, *Strong Experiences with Music: Music is Much More than Just Music*. Trans. R. Bradbury (Oxford: Oxford University Press, 2011).

18 Augustine, *Nicene and Post-Nicene Fathers. First Series*, Vol. 5. *St. Augustine: Anti-Pelagian Writings*, ed. by Philip Schaff (New York: Cosimo, 2007 [1887]), 19.

19 Walter Brueggemann, *Genesis* (Louisville, John Knox Press, 1982), 47–48.

20 Augustine, *City of God*, trans. H. Bettenson (London: Penguin, 2003), 513.

21 Ibid., 513–14; Augustine, *Nicene and Post-Nicene Fathers*, 176.

22 See V. Turner, *The Ritual Process: Structure and Anti-Structure* (Chicago: Aldine, 1969), vii, 201.

23 Ibid., 95. See also V. Turner, 'Variations on a Theme of Liminality'. In S. Moore & B. Myerhoff (eds), *Secular Ritual* (Amsterdam: Van Gorcum, 1977), 36–52.

24 Emilie Bresson, quoted in B. Bone, 'Monarch', *Rock-A-Rolla* 50 (2014), 11.

25   See E. Turner, 'The Literary Roots of Victor Turner's Anthopology'. In K. Ashley (ed.), *Victor Turner and the Construction of Cultural Criticism: Between Literature and Anthropology* (Bloomington: Indiana University Press, 1990), 167.

26   For a good recent collection of studies of Beat culture, which demonstrates this point perfectly, see J. Skerl (ed.), *Reconstructing the Beats* (New York: Palgrave Macmillan, 2004).

27   V. Turner, *Dramas, Fields and Metaphors* (Ithaca: Cornell University Press, 1974), 13–14.

28   D. Brill, 'Gender, Status and Subcultural Capital in the Goth Scene'. In P. Hodkinson & W. Deicke (eds), *Youth Cultures: Scenes, Subcultures and Tribes* (New York: Routledge, 2007), 117.

29   See, Turner, *Ritual Process*, 128–29.

30   See, Roland Boer, *Nick Cave: A Study of Love, Death and Apocalypse* (Sheffield: Equinox, 2012).

31   P. Bourdieu, *Distinction: A Social Critique of the Judgment of Taste*, trans. by R. Nice (Cambridge: Harvard University Press, 1984).

32   S. Thornton, *Club Cultures: Music, Media and Subcultural Capital* (Cambridge: Polity, 1995). It has since been helpful to a number of other popular music scholars. See, for example, Ryan Hibbett's discussion of 'indie', 'What is Indie Rock?', *Popular Music and Society* 28 (2005), 55–77.

33   Thornton, *Club Cultures*, 11–12.

34   See Hibbett, 'What is Indie Rock?', 55–77.

35   P. Townshend, *Who I Am* (London: HarperCollins, 2012), 87.

36   See ibid., 424, 448–49, 463, 517.

37   L. Goodlad & M. Bibby, 'Introduction'. In L. Goodlad & M. Bibby (eds), *Goth: Undead Subculture* (Durham: Yale University Press, 2007), 1.

38   K.E. Macfarlane, 'The Monstrous House of Gaga'. In J. Edwards & A.S. Monnet (eds), *The Gothic in Contemporary Literature and Popular Culture: Pop Goth* (New York: Routledge, 2012), 121.

39   F. Botting, 'Gothic Culture'. In C. Spooner & E. McEvoy (eds), The Routledge Companion to Gothic (London: Routledge, 2007), 203–04.

40   J. Baudrillard, *Simulacra and Simulation*, trans. by S.F. Glaser (Ann Arbor: University of Michigan Press, 1994).

41   N. Kilpatrick, *The Goth Bible: A Compendium for the Darkly Inclined* (London: Plexus, 2005).

42   E. Burke, *A Philosophical Enquiry into the Origins of the Sublime and Beautiful: And Other Pre-Revolutionary Writings* (New York: Penguin Classics, 1998), 86.

43   Ibid., 24.

44   A. Bennett, *Music, Style, and Aging: Growing Old Disgracefully?* (Philadelphia: Temple University Press, 2013), 22–23. See also, A. Bennett & J. Taylor, 'Popular Music and the Aesthetics of Ageing', *Popular Music* 13 (2012), 231–43.

45 Vampire Mike, quoted in N. Kilpatrick, *The Goth Bible: A Compendium for the Darkly Inclined* (London: Plexus, 2005), 1.

46 Nimue, quoted in Kilpatrick, *Goth Bible*, 2.

47 W.S.F. Pickering, *Durkheim's Sociology of Religion: Themes and Theories* (London: Routledge & Kegan Paul, 1984), 124–25.

48 Ibid., 125.

49 Lynch, *Sacred in the Modern World*, 19.

50 On music as a prosthetic technology, see Partridge, *Lyre of Orpheus*, 51–55.

51 P. Hegarty, *Noise/Music: A History* (New York: Continuum, 2007), 155.

52 Sacred Bones Records, 'Pharmakon, *Abandon*'. Available at: http://www.sacredbonesrecords.com/products/sbr099-pharmakon-abandon (accessed 24 May 2014).

53 Margaret Chardiet, quoted in D. Keenan, 'Pharmakon', *The Wire* 368 (October, 2014), 38.

54 Ibid.

55 For a short time, Bataille was closely associated with André Breton, with whom he founded the anti-Fascist group Contre-Attaque (1935–1936).

56 A. Riley, ' "Renegade Durkheimianism" and the Transgressive Left Sacred'. In J.C. Alexander & P. Smith (eds), *The Cambridge Companion to Durkheim* (Cambridge: Cambridge University Press, 2005), 285.

57 Ibid.

58 Pickering, *Durkheim's Sociology of Religion*, 124–25.

59 G. Bataille, *The Accursed Share*, Vol. I, trans. by R. Hurley (New York: Zone Books, 1991); *The Accursed Share*, Vols. II & III, trans. by R. Hurley (New York: Zone Books, 1991).

60 F. Botting & S. Wilson, 'Introduction: From Experience to Economy'. In F. Botting & S. Wilson (eds), *The Bataille Reader* (Oxford: Blackwell, 1997), 1–2.

61 G. Bataille, *Inner Experience*, trans. by L.A. Boldt (Albany: State University of New York Press, 1988), 3. It should be noted, as Bataille makes clear in this volume, he has an ambivalent attitude towards mysticism, particularly the way the experience is interpreted within Christianity, in that it is linked to a teleology, to a salvific process.

62 Adrenochrome is a compound produced in the human body by the oxidation or decomposition of adrenaline (epinephrine).

63 H.S. Thompson, *Fear and Loathing in Las Vegas* (London: Flamingo, 1993), 131.

64 Aldous Huxley, who was the first to posit the psychedelic effects of adrenochrome, claimed that it was able to 'produce many of the symptoms observed in mescaline intoxication'. This is, however, now known to be false. See A. Huxley, *The Doors of Perception and Heaven and Hell* (London: Flamingo, 1994), 2–3.

65 Thompson, *Fear and Loathing*, 130–32.

66 G. Bataille, *Eroticism: Death and Sensuality*, trans. by Mary Dalwood (San Francisco: City Lights Books, 1986), 67–68.

67   Boer, *Nick Cave*, 44.

68   See J. Baudrillard, 'Death in Bataille'. In F. Botting & S. Wilson (eds), *Bataille: A Critical Reader*, (Oxford: Blackwell, 1998), 139–45.

69   For an engaging, popular overview of the scene, see A. Mudrian, *Choosing Death: The Improbable History of Death Metal and Grindcore* (Los Angeles: Feral House, 2004).

70   On music as a channel for the construction of identities, see R. MacDonald, D. Hargreaves & D. Miell (eds), *Musical Identities* (Oxford: Oxford University Press, 2002).

71   V. Turner, 'Variations on a Theme of Liminality'. In S. Moore & B. Myerhoff (eds), *Secular Ritual* (Amsterdam: Van Gorcum, 1977), 37.

72   Ibid., 37. See also, V. Turner, 'Death and the Dead in the Pilgrimage Process'. In F.E. Reynolds & E.H. Waugh (eds), *Religious Encounters with Death: Insights from the History and Anthropology of Religions* (University Park: Pennsylvania State University Press, 1977), 24–39.

73   See Reynolds & Waugh, *Religious Encounters with Death*; J. Bowker, *The Meanings of Death* (Cambridge: Cambridge University Press, 1993).

74   A. Hanlan, quoted in Reynolds & Waugh, 'Introduction'. In Reynolds & Waugh (eds), *Religious Encounters with Death*, 7. See also, A. Hanlan, *Autobiography of Dying* (New York: Doubleday, 1979).

Chapter 3

1   R. Mintz, 'Gothic'. In M. Kehoss & B. Rein (eds), *Gothic* (Santa Ana: Orange County Centre for Contemporary Art, 2012), 1.

2   P. McGrath, 'Transgression and Decay'. In C. Grunenberg (ed.), *Gothic: Transmutations of Horror in Late Twentieth Century Art* (Boston: The Institute of Contemporary Art/MIT Press, 1997), 157–58.

3   For a good example of the influence of steampunk in heavy metal, see *Black Heart of Empire* (2011) by Imperial Vengeance (a luxury release of which includes a booklet inspired by Victorian penny dreadfuls).

4   I. van Elferen, *Gothic Music: The Sounds of the Uncanny* (Cardiff: University of Wales Press, 2012), 15.

5   Ibid., 1.

6   Bauman, *Mortality, Immortality*, 4.

7   Z. Bauman, quoted in M.H. Jacobsen, 'Sociology, Mortality and Solidarity ', 386.

8   See D. Punter, 'The Uncanny'. In C. Spooner & E. McEvoy (eds), *The Routledge Companion to Gothic* (London: Routledge, 2007), 129–36.

9   S. Freud, *The Uncanny*, Trans. by D. McLintock (London: Penguin, 2003), 121–62.

10   There have been a number of recent analyses of this most flexible of concepts. A good recent overview of the uncanny in contemporary critical theory is provided

by Matt Ffytche, 'Night of the Unexpected: A Critique of the "Uncanny" and Its Apotheosis Within Cultural and Social Theory', *New Formations* 75 (2012), 63–81.

11 Freud, *Uncanny*, 123.

12 N. Royle, *The Uncanny* (Manchester: Manchester University Press, 2003), 1.

13 Freud, *Uncanny*, 149.

14 Ibid., 148.

15 van Elferen, *Gothic Music*, 8, 10.

16 See Partridge, *Lyre of Orpheus*, 37–59; C. Partridge, 'Popular Music, Affective Space, and Meaning'. In G. Lynch, J. Mitchell & A. Strhan (eds), *Religion, Media and Culture: A Reader* (London: Routledge, 2012), 182–93.

17 J. Habermas, *The Theory of Communicative Action: A Critique of Functionalist Reason*, Vol. 2, Trans. T. McCarthy (London: Polity Press, 1987), 113–98.

18 T. DeNora, *Music in Everyday Life* (Cambridge: Cambridge University Press, 2000), 11.

19 See Partridge, *Lyre of Orpheus*; P.N. Juslin & J. Sloboda (eds), *Music and Emotion: Theory and Research* (Oxford: Oxford University Press, 2001).

20 Julia Kristeva, quoted in J. Culler, *The Pursuit of Signs: Semiotics, Literature, Deconstruction* (London: Routledge, 2001), 116. See also J. Kristeva, *Desire in Language: A Semiotic Approach to Literature and Art* (New York: Columbia University Press 1980).

21 Julia Kristeva, quoted in Culler, *The Pursuit of Signs*, 116. See also Kristeva, *Desire in Language*.

22 For a good introduction to Gregorian chant, see D. Hiley, *Gregorian Chant* (Cambridge: Cambridge University Press, 2009).

23 See S. Palmer, 'Purity and Danger in the Solar Temple'. In James R. Lewis (ed.), *The Order of the Solar Temple: The Temple of Death* (Aldershot: Ashgate, 2006), 48. J.R. Hall and P. Schuyler, 'The Mystical Apocalypse of the Solar Temple'. In James R. Lewis (ed.), *The Order of the Solar Temple: The Temple of Death* (Aldershot: Ashgate, 2006), 67.

24 The piece in which the backward chanting is used is Jocelyn Pook's 'Masked Ball', available on *Flood* (1999).

25 See, for example, Joseph Stannard's, worthwhile interview with Sunn O))): 'The Gathering Storm', *The Wire* 302 (April, 2009), 42–47. See also the video for 'Eulogy' by L.A. Vampires and Zola Jesus. The track is available on *LA Vampires Meets Zola Jesus* (Not Not Fun Records, 2010).

26 D. Laing, '"Sadeness", Scorpions and Single Markets: National and Transnational Trends in European Popular Music', *Popular Music* 11 (1992), 127.

27 S. Fish, *Is There a Text in This Class? The Authority of Interpretive Communities* (Cambridge: Harvard University Press, 1980), 14.

28 van Elferen, *Gothic Music*, 11.

29 'The tritone has long represented the Devil in music by negating a sense of modal or tonal stability. Originally, it acquired the name of *diabolus in musica* because

of its disruptive effect on the concordant fourths and fifths of Western European medieval music: the interval B to F needed to be "corrected" by flattening B or sharpening the F.' D.B. Scott, *From the Erotic to the Demonic: On Critical Musicology* (Oxford: Oxford University Press, 2003), 130.

30 For useful discussions of Herrmann's use of sound to evoke menace, see J. Wierzbicki, 'Psycho-Analysis: Form and Function in Bernard Herrmann's Music for Hitchcock's Masterpiece.' In P. Hayward (ed.), *Terror Tracks: Music, Sound and Horror Cinema* (London: Equinox, 2009), 14–46; R.J. Fenimore, 'Voices That Lie Within: The Heard and the Unheard in *Psycho*'. In N. Lerner (ed.), *Music in the Horror Film* (New York: Routledge, 2010), 88–89.

31 See J.M. Marzluff & T. Angell, *In the Company of Crows and Ravens* (New Haven: Yale University Press, 2005).

32 N. Richardson, 'In-between Worlds: Grouper', *The Wire* 334 (December, 2011), 28. Listen particularly to Grouper's albums *Wide* (Free Porcupine Society, 2006) and *Dragging a Dead Deer Up a Hill* (Type, 2008).

33 S. Frith, *Taking Popular Music Seriously: Selected Essays* (Aldershot: Ashgate, 2007), 263.

34 van Elferen, *Gothic Music*, 8, 10.

35 M. Schulkind, 'Is Memory for Music Special?', *Annals of the New York Academy of Sciences* 1169 (2009), 216.

36 D. Hesmondhalgh, *Why Music Matters* (Chichester: John Wiley & Sons, 2013), 53.

37 Schulkind, 'Is Memory for Music Special?', 216.

38 Ibid., 216.

39 For a useful general discussion of the significance of music for demented patients, see I. Vasionytė & G. Madison, 'Musical Intervention for Patients with Dementia: A Meta-analysis', *Journal of Clinical Nursing* 22 (2013), 1203–16.

40 M. Thaut, *Rhythm, Music, and the Brain: Scientific Foundations and Clinical Applications* (New York: Routledge, 2005), 76.

41 Ibid.

42 J.A. Sloboda & P.A. Juslin, 'At the Interface Between the Inner and Outer World: Psychological Perspectives'. In P.A. Juslin & J.A. Sloboda (eds), *Music and Emotion: Theory and Research* (Oxford: Oxford University Press, 2001), 88–89.

43 D. Toop, *Haunted Weather: Music, Silence and Memory* (London: Serpent's Tail, 2004), 42.

44 E. Levy, 'A Mix-Tape for Gus', *BBC Radio 4* (12 October 2014). Available at: http://emilylevy.co.uk (accessed: 12 October 2014).

45 L. Bernstein, *The Unanswered Question: Six Talks at Harvard* (Cambridge: Harvard University Press, 1976), 177.

46 Partridge, *Lyre of Orpheus*, 37–59.

47 D. Toop, *Sinister Resonance: The Mediumship of the Listener* (London: Continuum, 2010), xv.

48 van Elferen, *Gothic Music*, 9–10.

49 See, for example, Toop's discussion of sound and the uncanny: *Sinister Resonance*, 125–77.

50 See J. Derrida, 'Marx and Sons'. In M. Sprinker (ed.), *Ghostly Demarcations: A Symposium on Jacques Derrida's* Spectres of Marx (London: Verso, 1999), 213–69.

51 See Partridge, 'Haunted Culture, 39–50.

52 F. Jameson, 'Marx's Purloined Letter'. In M. Sprinker (ed.), *Ghostly Demarcations: A Symposium on Jacques Derrida's* Spectres of Marx (London: Verso, 1999), 39.

53 C. Davis, 'Hauntology, Spectres and Phantoms', *French Studies* 59 (2005), 376.

54 See, for example, Cary Wolfe's interesting analysis of Brian Eno and David Byrne's groundbreaking album *My Life in the Bush of Ghosts* (1981) in her book *What is Posthumanism?* (Minneapolis: University of Minnesota Press, 2010), 283–300; van Elferen, *Gothic Music*, 14–16. A particularly interesting and evocative use of 'hauntology' in relation to music and popular culture is provided by M. Fisher in *Ghosts of My Life: Depression, Hauntology and Lost Futures* (Alresford: Zero Books, 2014). See also the following release and accompanying book from Kode9 (Steve Goodman) and Toby Heys: AUDiNT, *Martial Hauntology* (2014).

55 Davis, 'Hauntology', 377.

56 Toop, *Sinister Resonance*, 24.

57 Ibid., 25.

58 S. Hill, *The Small Hand* (London: Profile Books, 2010), 6–7.

59 Davis, 'Hauntology', 377.

60 For a recent insider account of what is now often called instrumental transcommunication (ITC), see Anabela Cardoso's account of her own experiences, along with extracts of her conversations with the deceased, in *Electronic Voices: Contact With Another Dimension?* (Ropley: O Books, 2010).

61 G. Kieffer, 'Chasing Ghosts in the Dark: An Interview with Steve Wilson Regarding Bass Communion'. Available at: http://archive.today/onUxR (accessed 07 July 2014).

62 Wolfe, *What is Posthumanism?*, xxxiv.

63 D.N. Howard, *Sonic Alchemy: Visionary Music Producers and Their Maverick Recordings* (Milwaukee: Hal Leonard Corporation, 2004), 202.

64 J. Blacklow, 'What's Rihanna's Connection to Exorcisms?', *Yahoo Music* (15 November 2015). Available at: https://music.yahoo.com/blogs/yahoo-music/what-s-rihanna-s-connection-to-exorcisms-193920374.html (accessed 05 July 2014). See also the YouTube interview with JoJo Wright: 'Rihanna Tells JoJo About Seeing an Exorcism'. Available at: https://www.youtube.com/watch?v=ZGoNM1wdUnQ (accessed 05 July 2014).

65 V. Sage & A.L. Smith, quoted in van Elferen, *Gothic Music*, 14.

66 This point has been made by a number of contemporary theorists of Gothic: e.g. C. Spooner, 'Preface'. In B. Cherry, P. Howell & C. Ruddell (eds), *Twenty-First-Century Gothic* (Newcastle: Cambridge Scholars Publishing, 2010), xi.

67   On 'fields of discourse', see K. von Stuckrad, *Western Esotericism: A Brief History of Secret Knowledge*. Trans. N. Goodrick-Clarke (London: Equinox, 2005), 7.

68   See N. Gaiman, *Death: The Time of Your Life* (New York: DC/Time Warner, 1997).

69   Released in Scandinavia as 'Join Me in Death', because of the suicidal implications of the song, it had to be edited for the US market. As such, it is perhaps more widely known as simply 'Join Me'.

70   The idea of a 'Goth subculture' (although, oddly, not the notion of goth 'subcultural capital') is resisted by van Elferen, because not only is she nervous about using the term 'subculture' at a time when it is popular to use 'post-subcultural'/'neo-tribal' discourses, but also because 'there are too many Goth sub-styles that are each too different from one another to justify the unity and collectivity implied by the phrase'. These, of course, are points that can be contested, not least because the work done on 'subcultures' at the Birmingham Centre for Contemporary Cultural Studies has been interpreted rather narrowly and also that, while initially focusing heavily on class, should be allowed to evolve before we abandon it. Nevertheless, these points are worth noting, since they have attracted much discussion. See van Elferen, *Gothic Music*, 128–29.

71   See P. Hodkinson, *Goth: Identity, Style and Subculture* (Oxford: Berg, 2002).

72   See D. Shumway & H. Arnet, 'Playing Dress Up: David Bowie and the Roots of Goth'. In L. Goodlad & M. Bibby (eds), *Goth: Undead Subculture* (Durham: Yale University Press, 2007), 129–42.

73   D. Lockwood, 'Dead Souls: Post-Punk Music as Hauntological Trigger'. In B. Cherry, P. Howell & C. Ruddell (eds), *Twenty-First-Century Gothic* (Newcastle: Cambridge Scholars Publishing, 2010), 99–100.

74   Goodlad & Bibby, 'Introduction', 1–2.

75   Martin Hannet, quoted in S. Reynolds, *Rip It Up and Start Again: Post-punk 1978–1984* (London: Faber and Faber, 2005), 187.

76   D. Curtis, *Touching from a Distance: Ian Curtis and Joy Division* (London: Faber and Faber, 1995), 145–201.

77   See Reynolds, *Rip It Up*, 187.

78   S. Freud, quoted in Royle, *Uncanny*, 151.

79   Curtis, *Touching from a Distance*, 90.

80   D. Simpson, 'My Favourite Album: *Closer* by Joy Division', *The Guardian: Music Blog* (18 August 2011). Available at: http://www.theguardian.com/music/musicblog/2011/aug/18/joy-division-closer (accessed 09 July 2014).

81   Fisher, *Ghosts of My Life*, 50.

82   See Fisher's interesting interview and discussion in ibid., 98–108.

83   Ibid., 56.

84   The new romantics, of course, had been heavily influenced by David Bowie and Roxy Music, and influence which flowed through into goth culture. See, for example, D. Rimmer, *New Romantics: The Look* (London: Omnibus Press, 2003).

This new romantic influence is often ignored, even by those, such as David Shumway and Heather Arnet, who seek to make the connection with Bowie and Roxy Music: 'Playing Dress Up: David Bowie and the Roots of Goth', 129–42.

85   Nick Cave, *The Complete Lyrics, 1978–2007* (London: Penguin, 2007), 397.

86   See V. Nelson, *Gothicka: Vampire Heroes, Human Gods and the New Supernatural* (Cambridge: Harvard University Press, 2012), 117–67.

87   C. Spooner, *Contemporary Gothic* (London: Reaktion Books, 2006), 9.

88   van Elferen, *Gothic Music*, 131–32.

89   A.L. Smith, 'Postmodernism/Gothicism'. In V. Sage & A.L. Smith (eds), *Modern Gothic: A Reader* (Manchester: Manchester University Press, 1996), 8.

90   Walter Velez, quoted in P. Yglesias, *Cocinando!: Fifty Years of Latin Album Cover Art* (New York: Princeton Architectural Press, 2005), 7.

91   For an interesting insight into album cover design, see S. Thorgerson & A. Powell, *For the Love of Vinyl: The Album Art of Hipgnosis* (New York: PictureBox, 2008).

92   See J. Kristeva, *Powers of Horror: An Essay on Abjection*. Trans. by L.S. Roudiez (New York: Columbia University Press, 1982).

93   See R. Mighall, 'Gothic Cities'. In C. Spooner & E. McEvoy (eds), *The Routledge Companion to Gothic* (London: Routledge, 2007), 54–62.

94   C. Spooner, *Fashioning Gothic Bodies* (Manchester: Manchester University Press, 2004), 9.

95   Joel-Peter Witkin, quoted in J. Storck, 'Band of Outsiders: Williamsburg's Renegade Artists', *Billburg* (1 January 2002). Available at: http://www.billburg.com/community-affairs/archived/band-of-outsiders-williamsburg-s-renegade-artists?id=134 (accessed 18 July 2014).

96   See M. Brown, *Debussy Redux: The Impact of His Music on Popular Culture* (Bloomington: Indiana University Press, 2012), 110–12.

97   Spooner, *Contemporary Gothic*, 85.

98   C. Hagen, 'A Career's Worth of Corpses and Severed Limbs', *New York Times* (20 October 1995). Available at: http://www.nytimes.com/1995/10/20/arts/photography-review-a-career-s-worth-of-corpses-and-severed-limbs.html (accessed 20 July 2014).

99   See C. Siegel, 'The Obscure Object of Desire Revisited: Poppy Z. Brite and the Goth Hero as Masochist'. In Goodlad & Bibby, *Goth*, 342.

100 Bataille, *Inner Experience*, 3.

101 Ibid., 3.

102 Spooner, *Contemporary Gothic*, 63.

103 P. Stallybrass & A. White, *The Politics and Poetics of Transgression* (London: Methuen & Co., 1986), 21.

104 See ibid., 21–22.

105 See Bauman, *Mortality, Immortality*, 167–70.

106   M. Bakhtin, *Rabelais and His World*, Trans. by Hélène Iswolsky (Bloomington: Indiana University Press, 1984), 319.

107   G. Baddeley, *Goth Chic: A Connoisseur's Guide to Dark Culture* (London: Plexus, 2002), 19.

108   E. Becker, *The Denial of Death* (New York: The Free Press, 1973).

109   R. Schraffenberger, 'This Modern Goth (Explains Herself)'. In L. Goodlad & M. Bibby (eds), *Goth: Undead Subculture* (Durham: Yale University Press, 2007), 124.

110   Nick Cave, quoted in Boer, *Nick Cave*, 44.

111   Schraffenberger, 'This Modern Goth', 124.

Chapter 4

1   Nelson, *Gothicka*, 204.

2   See J. Kendrick, *Film Violence: History, Ideology, Genre* (New York: Columbia University Press, 2010); J.T. Brink & J. Oppenheimer (eds), *Killer Images: Documentary Film, Memory and the Performance of Violence* (New York: Columbia University Press, 2012); E. Christianson & C. Partridge (eds), *Holy Terror: Understanding Religion and Violence in Popular Culture* (London: Equinox, 2010).

3   See Kristeva, *Powers of Horror*, 1–10.

4   See Thornton, *Club Cultures*, 135–36.

5   Audrey Sylvain, quoted in Todestrieb Records, 'Amesoeurs Interview' (03 January 2007). Available at: http://label.todestrieb.co.uk/2007/01/03/amesoeurs-interview/ (accessed 12 August 2014).

6   B. Johnson & M. Cloonan, *Dark Side of the Tune: Popular Music and Violence* (Aldershot: Ashgate, 2009), 105–16.

7   See K.S. Long, 'Rock Lyrics, Advertising, and the Parents' Music Resource Center'. In K.S. Long & M. Nadelhaft (eds), *America Under Construction: Boundaries and Identities in Popular Culture* (New York: Routledge, 1997), 149–68.

8   See S. Anderson & G. Howard, 'Crime, Criminal Justice, and Popular Culture', *Journal of Criminal Justice Education* 5 (1994), 123–31; M. Sampar, 'Rock "n" Roll Suicide: Why Heavy Metal Musicians Cannot Be Held Responsible for the Violent Acts of Their Listeners', *Seton Hall Journal of Sports and Entertainment Law* 15 (2005), 173–96; R. Walser, *Running with the Devil: Power, Gender and Madness in Heavy Metal Music* (Middletown: Wesleyan University Press, 1993), 145–47.

9   The Columbine High School massacre on 20 April 1999, was carried out by two students, Eric Harris and Dylan Klebold, who embarked on a shooting spree, which resulted in the deaths of twelve students and one teacher. That they were both fans of German industrial bands, such as Rammstein, was interpreted by the

media to be a contributory factor. See David Altheide, 'The Columbine Shootings and the Discourse of Fear', *American Behavioral Scientist* 52 (2009), 1354–70; R.W. Larkin, *Comprehending Columbine* (Philadelphia: Temple University Press, 2007); Johnson & Cloonan, *Dark Side of the Tune*. See also the comments by Lou Koller of the band Sick Of It All regarding the killings by Wayne Lo, who was wearing a Sick Of It All shirt. Mörat, 'Dark Recollections: Sick of It All, *Scratch the Surface*', *Terrorizer* 214 (2011), 72.

10 See D. Weinstein, *Heavy Metal: The Music and Its Culture*, revised edition (New York: Da Capo Press, 2000), 238–75; K. Kahn-Harris, *Extreme Metal: Music and Culture on the Edge* (Oxford: Berg, 2007).

11 M. Phillipov, 'Extreme Music for Extreme People? Norwegian Black Metal and Transcendent Violence'. In T. Hjelm, K. Kahn-Harris, & M. Levine (eds), *Heavy Metal: Controversies and Countercultures* (Sheffield: Equinox, 2013), 152.

12 Ibid., 152.

13 See Partridge, *The Lyre of Orpheus*, 201–09.

14 Phillipov, 'Extreme Music', 152–53.

15 Sampar, 'Rock "n" Roll Suicide', 195.

16 See DeNora, *Music in Everyday Life*; S. Frith, 'Music and Everyday Life'. In M. Clayton, T. Herbert, & R. Middleton (eds), *The Cultural Study of Music: A Critical Introduction* (New York: Routledge, 2003), 92–101.

17 Kristeva, *Powers of Horror*, 1.

18 S. Pinker, *The Better Angels of Our Nature: Why Violence Has Declined* (New York: Viking, 2011).

19 Kristeva, *Powers of Horror*, 3.

20 Ibid., 4.

21 Ibid., 3–4.

22 Ibid., 12–13.

23 S. Freud, 'Beyond the Pleasure Principle'. In J. Strachey (ed.), *The Standard Edition of the Complete Psychological Works of Sigmund Freud*, Vol. 18 (London: Vintage, 2001), 7–64.

24 Ibid., 12–13.

25 Ibid., 9.

26 Ibid., 38.

27 Freud went on to develop his thesis more broadly, seeing the death drive manifested in masochism and, when turned away from the self, in sadism, violence and war.

28 See L. Razinsky, *Freud, Psychoanalysis and Death* (Cambridge: Cambridge University Press, 2013).

29 See B. Creed, *The Monstrous-Feminine: Film, Feminism, Psychoanalysis* (New York: Routledge, 1993).

30 S. Žižek, *The Parallax View* (Cambridge: MIT Press, 2006), 62.

31 Ibid.

32 Kristeva, *Powers of Horror*, 1.

33 Neige, quoted in Todestrieb Records, 'Amesoeurs Interview'.

34 Z. Bauman, *Mortality, Immortality and Other Life Strategies* (Cambridge: Polity Press, 1992), 33.

35 The popularity of *Edge of the Century* was largely the result of Dennis DeYoung's song 'Show Me the Way'.

36 Bauman, *Mortality, Immortality*, 34.

37 R. Layard, *Happiness: Lessons From a New Science* (London: Penguin, 2006), 42.

38 Bauman, *Mortality, Immortality*, 34.

39 J. Donne, *Devotions upon Emergent Occasions and Death's Duel* (New York: Vintage Books, 1999), 103.

40 A. Stone, 'Natality and Mortality: Rethinking Death with Cavarero', *Continental Philosophy Review* 43 (2010), 370.

41 Bauman, *Mortality, Immortality*, 35.

42 E. Canetti, quoted in Bauman, *Mortality, Immortality*, 34.

43 See C. Baudelot & R. Establet, *Suicide: The Hidden Side of Modernity* (Cambridge: Polity Press, 2008), 1.

44 See O. Kernberg, 'The Concept of the Death Drive: A Clinical Perspective', *The International Journal of Psychoanalysis* 90 (2009), 1009–23.

45 É. Durkheim, *Suicide: A Study in Sociology*. Trans. by J.A. Spaulding & G. Simpson (London: Routledge & Kegan Paul, 1952).

46 See W.S.F. Pickering & G. Walford (eds), *Durkheim's Suicide: A Century of Research and Debate* (London: Routledge, 2000).

47 Baudelot & Establet, *Suicide*.

48 H.H. Farmer, *Experience of God: A Brief Enquiry into the Grounds of Christian Conviction* (London: SCM Press, 1929), 32.

49 Durkheim, *Suicide*, 276.

50 D. Gaines, *Teenage Wasteland: Suburbia's Dead End Kids* (Chicago: Chicago University Press, 1998), 252–53.

51 Ibid., 253.

52 K. Sellgren, 'Young People "Feel They Have Nothing to Live For"', *BBC News* (02 January 2014). Available at: http://www.bbc.co.uk/news/education-25559089 (accessed 28 September 2014).

53 See, for example, the DVD directed by Paul Rachman, *American Hardcore* (2006) and the book by Steven Blush on which it was based, *American Hardcore: A Tribal History* (Los Angeles: Feral House, 2010).

54 Durkheim, *Suicide*, 278–79.

55 Sellgren, 'Young People'.

56 Durkheim, *Suicide*, 279.

57 See http://twloha.com/home (accessed 29 August 2014).

58 R. Young, H. Sweeting, & P. West, 'Prevalence of Deliberate Self Harm and Attempted Suicide Within Contemporary Goth Youth Subculture: Longitudinal Cohort Study', *British Medical Journal* 332 (2006), 1060. Although a little idiosyncratic, see also J. Silk, 'Open a Vein: Suicidal Black Metal and Enlightenment', *Helvete: A Journal of Black Metal Theory* 1 (Winter, 2013), 5–20.

59 M. Phillipov, 'Self Harm in Goth Youth Subculture: Study Merely Reinforces Popular Stereotypes', *British Medical Journal* 332 (2006), 1215. M. Taubert & J. Kandasamy, 'Self Harm in Goth Youth Subculture: Conclusion Relates Only to Small Sample', *British Medical Journal* 332 (2006), 1215. R. Young, H. Sweeting, & P. West, 'Self Harm in Goth Youth Subculture: Author's Reply', *British Medical Journal* 332 (2006), 1335.

60 Some researchers have found that, for example, the music nurtures suicidal tendencies already present in the heavy metal subculture: S. Stack, 'Heavy Metal, Religiosity, and Suicide', *Suicide and Life-Threatening Behavior* 28 (1998), 388–94; S. Stack, J. Gundlach, & J.L. Reeves, 'The Heavy Metal Subculture and Suicide', *Suicide and Life-Threatening Behavior* 24 (1994), 15–23. See also, R.J. Peterson, M.A. Safer, & D.A. Jobes, 'The Impact of Suicidal Rock Music Lyrics on Youth: An Investigation of Individual Differences', *Archives of Suicide Research* 12 (2008), 161–69.

61 For a recent study of the impact of suicidal lyrics on listeners, see Peterson, Safer, & Jobes, 'The Impact of Suicidal Rock Music Lyrics on Youth', 161–69.

62 See Partridge, *Lyre of Orpheus*. See also M. Definis-Gojanović, D. Gugić, & D. Sutlović, 'Suicide and Emo Youth Subculture: A Case Analysis', *Collegium Antropologicum: Journal of the Croatian Anthropological Society* 33, Supplement 2 (2009), 173–75.

63 L. Grossberg, *We Gotta Get Out of This Place: Popular Conservatism and Postmodern Culture* (London: Routledge, 1992), 83–84.

64 J. Hval, 'The Inner Sleeve', *The Wire* 366 (August 2014), 71.

65 Durkheim, *Suicide*, 241.

66 N. Antonakakis & A. Collins, 'The Impact of Fiscal Austerity on Suicide: On the Empirics of a Modern Greek Tragedy', *Social Science & Medicine* 112 (2014), 39–50.

67 Durkheim, *Suicide*, 246.

68 Ibid.

69 Ibid., 247.

70 Ibid., 247–48.

71 É. Durkheim, 'Individualism and the Intellectuals'. In R.N. Bellah (ed.), *Emile Durkheim: On Morality and Society* (Chicago: University of Chicago Press, 1973), 44.

72 See Z. Bauman, *Work, Consumerism and the New Poor* (Buckingham: Open University Press, 1998), 23–41.

73 See also Layard, *Happiness*.

74 Tori Amos, quoted in Polari, 'From the Fringes of the Milky Way: Tori Amos', *Polari Magazine* (09 May 2009). Available at: http://www.polarimagazine.com/ interviews/fringes-of-milky-way-interview-tori-amos/ (accessed 07 August 2014).

75 Durkheim, *Suicide*, 246.

76 Gaines, *Teenage Wasteland*, 253.

77 Layard, *Happiness*, 48.

78 Ibid.

79 David Gilmour, quoted in J. Robb, 'Syd Barrett, the Swinging 60', *The Independent* (07 January 2006). Available at: http://www.independent.co.uk/arts-entertainment/ music/features/syd-barrett-the-swinging-60-521928.html (accessed 06 August 2014).

80 M. Celmins, *Peter Green: The Authorised Biography* (London: Sanctuary Publishing, 2003), 139.

81 H. Watts, 'James Arthur Reveals His Spiral Into Drugs and Panic Attacks After *X Factor* Win', *Mirror* (25 October 2013). Available at: http://www.mirror.co.uk/3am/celebrity-news/james-arthur-took-drugs-suffered-2528670 (accessed 29 September 2014).

82 See C.R. Cross, *Heavier Than Heaven: The Biography of Kurt Cobain* (London: Hodder & Stoughton, 2001).

83 For a scanned image of the suicide note, see http://kurtcobainssuicidenote.com/ kurt_cobains_suicide_note_scan.html (accessed 08 August 2014).

84 Available on, Johnny Mandel, *M*A*S*H (Original Soundtrack Recording)*. Columbia Masterworks, 1970.

85 The self-harming incident followed an argument with the *New Musical Express* journalist, Steve Lamacq, on 15 May 1991, after a concert at the Norwich Arts Centre. Lamacq had challenged the band about their 'punk' authenticity and values. In particular, he asked Edwards whether he was serious about his music. His response was to take a razor blade and carve the words '4 Real' into his forearm, inflicting an injury that required eighteen stitches.

86 J.E. Pirkis, P.M. Burgess, C. Francis, R.W. Blood, D.J. Jolley, 'The Relationship Between Media Reporting of Suicide and Actual Suicide in Australia', *Social Science & Medicine* 62 (2006), 2874. See also A. Yang, S-J. Tsai, C-H. Yang, B-C. Shia, J-L. Fuh, S-J. Wang, C-K. Peng, N. Huang, 'Suicide and Media Reporting: A Longitudinal and Spatial Analysis', *Social Psychiatry and Psychiatric Epidemiology* 48 (2013), 427–35.

87 See G. Gorer, 'The Pornography of Death', *Encounter* (October, 1955), 49–52.

88 See, for example, D. MacLeod, '"Social Distortion": The Rise of Suburban Punk Rock in Los Angeles'. In Long & Nadelhaft, *America Under Construction*, 123–48; A. Branch, '"Stop Flexing Your Roots, Man": Reconversion Strategies, Consecrated Heretics and the Violence of UK First-wave Punk', *Punk and Post Punk* 3 (2014), 21–39.

89 See B. Mullen, *Lexicon Devil: The Fast Times and Short Life of Darby Crash and The Germs* (Los Angeles: Feral House, 2002).

90 Mick Farren, quoted in N. Rombes, *A Cultural Dictionary of Punk: 1974–1982* (New York: Continuum, 2009), 135. This point is made forcefully in the documentary directed by Paul Rachman, *American Hardcore* (2006).

91 Mick Farren, quoted in Rombes, *Cultural Dictionary*, 135.

92 Justin Broadrick, quoted in D. Stubbs, 'Invisible Jukebox: Justin Broadrick', *The Wire* 367 (2014), 25.

93 Henry Rollins, quoted in M. Azerrad, *Our Band Could Be Your Life: Scenes from the American Indie Underground, 1981–1991* (Boston: Little Brown and Company, 2001), 25

94 Azerrad, *Our Band Could Be Your Life*, 32.

95 See the documentary, *American Hardcore* (2006).

96 Tobi Vail, quoted in J. Jordan-Wrench, 'Interview: Bikini Kill', *The Stool Pigeon* (24 October 2012). Available at: http://www.thestoolpigeon.co.uk/features/interview-bikini-kill.html (accessed 22 August 2014).

97 Azerrad, *Our Band Could Be Your Life*, 32.

98 See A. Larson, 'Fast, Cheap and Out of Control: The Graphic Symbol in Hardcore Punk', *Punk and Post Punk* 2 (2013), 91–106.

99 Blush, *American Hardcore*, 39. See also Azerrad, *Our Band Could Be Your Life*, 30–32; N. Levine, *Dharma Punx: A Memoir* (New York: HarperCollins, 2003), 43–84.

100 Azerrad, *Our Band Could Be Your Life*, 24. See also, J. Parker, *Turned on: A Biography of Henry Rollins* (New York: Cooper Square Press, 2000), 2–3

101 H. Rollins, *Eye Scream* (Los Angeles: 2.13.61, 1996), 129.

102 See Gaines, *Teenage Wasteland*.

103 Husker Dü, quoted in Blush, *American Hardcore*, 39.

104 See B. Mould, *See a Little Light: The Trail of Rage and Melody* (New York: Little Brown and Company, 2011).

105 Ibid., 90.

106 Steve Albini, quoted in M. Prindle, 'Steve Albini: 2005', *Mark's Record Reviews*. Available at: http://www.markprindle.com/albini-i.htm (accessed 22 August 2014).

107 A useful, but rather too sanguine description of mosh pit violence is provided by Randall Collins, *Violence: A Micro-Sociological Theory* (Princeton: Princeton University Press, 2008), 277–81.

108 See W. Tsitsos, 'Rules of Rebellion: Slamdancing, Moshing, and the American Alternative Scene'. In A. Bennett, B. Shank, & J. Toynbee (eds), *The Popular Music Studies Reader* (Abingdon: Routledge, 2006), 121–27.

109 Durkheim, *The Elementary Forms of Religious Life*, 171.

110 See B. Hutcherson & R. Haenfler, 'Musical Genre as a Gendered Process: Authenticity in Extreme Metal'. In N.K. Denzin (ed.), *Studies in Symbolic Interaction*, Vol. 35 (Bingley: Emerald Group Publishing, 2010), 110–14.

111   See Tsitsos, 'Rules of Rebellion', 125.

112   R. Caillois, *Man and the Sacred*. Trans. by M. Barash (Urbana: University of Illnois Press, 2001), 97–127.

113   R. Arya, 'The Religious Significance of Violence in Football'. In E. Christianson & C. Partridge (eds), *Holy Terror: Understanding Religion and Violence in Popular Culture* (London: Equinox, 2010), 130.

114   Ibid., 130.

115   Ibid., 130.

116   G. Bataille, *Inner Experience*. Trans. by L.A. Boldt (Albany: State University of New York Press, 1988).

117   Azerrad, *Our Band Could Be Your Life*, 22.

118   Mörat, 'Dark Recollections', 72.

119   R. Girard, *Violence and the Sacred*. Trans. by P. Gregory (Baltimore: John Hopkins University Press, 1977), 4.

120   Ibid., 4.

121   See P. Brannigan, 'Just Say No', *Mojo* 217 (December, 2011), 52–56; and A. Earles, *Hüsker Dü: The Story of the Noise-Pop Pioneers Who Launched Modern Rock* (Minneapolis: Voyageur Press, 2010), 103.

122   Arya, 'Religious Significance of Violence', 132.

123   Girard, *Violence and the Sacred*, 30.

124   Bauman & Tester, *Conversations with Zygmunt Bauman*, 126.

125   Ibid., 187.

126   Ibid., 164.

127   Ibid., 127.

128   See Partridge, *Lyre of Orpheus*, 68–74.

129   Turner, 'Variations on a Theme of Liminality', 37.

130   See Partridge, *Lyre of Orpheus*, 63–114.

131   M. Phillipov, *Death Metal and Music Criticism: Analysis at the Limits* (Plymouth: Lexington Books, 2012), 128.

132   Ibid., 128.

133   Frith & McRobbie, 'Rock and Sexuality', 374.

134   Phillipov, *Death Metal*, 108–13.

135   For useful comments of the issues surrounding such discourses, see Phillipov, *Death Metal*, 134–35; K. Kahn-Harris, 'Death Metal and the Limits of Musical Expression'. In M. Cloonan & R. Garofalo (eds), *Policing Pop* (Philadelphia: Temple University Press, 2003), 81–99.

136   B.A. Primack, M.A. Gold, E.B. Schwarz, & M.A. Dalton, 'Degrading and Non-Degrading Sex in Popular Music: A Content Analysis', *Public Health Reports* 123 (2008), 593–600.

137 B. Bretthauer, T.S. Zimmerman, & J. Banning, 'A Feminist Analysis of Popular Music: Power Over, Objectification of, and Violence Against Women', *Journal of Feminist Family Therapy* 18 (2007), 30–31.

138 See E.G. Armstrong, 'Gangsta Misogyny: A Content Analysis of the Portrayals of Violence Against Women in Rap Music, 1987-1993', *Journal of Criminal Justice and Popular Culture*, 8 (2001), 96–126.

139 Adam Horowitz, quoted in D. Porter, *Rapcore: The Nu-Metal Rap Fusion* (London: Plexus, 2003), 37.

140 Chuck D, quoted in B. Myers, *American Heretics: Rebel Voices in Music* (Hove: Codex, 2002), 110.

141 See E. Quinn, *Nuthin' But a G Thang: The Culture and Commerce of Gangsta* (New York: Columbia University Press, 2005).

142 Although performed at concerts, Lauryn Hill did not release 'Black Rage' as a single or on an album. However, she has made it available on Soundcloud: https://soundcloud.com/mslaurynhill/black-rage-sketch (accessed 12 September 2104).

143 T. Rose, 'Voices from the Margins: Rap Music and Contemporary Cultural Production'. In A. Bennett, B. Shank, & J. Toynbee (eds), *The Popular Music Studies Reader* (Abingdon: Routledge, 2006), 216.

144 J. Hagedorn, *A World of Gangs: Armed Young Men and Gangsta Culture* (Minneapolis: University of Minnesota Press, 2009), 53. See also G. Harkness, *Chicago Hustle and Flow: Gangs, Gangsta Rap, and Social Class* (Minneapolis: University of Minnesota Press, 2014).

145 Tupac Shakur, 'When Ure Heart Turns Cold', *The Rose That Grew from Concrete* (London: Pocket Books, 2006), 13.

146 See Hagedorn, *World of Gangs*, 53–64, 85–91.

147 Camus, *Myth of Sisyphus*, 7.

148 Shakur, 'When Ure Heart Turns Cold', 13.

149 S. Taylor, *People's Instinctive Travels and the Paths of Rhythm* (New York: Continuum, 2007), 1–5.

150 See T.L. McQuillar & F. Johnson, *Tupac Shakur: The Life and Times of an American Icon* (Cambridge: Da Capo Press, 2010).

151 See S.G. Anso & C. Rappleye, 'Rap Sheet'. In D. Brackett (ed.), *The Pop, Rock, and Soul Reader: Histories and Debates*, second edition (New York: Oxford University Press, 2009), 484–86; S.S. Hinds, 'Party Over'. In D. Brackett (ed.), *The Pop, Rock, and Soul Reader: Histories and Debates*, second edition (New York: Oxford University Press, 2009), 486.

152 See T. Rose, *Black Noise: Rap Music and Black Culture in Contemporary America* (Middletown: Wesleyan University Press, 1994); T. Rose, *The Hip-Hop Wars: What We Talk About When We Talk About Hip-hop and Why It Matters* (New York: Basic Books, 2008). See also M.R. Miller, *Religion and Hip Hop* (New York: Routledge,

2013), 24–44; M.E. Dyson, *Between God and Gangsta Rap: Bearing Witness to Black Culture* (New York: Oxford University Press, 1996). See also M.R. Miller, A.B. Pinn, & B. Freeman, *Religion in Hip Hop: Mapping the New Terrain* (London: Bloomsbury, 2014).

153 See Durkheim, *Suicide*, 241–76.

154 M.E. Dyson, *Between God and Gangsta Rap: Bearing Witness to Black Culture* (New York: Oxford University Press, 1996), ix.

155 Miller, *Religion and Hip Hop*, 176.

156 See J. Brown, *Suge Knight: The Rise, Fall, and Rise of Death Row Record* (Phoenix: Colossus Books, 2002).

157 Rose, *Hip-Hop Wars*, 1.

158 For a useful discussion of 'rap realism', see I. Perry, *Prophets of the Hood: Politics and Poetics in Hip Hop* (Durham: Duke University Press, 2004) and, with critical reference to that work, L.K. Spence, *Stare in the Darkness: The Limits of Hip-hop and Black Politics* (Minneapolis: University of Minnesota Press, 2011).

159 Taylor, *People's Instinctive Travels*, 64.

160 Bauman, *Mortality, Immortality*, 166.

161 Ibid., 165.

162 Ibid., 168.

163 See Myers, *American Heretics*, 102–03. See also D. Chuck (with Y.. Jah), *Fight the Power: Rap, Race and Reality* (Edinburgh: Payback Press, 1997).

164 D. Cooke, *The Language of Music* (Oxford: Oxford University Press, 1959), 272. See also Partridge, *Lyre of Orpheus*, 37–59.

165 F. Nietzsche, *The Will to Power: In Science, Nature, Society and Art*. Trans. by W.A. Kaufmann & R.J. Hollingdale (New York: Vintage Books, 1968), 428.

166 T. Turino, *Music as Social Life: The Politics of Participation* (Chicago: University of Chicago Press, 2008), 1.

167 See R. MacDonald, D. Hargreaves, & D. Miell (eds), *Musical Identities* (Oxford: Oxford University Press, 2002).

168 See Turino, *Music as Social Life*.

Chapter 5

1 Quoted in G. Marcus, *Dead Elvis: A Chronicle of a Cultural Obsession* (New York: Viking, 1992), xii.

2 See R. Bultmann, 'The New Testament and Mythology: The Mythological Element in the Message of the New Testament and the Problem of Its Re-interpretation'. In H.W. Bartsch (ed.) *Kerygma and Myth: A Theological Debate* (New York: Harper & Row, 1961), 1–44.

3   See G.B. Rodman, *Elvis After Elvis: The Posthumous Career of a Living Legend* (Abingdon: Routledge, 1996).

4   C. Rojek, *Fame Attack: The Inflation of Celebrity and Its Consequences* (London: Bloomsbury, 2012), 180.

5   See ibid., 50–53.

6   See, for example, Pirkis et al., 'The Relationship Between Media Reporting of Suicide and Actual Suicide in Australia', 2874–86; J.E. Pirkis & R.W. Blood, 'Suicide and the Media: Part I: Reportage in Nonfictional Media', *Crisis: The Journal of Crisis Intervention and Suicide Prevention* 22 (2001), 146–54; Yang et al., 'Suicide and Media Reporting: A Longitudinal and Spatial Analysis', 427–35.

7   See, for example, A.T.A. Cheng, K. Hawton, T.H.H. Chen, A.M.F. Yen, J.-C. Chang, M.-Y. Chong, C.-Y. Liu, Y. Lee, P.R. Teng & L.-C. Chen, 'The Influence of Media Reporting of a Celebrity Suicide on Suicidal Behavior in Patients with a History of Depressive Disorder', *Journal of Affective Disorders* 103 (2007), 69–75; J. Jeong, S. Shin, H. Kim, Y. Hong, S. Hwang & E. Lee, 'The Effects of Celebrity Suicide on Copycat Suicide Attempt: A Multi-center Observational Study', *Social Psychiatry and Psychiatric Epidemiology* 47 (2012), 957–65.

8   Jeong et al., 'The Effects of Celebrity Suicide on Copycat Suicide Attempt', 957.

9   K.W. Fu & P.S.F. Yip, 'Long-term Impact of Celebrity Suicide on Suicidal Ideation: Results from A Population-based Study', *Journal of Epidemiology and Community Health* 61 (2007), 540–46.

10   See C. Bottici, *A Philosophy of Political Myth* (Cambridge: Cambridge University Press, 2007); A. Dundes (ed.), *Sacred Narrative: Readings in the Theory of Myth* (Berkeley: University of California Press, 1884); J.S. Jensen (ed.), *Myths and Mythologies: A Reader* (London: Equinox, 2009); R. Segal, *Theorizing about Myth* (Amherst: University of Massachusetts Press, 1999). See also Bultmann, 'The New Testament and Mythology', 1–44.

11   Bultmann, 'The New Testament and Mythology', 10.

12   A. Camus, *The Myth of Sisyphus*, trans. by J. O'Brien (Harmondsworth: Penguin Books, 1975), 108.

13   E. Bailey, 'Implicit Religion'. In P.B. Clarke (ed.), *The Oxford Handbook of the Sociology of Religion* (New York: Oxford University Press, 2009), 802.

14   See, for example, ibid., 801–16.

15   In using the notion of 'fields of discourse', I am drawing on Kocku von Stuckrad's useful articulation of Foucauldian discourse theory, in *Western Esotericism*, trans. N. Goodrick-Clarke (London: Equinox, 2005).

16   Several key studies of celebrity culture, for example, fail to make this distinction in their efforts to argue that it has replaced institutional religion as a space within which meaning and devotion are constructed in secular societies. See, for example, C. Rojek, *Celebrity* (London: Reaktion Books, 2001), 51–100.

17 D. Austin-Broos, 'The Anthropology of Conversion: An Introduction'. In
    A. Buckser & S.D. Glazier (eds), *The Anthropology of Religious Conversion* (Lanham:
    Rowman & Littlefield, 2003), 1.

18 See J. Richards, S. Wilson & L. Woodhead (eds), *Diana: The Making of a Media
    Saint* (London: I.B. Tauris, 1999).

19 R. Eide, *The Celestial Voice of Diana: Her Spiritual Guidance to Finding Love*
    (Forres: Findhorn Press, 2001); M. McMahon, *Princess Diana's Message of Peace:
    An Extraordinary Message of Peace for Our Current World* (La Vergne: Write to
    Print, 2003); C. Tooney, *In Her Own Words: The After Death Journal of Princess
    Diana* (Mt. Pleasant: English Rose Press, 1999).

20 E. Harrison, 'Princess Diana Speaks', *PlanetLightworker.com* (October/November
    1999). Available at: http://www.planetlightworker.com/articles/interviews/ritaeide/
    interview1.htm (accessed 14 February 2014).

21 M. McMahon, *Notes from John: Messages from Across the Universe* (Taylorville:
    Eternal Rose Publishing, 2012), 136–37.

22 V. Turner, 'The Center Out There: Pilgrim's Goal', *History of Religions* 12.3 (1973),
    223.

23 Partridge, *Lyre of Orpheus*, 236–43. Building on the initial thoughts in this book,
    the ideas in the current chapter were first developed in C. Partridge, 'Fandom, Pop
    Devotion, and the Transfiguration of Dead Celebrities'. In F. Metzger & E. Pahud de
    Mortanges (eds), *Orte und Räume des Religiösen (19–21 Jahrhundert)* (Paderborn:
    Schöningh Verlag, forthcoming).

24 A. Danto, *The Transfiguration of the Commonplace: A Philosophy of Art*
    (Cambridge: Harvard University Press, 1981).

25 I am here, of course, referencing M. Polanyi's famous discussion in *Personal Knowledge:
    Towards a Post-Critical Philosophy* (Chicago: Chicago University Press, 1962).

26 Luciano Pavarotti, quoted in L. Woodhead, 'Diana and the Religion of the Heart'.
    In J. Richards, S. Wilson & L. Woodhead (eds), *Diana: The Making of a Media Saint*
    (London: I.B. Tauris, 1999), 135.

27 Lauren Laverne, quoted in R. Till, *Pop Cult: Religion and Popular Music* (London:
    Continuum, 2010), 119.

28 D. Halberstam, 'Foreword'. In G. DePaoli (ed.), *Elvis + Marilyn: 2 x Immortal*
    (New York: Rizzoli, 1994), 8.

29 C. King, 'His Truth Goes Marching On: Elvis Presley and the Pilgrimage
    to Graceland'. In I. Reader & T. Walter (eds), *Pilgrimage in Popular Culture*
    (Houndmills: Macmillan, 1993), 103.

30 E. Doss, 'Believing in Elvis: Popular Piety in Material Culture'. In Stewart M.
    Hoover & Lynn Schofield Clark (eds), *Religion in the Age of the Media: Explorations
    in Media, Religion and Culture* (New York: Columbia University Press, 2002),
    63–86; E. Doss, 'Rock and Roll Pilgrims: Reflections on Ritual, Religiosity and Race
    at Graceland'. In P.J. Margry (ed.), *Shrines and Pilgrimage in the Modern World:*

New Itineraries Into the Sacred (Amsterdam: Amsterdam University Press, 2008), 130–34; King, 'His Truth Goes Marching On'', 103; J.P. Margry, 'The Pilgrimage to Jim Morrison's Grave at Père Lachaise Cemetery: The Social Construction of Sacred Space'. In P.J. Margry (ed.), *Shrines and Pilgrimage in the Modern World: New Itineraries Into the Sacred* (Amsterdam: Amsterdam University Press, 2008), 143–72.

31 See J.D. Reed & M. Miller, *Stairway to Heaven: The Final Resting Places of Rock's Legends* (New York: Wenner Books, 2005).

32 See O. Riis & L. Woodhead, *A Sociology of Religious Emotion* (Oxford: Oxford University Press, 2010), 133.

33 Ibid., 133–34.

34 Mark Duffett's forthright rejection of analyses of 'fandom' in terms of 'religion' (some of which are admittedly crude) misunderstands this process, as well as the complex nature of 'religion' and the 'sacred'. M. Duffett, 'False Faith or False Comparison? A Critique of the Religious Interpretation of Elvis Fan Culture', *Popular Music and Society* 26 (2003), 514–22.

35 See G. Schopen, 'Relic'. In Mark C. Taylor (ed.), *Critical Terms for Religious Studies* (Chicago: Chicago University Press, 1998), 256–68.

36 Quoted in King, 'His Truth Goes Marching On', 103; see also Bono, 'Elvis: American David'. In G. DePaoli (ed.), *Elvis + Marilyn: 2 x Immortal* (New York: Rizzoli, 1994), 18.

37 Kiki Apostolakos, an Elvis fan, quoted in Doss, 'Believing in Elvis', 63–64.

38 G. Reece, *Elvis Religion: The Cult of the King* (London: I.B. Tauris, 2006), 2.

39 See, for example, J. Riordan & J. Prochnicky, *Break on Through: The Life and Death of Jim Morrison* (London: Plexus, 1991), 462–72.

40 Margry, 'The Pilgrimage to Jim Morrison's Grave', 168.

41 Ibid., 163.

42 Riordan & Prochnicky, *Break on Through*, 465–66.

43 Ibid., 466.

44 Ibid., 466–67.

45 See Partridge, *Lyre of Orpheus*.

46 For a discussion of the notion of occulture, see C. Partridge, 'Occulture is Ordinary'. In K. Granholm & E. Asprem (eds), *Contemporary Esotericism* (Sheffield: Equinox, 2013), 113–33; C. Partridge, *The Re-enchantment of the West: Alternative Spiritualities, Sacralization, Popular Culture and Occulture*, 2 vols. (London: Continuum, 2004, 2005).

47 On Oliver Stone's fascination with Jim Morrison, see S. Talbot, 'Sixties Something', *Mother Jones Magazine* 16:2 (March–April 1991), 47–49, 69–70.

48 Margry, 'The Pilgrimage to Jim Morrison's Grave', 146.

49 Ibid., 146.

50   Another compilation album, *The Best of the Doors*, released in 2000 by Elektra, uses
     another photograph of Brodsky's photographs from *Young Lion* series. See also The
     Morrison Hotel Gallery: https://www.morrisonhotelgallery.com/photographer/
     default.aspx?photographerID=22 (accessed 18 February 2014).
51   Margry, 'The Pilgrimage to Jim Morrison's Grave', 147.
52   See DePaoli, *Elvis + Marilyn*; for Bar-min-ski's portrait *Elvis Christ*, see the cover of
     Death Ride '69, *Elvis Christ* (1988).
53   Rojek, *Fame Attack*, 3.
54   See Partridge, *Lyre of Orpheus*.
55   Rojek, *Fame Attack*, 3.
56   T. Day, *A Century of Recorded Music: Listening to Musical History* (New Haven: Yale
     University Press, 2000).
57   Ibid., 216.
58   Ibid.
59   Ibid.
60   K. Barth, *Wolfgang Amadeus Mozart*. Trans. by C.K. Pott (Grand Rapids: Eerdmans,
     1986), 16–17.
61   Reed & Miller, *Stairway to Heaven*, 9.
62   See Reader & Walter, *Pilgrimage in Popular Culture*.
63   See Reed & Miller, *Stairway to Heaven*.
64   Riis & Woodhead, *Sociology of Religious Emotion*, 133–34.
65   See particularly P. Tillich, *Dynamics of Faith* (New York: Harper & Row, 1957),
     1–4.
66   J. Eade & M.J. Sallnow, 'Introduction'. In J. Eade & M.J. Sallnow (eds), *Contesting
     the Sacred: The Anthropology of Christian Pilgrimage* (Urbana: University of Illinois
     Press, 2000), 6.
67   See C. Morris, 'Introduction'. In C. Morris & P. Roberts (eds), *Pilgrimage:
     The English Experience from Becket to Bunyan* (Cambridge: Cambridge University
     Press, 2002), 1.
68   B.E. Whalen, *Pilgrimage in the Middle Ages: A Reader* (Toronto: University of
     Toronto Press, 2011), xi.
69   P.J. Margry, 'Secular Pilgrimage: A Contradiction in Terms?' In P.J. Margry
     (ed.), *Shrines and Pilgrimage in the Modern World: New Itineraries in the Sacred*
     (Amsterdam: Amsterdam University Press, 2008), 17. See also L. Tomasi, '*Homo
     Viator*: From Pilgrimage to Religious Tourism via the Journey'. In W.H. Swatos &
     L. Tomasi (eds), *From Medieval Pilgrimage to Religious Tourism. The Social and
     Cultural Economics of Piety* (Westport: Praeger, 2002), 1–24.
70   A.D. Bemborg, 'Creating Sacred Space by Walking in Silence: Pilgrimage in a Late
     Modern Lutheran Context', *Social Compass* 60 (2013), 544–60.
71   Again, for a concise and helpful analysis, see ibid., 546–48.

72 See Margry, *Shrines and Pilgrimage in the Modern World*; Reader & Walter, *Pilgrimage in Popular Culture*; W.H. Swatos (ed.), *On the Road to Being There: Studies in Pilgrimage and Tourism in Late Modernity* (Leiden: Brill, 2006).

73 S. Coleman & J. Eade, 'Reframing Pilgrimage'. In S. Coleman & J. Eade (eds), *Reframing Pilgrimage: Cultures in Motion* (London: Routledge, 2004), 9. See also N. Collins-Kreiner, 'Researching Pilgrimage: Continuity and Transformations', *Annals of Tourism Research* 37: 2 (2010), 440–56.

74 See E. Cohen, 'Pilgrimage and Tourism: Convergence and Divergence'. In E.A. Morinis (ed.), *Sacred Journeys: The Anthropology of Pilgrimage* (New York: Greenwood, 1992), 47–61.

75 There is always profit to be gained from re-reading, Clifford Geertz's influential essay, 'Thick Description: Toward and Interpretive Theory of Culture', in his collection of essays, *The Interpretation of Cultures: Selected Essays* (New York: Basic Books, 1973), 3–30.

76 E. Turner, 'Preface'. In V. Turner & E. Turner, *Image and Pilgrimage in Christian Culture* (New York: Columbia University Press, 1978), xiii–xiv.

77 Turner, *Ritual Process*.

78 N.L. Frey, *Pilgrim Stories: On and Off the Road to Santiago* (Berkeley: University of California Press, 1998), 230.

79 Ibid., 224–25.

80 Turner, 'Preface', xiii.

81 See Turner & Turner, *Image and Pilgrimage*; E. Turner, *Communitas: The Anthropology of Collective Joy* (New York: Palgrave Macmillan, 2012).

82 Turner, *Communitas*, 1.

83 Ibid., 1; see also, Partridge, *Lyre of Orpheus*, 73–78, 95–102.

84 Turner, *Communitas*, 31. See also Frey's interesting discussion of the sexual feelings experienced between pilgrims, in *Pilgrim Stories*, 115–17, 124–25.

85 Turner & Turner, *Image and Pilgrimage*, 34.

86 See Turner, *Ritual Process*, vii, 201.

87 E. Turner, *Heart of Lightness: The Life Story of an Anthropologist* (Oxford: Berghahn Books, 2005), 264.

88 V. Turner, *Dramas, Fields and Metaphors* (Ithaca: Cornell University Press, 1974), 13–14; see also, Turner, *Communitas*.

89 Turner & Turner, *Image and Pilgrimage*, 34.

90 W. Brooker, ' "It is love": The Lewis Carroll Society as Fan Community', *American Behavioral Scientist* 48 (2005), 868.

91 A similar point is made by Tony Walter regarding war grave 'tourism' as opposed to war grave 'pilgrimage': 'War Grave Pilgrimage'. In I. Reader and T. Walter (eds), *Pilgrimage in Popular Culture* (Houndmills: Macmillan, 1993), 82.

92 Brooker, ' "It is love" ', 48, 868–69.

93   See W. Brooker, 'A Sort of Homecoming: Fan Viewing and Symbolic Pilgrimage'. In J. Gray, C. Sandvoss & C.L. Harrington (eds), *Fandom: Identities and Communities in a Mediated World* (New York: New York University Press, 2007), 149–64.

94   Turner, 'The Center Out There', 223.

95   L. Lewis, 'Introduction'. In L. Lewis (ed.), *The Adoring Audience: Fan Culture and Popular Media* (London: Routledge, 1992), 1.

96   See L. Grossberg, 'Is There a Fan in the House? The Affective Sensibility of Fandom'. In L. Lewis (ed.), *The Adoring Audience: Fan Culture and Popular Media* (London: Routledge, 1992), 50–65.

97   Ibid., 63.

98   Austin-Broos, 'The Anthropology of Conversion', 2.

99   S. Pattison, 'Living Relations with Visual and Material Artefacts'. In G. Lynch, J. Mitchell & A. Strhan (eds), *Religion, Media and Culture: A Reader* (London: Routledge, 2012), 197.

100 Nick Drake was clearly not thinking of dead celebrities when he wrote these lyrics, but, as they are engraved on his gravestone and describe well the growth of his own posthumous significance, they are worth quoting. They are also taken from the last song on his final album prior to his suicide.

101 Barth, *Wolfgang Amadeus Mozart*, 15–16.

102 Ibid., 19 (original emphasis).

103 Ibid.

104 Ibid., 27.

105 Z. Bauman, quoted in Jacobsen, 'Sociology, Mortality and Solidarity', 382 (original emphasis).

Bibliography

Abrahamsson, Carl, 'Changing Compositions'. In Genesis P-Orridge (ed.), *Painful but Fabulous: The Lives and Art of Genesis P-Orridge* (New York: Soft Skull Shortwave, 2002), 29–39.

Acoustic Nation, 'Kansas's Kerry Livgren Shares the Story Behind "Dust In The Wind"': http://www.guitarworld.com/acoustic-nation-kansas-ken-livgren-shares-story-behind-dust-wind (accessed 25 March 2014).

Alexander, J., *The Meanings of Social Life: A Cultural Sociology* (New York: Oxford University Press, 2003).

Allen, H., 'Last Words: A Testament to Hunter Thompson', *The Washington Post* (09 September 2005): http://www.washingtonpost.com/wp-dyn/content/article/2005/09/08/AR2005090801993.html (accessed 09 April 2014).

Almond, M., *Tainted Life: The Autobiography* (London: Sidgwick & Jackson, 1999).

Altheide, D., 'The Columbine Shootings and the Discourse of Fear', *American Behavioral Scientist* 52 (2009), 1356–57.

Anderson, S. & G. Howard, 'Crime, Criminal Justice, and Popular Culture', *Journal of Criminal Justice Education* 5 (1994), 123–31.

Anso, S.G. & C. Rappleye, 'Rap Sheet'. In D. Brackett (ed.), *The Pop, Rock, and Soul Reader: Histories and Debates*, second edition (New York: Oxford University Press, 2009), 484–86.

Antonakakis N. & A. Collins, 'The Impact of Fiscal Austerity on Suicide: On the Empirics of a Modern Greek Tragedy', *Social Science & Medicine* 112 (2014), 39–50.

Ariès, P., *The Hour of Our Death*, trans. by H. Weaver (New York: Alfred A. Knopf, 1981).

Armstrong, E.G., 'Gangsta Misogyny: A Content Analysis of the Portrayals of Violence Against Women in Rap Music, 1987-1993', *Journal of Criminal Justice and Popular Culture*, 8 (2001), 96–126.

Armstrong, R., *Mourning Films: A Critical Study of Loss and Grieving in Cinema* (Jefferson: McFarland & Company, 2012).

Arnds, P., 'Innocence Abducted: Youth, War, and the Wolf in Literary Adaptations of the Pied Piper Legend from Robert Browning to Michel Tournier', *Jeunesse: Young People, Texts, Cultures* 4/1 (2012), 61–84.

Arya, R., 'The Religious Significance of Violence in Football'. In E. Christianson & C. Partridge (eds), *Holy Terror: Understanding Religion and Violence in Popular Culture* (London: Equinox, 2010), 122–34.

Augustine, *City of God*, trans. H. Bettenson (London: Penguin, 2003).

Augustine, *Nicene and Post-Nicene Fathers. First Series, Vol. 5. St. Augustine: Anti-Pelagian Writings*. Ed. by Philip Schaff (New York: Cosimo, 2007).

Aurelius, M., *Meditations* (Ware: Wordsworth, 1997).

Austin-Broos, D., 'The Anthropology of Conversion: An Introduction'. In A. Buckser & S.D. Glazier (eds), *The Anthropology of Religious Conversion* (Lanham: Rowman & Littlefield, 2003), 1–12.

Azerrad, M., *Our Band Could Be Your Life: Scenes from the American Indie Underground, 1981–1991* (Boston: Little Brown and Company, 2001).

Baddeley, G., *Goth Chic: A Connoisseur's Guide to Dark Culture* (London: Plexus, 2002).

Bailey, E., 'Implicit Religion'. In P.B. Clarke (ed.), *The Oxford Handbook of the Sociology of Religion* (New York: Oxford University Press, 2009), 801–16.

Bakhtin, M., *Rabelais and His World*, trans. by Hélène Iswolsky (Bloomington: Indiana University Press, 1984).

Barth, K., *Wolfgang Amadeus Mozart*, trans. by C.K. Pott (Grand Rapids: Eerdmans, 1986).

Bataille, G., *Eroticism: Death and Sensuality*, trans. by M. Dalwood (San Francisco: City Lights Books, 1986).

Bataille, G., *Visions of Excess: Selected Writings 1927–1939*, ed. and trans. by Allan Stoekl (Manchester: Manchester University Press, 1985).

Bataille, G., *Inner Experience*, trans. by L.A. Boldt (Albany, New York: State University of New York Press, 1988).

Bataille, G., *Theory of Religion*, trans. by R. Hurley (New York: Zone Books, 1989).

Bataille, G., *The Accursed Share*, Vol. I, trans. by R. Hurley (New York: Zone Books, 1991).

Bataille, G., *The Accursed Share*, Vols. II & III, trans. by R. Hurley (New York: Zone Books, 1991).

Bataille, G., *The Absence of Myth*, trans. by M. Richardson (London: Verso, 1994).

Bataille, G., 'Hegel, Death and Sacrifice'. In F. Botting & S. Wilson (eds), *The Bataille Reader* (Oxford: Blackwell, 1997), 279–95.

Baudelot, C. & R. Establet, *Suicide: The Hidden Side of Modernity* (Cambridge: Polity Press, 2008).

Baudrillard, J., 'Death in Bataille'. In F. Botting and S. Wilson (eds), *Bataille: A Critical Reader* (Oxford: Blackwell, 1998), 139–45.

Baudrillard, J., *Simulacra and Simulation*, trans. by S.F. Glaser (Ann Arbor: University of Michigan Press, 1994).

Baudrillard, J., *Symbolic Exchange and Death*, trans. by Iain Hamilton Grant (London: Sage, 1993).

Bauman, Z., *Intimations of Postmodernity* (London: Routledge, 1992).

Bauman, Z., *Mortality, Immortality and Other Life Strategies* (Cambridge: Polity Press, 1992).

Bauman, Z., *Work, Consumerism and the New Poor* (Buckingham: Open University Press, 1998).

Bauman, Z. & K. Tester, *Conversations with Zygmunt Bauman* (Cambridge: Polity Press, 2001).

Becker, E., *The Denial of Death* (New York: The Free Press, 1973).

Bemborg, A.D., 'Creating Sacred Space by Walking in Silence: Pilgrimage in a Late Modern Lutheran Context', *Social Compass* 60 (2013), 544–60.

Bennett, A., *Music, Style, and Ageing: Growing Old Disgracefully?* (Philadelphia: Temple University Press, 2013).

Bennett A. & J. Taylor, 'Popular Music and the Aesthetics of Ageing', *Popular Music* 13 (2012), 231–43.

Bernstein, L., *The Unanswered Question: Six Talks at Harvard* (Cambridge: Harvard University Press, 1976).

Bivins, J.C., *Religion of Fear: The Politics of Horror in Conservative Evangelicalism* (New York: Oxford University Press, 2008).

Blacklow, J., 'What's Rihanna's Connection to Exorcisms?', *Yahoo Music* (15 November 2015): https://music.yahoo.com/blogs/yahoo-music/what-s-rihanna-s-connection-to-exorcisms-193920374.html (accessed 05 July 2014).

Blush, S., *American Hardcore: A Tribal History* (Los Angeles: Feral House, 2010).

Boer, R., *Nick Cave: A Study of Love, Death and Apocalypse* (Sheffield: Equinox, 2012).

Bone, B., 'Monarch', *Rock-A-Rolla* 50 (2014), 11.

Bono, 'Elvis: American David'. In G. DePaoli (ed.), *Elvis + Marilyn: 2 x Immortal* (New York: Rizzoli, 1994), 18.

Bottici, C., *A Philosophy of Political Myth* (Cambridge: Cambridge University Press, 2007).

Botting, F., 'Gothic Culture'. In C. Spooner & E. McEvoy (eds), *The Routledge Companion to Gothic* (London: Routledge, 2007), 199–213.

Botting, F. & S. Wilson, 'Introduction: From Experience to Economy'. In F. Botting & S. Wilson (eds), *The Bataille Reader* (Oxford: Blackwell, 1997), 1–34.

Bourdieu, P., *Distinction: A Social Critique of the Judgment of Taste*, trans. by R. Nice (Cambridge: Harvard University Press, 1984).

Bowker, J., *The Meanings of Death* (Cambridge: Cambridge University Press, 1993).

Branch, A., '"Stop Flexing Your Roots, Man": Reconversion Strategies, Consecrated Heretics and the Violence of UK First-wave Punk', *Punk and Post Punk* 3 (2014), 21–39.

Brannigan, P., 'Just Say No', *Mojo* 217 (December 2011), 52–56.

Bretthauer, B., T.S. Zimmerman & J. Banning, 'A Feminist Analysis of Popular Music: Power Over, Objectification of, and Violence Against Women', *Journal of Feminist Family Therapy* 18 (2007), 29–51.

Brill, D., 'Gender, Status and Subcultural Capital in the Goth Scene'. In P. Hodkinson & W. Deicke (eds), *Youth Cultures: Scenes, Subcultures and Tribes* (New York: Routledge, 2007), 111–26

Brink, J.T. & J. Oppenheimer (eds), *Killer Images: Documentary Film, Memory and the Performance of Violence* (New York: Columbia University Press, 2012).

Brooker, W., '"It is love": The Lewis Carroll Society as Fan Community', *American Behavioral Scientist* 48 (2005), 859–80.

Brooker, W., 'A Sort of Homecoming: Fan Viewing and Symbolic Pilgrimage'. In J. Gray, C. Sandvoss & C.L. Harrington (eds), *Fandom: Identities and Communities in a Mediated World* (New York: New York University Press, 2007), 149–64.

Brown, J., *Suge Knight: The Rise, Fall, and Rise of Death Row Records* (Phoenix: Colossus Books, 2002).

Brown, M., *Debussy Redux: The Impact of His Music on Popular Culture* (Bloomington: Indiana University Press, 2012).

Brueggemann, W., *Genesis* (Louisville: John Knox Press, 1982).

Bryant, T., *The True Lives of My Chemical Romance* (London: Sidgwick & Jackson, 2014).

Bultmann, R., 'The New Testament and Mythology: The Mythological Element in the Message of the New Testament and the Problem of Its Re-interpretation'. In H.W. Bartsch (ed.) *Kerygma and Myth: A Theological Debate* (New York: Harper & Row, 1961), 1–44.

Burke, E., *A Philosophical Enquiry into the Origins of the Sublime and Beautiful: And Other Pre-Revolutionary Writings* (New York: Penguin Classics, 1998).

Bynum, C.W. & P. Freedman, 'Introduction'. In C.W. Bynum and P. Freedman (eds), *Last Things: Death and the Apocalypse in the Middle Ages* (Philadelphia: University of Pennsylvania Press, 2000), 1–17.

Caillois, R., *Man and the Sacred*, trans. by M. Barash (Urbana: University of Illnois Press, 2001).

Campbell, J., *The Power of Myth* (New York: Anchor Books, 1991).

Camus, A., *The Myth of Sisyphus*, trans. by J. O'Brien (Harmondsworth: Penguin Books, 1975).

Cardoso, A., *Electronic Voices: Contact with Another Dimension?* (Ropley: O Books, 2010).

Carpenter, A., 'The "Ground Zero" of Goth: Bauhaus, "Bela Lugosi's Dead" and the Origins of Gothic Rock', *Popular Music and Society* 35 (2012), 25–52.

Cate, Hans ten, ' "Always Look on the Bright Side of Life" Among Funeral Favorites', *PythOnline's Daily Llama* (13 March 2005): http://www.dailyllama.com/news/2005/llama276.html (accessed 09 May 2014).

Cave, N., *The Complete Lyrics, 1978-2007* (London: Penguin, 2007).

Celmins, M., *Peter Green: The Authorised Biography* (London: Sanctuary Publishing, 2003).

Cheng, A.T.A., K. Hawton, T.H.H. Chen, A.M.F. Yen, J.-C. Chang, M.-Y. Chong, C.-Y. Liu, Y. Lee, P.R. Teng & L.-C. Chen, 'The Influence of Media Reporting of a Celebrity Suicide on Suicidal Behavior in Patients with a History of Depressive Disorder', *Journal of Affective Disorders* 103 (2007), 69–75.

Christgau, R., *Grown Up All Wrong: 75 Great Rock and Roll Artists from Vaudeville to Techno* (Cambridge: Harvard University Press, 1998).

Christianson, E. & C. Partridge (eds), *Holy Terror: Understanding Religion and Violence in Popular Culture* (London: Equinox, 2010).

Chuck, D. (with Y. Jah), *Fight the Power: Rap, Race and Reality* (Edinburgh: Payback Press, 1997).

Clack, B., *Sex and Death: A Reappraisal of Human Mortality* (Cambridge: Polity Press, 2002).

Cobain, K. 'Suicide Note'. Available at: http://kurtcobainssuicidenote.com/ (accessed 09 April 2014).

Cohen, E., 'Pilgrimage and Tourism: Convergence and Divergence'. In E.A. Morinis (ed.), *Sacred Journeys: The Anthropology of Pilgrimage* (New York: Greenwood, 1992), 47–61.

Coleman, S. & J. Eade, 'Reframing Pilgrimage'. In S. Coleman & J. Eade (eds), *Reframing Pilgrimage: Cultures in Motion* (London: Routledge, 2004), 1–26.

Collins, R., *Violence: A Micro-Sociological Theory* (Princeton: Princeton University Press, 2008).

Collins-Kreiner, N., 'Researching Pilgrimage: Continuity and Transformations', *Annals of Tourism Research* 37: 2 (2010), 440–56.

Cooke, D., *The Language of Music* (Oxford: Oxford University Press, 1959).

Creed, B., *The Monstrous-Feminine: Film, Feminism, Psychoanalysis* (New York: Routledge, 1993).

Cross, C., *Heavier Than Heaven: A Biography of Kurt Cobain* (London: Hodder & Stoughton, 2001).

Culler, J., *The Pursuit of Signs: Semiotics, Literature, Deconstruction* (London: Routledge, 2001).

Curtis, D., *Touching from a Distance: Ian Curtis and Joy Division* (London: Faber and Faber, 1995).

Danto, A., *The Transfiguration of the Commonplace: A Philosophy of Art* (Cambridge: Harvard University Press, 1981).

Dastur, F., *How Are We to Confront Death: An Introduction to Philosophy*, trans. R. Vallier (New York: Fordham University Press, 2012).

Dastur, F., *Death: An Essay on Finitude*, trans. J. Llewelyn (London: Athlone, 1996).

Davies, D.J., *Death, Ritual and Belief: The Rhetoric of Funerary Rites*, second edition (London: Continuum, 2002).

Davies, D.J., *A Brief History of Death* (Oxford: Blackwell, 2005).

Davies, D.J., *The Theology of Death* (London: T&T Clark, 2008).

Davis, C., 'Hauntology, Spectres and Phantoms', *French Studies* 59 (2005), 373–79.

Day, T., *A Century of Recorded Music: Listening to Musical History* (New Haven: Yale University Press, 2000).

Dean, M., 'Christian Death Interview'. Available at: http://www.vamp.org/Gothic/Text/cd-interview.html (accessed 31 March 2014).

de Botton, A. & J. Armstrong, *Art As Therapy* (London: Phaidon Press, 2013).

Definis-Gojanović, M., D. Gugić & D. Sutlović, 'Suicide and Emo Youth Subculture: A Case Analysis', *Collegium Antropologicum: Journal of the Croatian Anthropological Society* 33, Supplement 2 (2009), 173–75.

DeNora, T., *Music in Everyday Life* (Cambridge: Cambridge University Press, 2000).

DeNora, T., 'Aesthetic Agency and Musical Practice: New Directions in the Sociology of Music'. In Patrik Juslin & John Sloboda (eds), *Music and Emotion: Theory and Research* (Oxford: Oxford University Press, 2001), 161–80.

DePaoli, G. (ed.), *Elvis + Marilyn: 2 x Immortal* (New York: Rizzoli, 1994).

Derrida, J., 'Marx and Sons'. In M. Sprinker (ed.), *Ghostly Demarcations: A Symposium on Jacques Derrida's* Spectres of Marx (London: Verso, 1999), 213–69.

DeSpelder, L.A. & A.L. Strickland, *The Last Dance: Encountering Death and Dying* (Palo Alto: Mayfield Publishing Company, 1983).

Dollimore, J., *Death, Desire and Loss in Western Culture* (London: Allen Lane, 1998).

Donne, J., *Devotions upon Emergent Occasions and Death's Duel* (New York: Vintage Books, 1999). Also available at: http://www.gutenberg.org/files/23772/23772-h/23772-h.htm (accessed 15 October 2010).

Doss, E., 'Believing in Elvis: Popular Piety in Material Culture'. In Stewart M. Hoover & Lynn Schofield Clark (eds), *Religion in the Age of the Media: Explorations in Media, Religion and Culture* (New York: Columbia University Press, 2002), 63–86.

Doss, E., 'Rock and Roll Pilgrims: Reflections on Ritual, Religiosity and Race at Graceland'. In P.J. Margry (ed.), *Shrines and Pilgrimage in the Modern World: New Itineraries into the Sacred* (Amsterdam: Amsterdam University Press, 2008), 130–34

Douglas, M., *Purity and Danger: An Analysis of the Concept of Pollution and Taboo* (London: Routledge, 2002).

Duffett, M., 'False Faith or False Comparison? A Critique of the Religious Interpretation of Elvis Fan Culture', *Popular Music and Society* 26 (2003), 514–22.

Dundes, A. (ed.), *Sacred Narrative: Readings in the Theory of Myth* (Berkeley: University of California Press, 1884).

Durkheim, É., *Suicide: A Study in Sociology*, trans. by J.A. Spaulding & G. Simpson (London: Routledge & Kegan Paul, 1952).

Durkheim, É., 'Individualism and the Intellectuals'. In R.N. Bellah (ed.), *Emile Durkheim: On Morality and Society* (Chicago: University of Chicago Press, 1973), 43–57.

Durkheim, É., *The Elementary Forms of Religious Life*, trans. by C. Cosman (Oxford: Oxford University Press, 2001).

Dyson, M.E., *Between God and Gangsta Rap: Bearing Witness to Black Culture* (New York: Oxford University Press, 1996).

Eade, J. & M.J. Sallnow, 'Introduction'. In J. Eade & M.J. Sallnow (eds), *Contesting the Sacred: The Anthropology of Christian Pilgrimage* (Urbana: University of Illinois Press, 2000), 1–29.

Earles, A., *Hüsker Dü: The Story of the Noise-Pop Pioneers Who Launched Modern Rock* (Minneapolis: Voyageur Press, 2010).

Eck, D., *Banaras: City of Light* (New York: Columbia University Press, 1999).

Edwards, P., 'Existentialism and Death: A Survey of Some Confusions and Absurdities'. In J. Donnelly (ed.), *Language, Metaphysics, and Death* (New York: Fordham University Press, 1978), 32–61.

Eide, R., *The Celestial Voice of Diana: Her Spiritual Guidance to Finding Love* (Forres: Findhorn Press, 2001).

Elferen, I. van, *Gothic Music: The Sounds of the Uncanny* (Cardiff: University of Wales Press, 2012).

Farmer, H.H., *Experience of God: A Brief Enquiry into the Grounds of Christian Conviction* (London: SCM Press, 1929).

Farmer, H.H., *Reconciliation and Religion*. Gifford Lectures, 1951. Ed. by C.H. Partridge (Lewiston: Edwin Mellen, 1998).

Fenimore, R.J., 'Voices That Lie Within: The Heard and the Unheard in *Psycho*'. In
N. Lerner (ed.), *Music in the Horror Film* (New York: Routledge, 2010), 80–97.

Feuerbach, L., *Thoughts on Death and Immortality*, trans. J.A. Massey (Berkeley:
University of California Press, 1980).

Ffytche, M., 'Night of the Unexpected: A Critique of the 'Uncanny' and Its Apotheosis
Within Cultural and Social Theory', *New Formations* 75 (2012), 63–81.

Fish, M., *Industrial Evolution: Through the Eighties with Cabaret Voltaire* (London:
SAF Publishing, 2002).

Fish, S., *Is There a Text in This Class? The Authority of Interpretive Communities*
(Cambridge: Harvard University Press, 1980).

Fisher, M., *Ghosts of My Life: Depression, Hauntology and Lost Futures* (Alresford: Zero
Books, 2014).

Fonseca, T., 'Bela Lugosi's Dead but Vampire Music Stalks the Airwaves'. In J.C. Holte
(ed.), *The Fantastic Vampire: Studies in the Children of the Night – Selected Essays
from the Eighteenth International Conference on the Fantastic in the Arts* (Westport:
Greenwood Press, 2002), 59–68.

Foucault, M., *The Birth of the Clinic: An Archaeology of Medical Perception*, trans.
A.M. Sheridan Smith (New York: Sheridan Books, 1972).

Freud, S., 'Beyond the Pleasure Principle'. In S. Freud (ed.), *The Standard Edition of the
Complete Psychological Works of Sigmund Freud*, Vol. 18. Ed. by J. Strachey (London:
Vintage, 2001), 7–64.

Freud, S., 'The Future of an Illusion'. In S. Freud (ed.), *The Standard Edition of the
Complete Psychological Works of Sigmund Freud*, Vol. 21. Ed. by J. Strachey (London:
Vintage, 2001), 5–56.

Freud, S., 'Thoughts for the Times on War and Death'. In S. Freud (ed.), *The Standard
Edition of the Complete Psychological Works of Sigmund Freud*, Vol. 14. Ed. by
J. Strachey (London: Vintage, 2001), 273–300.

Freud, S., *The Uncanny*, trans. by D. McLintock (London: Penguin, 2003).

Frey, N.L., *Pilgrim Stories: On and Off the Road to Santiago* (Berkeley: University of
California Press, 1998).

Fricke, D., 'Lou Reed, *Magic and Loss*', *Rolling Stone* (23 January 1992): http://www.
rollingstone.com/music/albumreviews/magic-and-loss-19920123 (accessed 23
August 2013).

Frith, S., 'Pop Music'. In S. Frith, W. Straw, & J. Street (eds), *The Cambridge Companion
to Pop and Rock* (Cambridge: Cambridge University Press, 2001), 93–108.

Frith, S., 'Music and Everyday Life'. In M. Clayton, T. Herbert & R. Middleton (eds), *The
Cultural Study of Music: A Critical Introduction* (New York: Routledge, 2003), 92–101.

Frith, S., *Taking Popular Music Seriously: Selected Essays* (Aldershot: Ashgate, 2007).

Frith, S. & A. McRobbie, 'Rock and Sexuality'. In S. Frith & A. Goodwin (eds), *On
Record: Rock, Pop, and the Written Word* (New York: Pantheon Books, 1990), 371–89.

Fu, K.W. & P.S.F. Yip, 'Long-term Impact of Celebrity Suicide on Suicidal Ideation:
Results from A Population-based Study', *Journal of Epidemiology and Community
Health* 61 (2007), 540–46.

Gabrielsson, A., *Strong Experiences with Music: Music is Much More than Just Music.* Trans. R. Bradbury (Oxford: Oxford University Press, 2011).

Gaiman, N., *Death: The Time of Your Life* (New York: DC/Time Warner, 1997).

Gaines, D., *Teenage Wasteland: Suburbia's Dead End Kids* (Chicago: Chicago University Press, 1998).

Garces-Foley, K. (ed.), *Death and Religion in a Changing World* (Armonk: M.E. Sharpe, 2006), 207–27.

Gawande, A., *Being Mortal: Illness, Medicine and What Matters in the End* (London: Profile Books, 2014).

Geertz, C., *The Interpretation of Cultures: Selected Essays* (New York: Basic Books, 1973).

Gibb, R., 'Unholy Matrimony: An Interview With Demdike Stare', *The Quietus* (17 February 2011): http://thequietus.com/articles/05699-demdike-stare-interview (accessed 20 June 2014).

Giddens, A., *Modernity and Self-Identity: Self and Society in a Late Modern Age* (Oxford: Polity Press, 1991).

Giddens, A., *The Transformation of Intimacy* (Stanford: Stanford University Press, 1993).

Girard, R., *Violence and the Sacred.* trans. by P. Gregory (Baltimore: John Hopkins University Press, 1977).

Goodlad, L. & M. Bibby, 'Introduction'. In L. Goodlad & M. Bibby (eds), *Goth: Undead Subculture* (Durham: Yale University Press, 2007), 1–37.

Gorer, G., 'The Pornography of Death', *Encounter* (October 1955), 49–52.

Gragnolati, M., 'From Decay to Splendor: Body and Pain in Bonvesin de la Riva's *Book of the Three Scriptures*'. In C.W. Bynum & P. Freedman (eds), *Last Things: Death and the Apocalypse in the Middle Ages* (Philadelphia: University of Pennsylvania Press, 2000), 83–97.

Green, J.W., *Beyond the Good Death: The Anthropology of Modern Dying* (Philadelphia: University of Pennsylvania Press, 2008).

Grossberg, L., 'Is There a Fan in the House? The Affective Sensibility of Fandom'. In L. Lewis (ed.), *The Adoring Audience: Fan Culture and Popular Media* (London: Routledge, 1992), 50–65.

Grossberg, L., *We Gotta Get Out of This Place: Popular Conservatism and Postmodern Culture* (London: Routledge, 1992).

Habermas, J., *The Theory of Communicative Action: A Critique of Functionalist Reason,* Vol. 2. Trans. T. McCarthy (London: Polity Press, 1987).

Hagedorn, J., *A World of Gangs: Armed Young Men and Gangsta Culture* (Minneapolis: University of Minnesota Press, 2009).

Hagen, C., 'A Career's Worth of Corpses and Severed Limbs', *New York Times* (20 October 1995): http://www.nytimes.com/1995/10/20/arts/photography-review-a-career-s-worth-of-corpses-and-severed-limbs.html (accessed 20 July 2014).

Halberstam, D., 'Foreword'. In G. DePaoli (ed.), *Elvis + Marilyn: 2 x Immortal* (New York: Rizzoli, 1994), 8–9.

Hall, J.R. & P. Schuyler, 'The Mystical Apocalypse of the Solar Temple'. In J.R. Lewis (ed.), *The Order of the Solar Temple: The Temple of Death* (Aldershot: Ashgate, 2006), 55–90.

Hanlan, A., *Autobiography of Dying* (New York: Doubleday, 1979).

Harkness, G., *Chicago Hustle and Flow: Gangs, Gangsta Rap, and Social Class* (Minneapolis: University of Minnesota Press, 2014).

Harrison, E., 'Princess Diana Speaks', *PlanetLightworker.com* (October/November 1999): http://www.planetlightworker.com/articles/interviews/ritaeide/interview1.htm (accessed 14 February 2014).

Hesmondhalgh, D., *Why Music Matters* (Chichester: John Wiley & Sons, 2013).

Hegarty, P., *Noise/Music: A History* (New York: Continuum, 2007).

Hibbett, R., 'What is Indie Rock?', *Popular Music and Society* 28 (2005), 55–77.

Hick, J., *The Metaphor of God Incarnate*, second edition (London: SCM Press, 2005).

Hiley, D., *Gregorian Chant* (Cambridge: Cambridge University Press, 2009).

Hinds, S.S., 'Party Over'. In D. Brackett (ed.), *The Pop, Rock, and Soul Reader: Histories and Debates*, second edition (New York: Oxford University Press, 2009), 486.

Hobsbawm, E., *Age of Extremes* (London: Abacus, 1995).

Hodkinson, P., *Goth: Identity, Style and Subculture* (Oxford: Berg, 2002).

Howard, D.N., *Sonic Alchemy: Visionary Music Producers and Their Maverick Recordings* (Milwaukee: Hal Leonard Corporation, 2004).

Hull Daily Mail, 'Yorkshire's Top Ten Funeral Songs', *Hull Daily Mail* (29 October 2012): http://www.hulldailymail.co.uk/Revealed-Yorkshire-s-funeral-songs/story-17194566-detail/story.html (accessed 09 May 2014).

Hutcherson, B. & R. Haenfler, 'Musical Genre as a Gendered Process: Authenticity in Extreme Metal'. In N.K. Denzin (ed.), *Studies in Symbolic Interaction*, Vol. 35 (Bingley: Emerald Group Publishing, 2010), 101–22.

Huxley, A., *The Doors of Perception and Heaven and Hell* (London: Flamingo, 1994).

Hval, J., 'The Inner Sleeve', *The Wire* 366 (August 2014), 71.

Jacobsen, M.H., 'Sociology, Mortality and Solidarity. An Interview with Zygmunt Bauman on Death, Dying and Immortality', *Mortality* 16: 4 (2011), 380–93.

Jalland, P., *Death in the Victorian Family* (Oxford: Oxford University Press, 1996).

Jameson, F., 'Marx's Purloined Letter'. In M. Sprinker (ed.), *Ghostly Demarcations: A Symposium on Jacques Derrida's* Spectres of Marx (London: Verso, 1999), 26–67.

Jenks, C., *Transgression* (London: Routledge, 2003).

Jensen, J.S. (ed.), *Myths and Mythologies: A Reader* (London: Equinox, 2009).

Jeong, J., S. Shin, H. Kim, Y. Hong, S. Hwang & E. Lee, 'The Effects of Celebrity Suicide on Copycat Suicide Attempt: A Multi-center Observational Study', *Social Psychiatry and Psychiatric Epidemiology* 47 (2012), 957–65.

Johnson, B. & M. Cloonan, *Dark Side of the Tune: Popular Music and Violence* (Aldershot: Ashgate, 2009).

Jordan-Wrench, J., 'Interview: Bikini Kill', *The Stool Pigeon* (24 October 2012): http://www.thestoolpigeon.co.uk/features/interview-bikini-kill.html (accessed 22 August 2014).

Juslin, P.N. & J. Sloboda (eds), *Music and Emotion: Theory and Research* (Oxford: Oxford University Press, 2001).

Kahl, A., ' "Our Dead are the Ultimate Teachers of Life": The Corpse as an Intermediator of Transcendence: Spirituality in the German Funeral Market', *Fieldwork in Religion* 8 (2013), 223–40.

Kahn-Harris, K., 'Death Metal and the Limits of Musical Expression'. In M. Cloonan & R. Garofalo (eds), *Policing Pop* (Philadelphia: Temple University Press, 2003), 81–99.

Kahn-Harris, K., *Extreme Metal: Music and Culture on the Edge* (Oxford: Berg, 2007).

Kanter, J., *Performing Loss: Rebuilding Community Through Theatre and Writing* (Carbondale: Southern Illinois University Press, 2007).

Keenan, D., 'Pharmakon', *The Wire* 368 (October 2014), 36–39.

Kendrick, J., *Film Violence: History, Ideology, Genre* (New York: Columbia University Press, 2010).

Kernberg, O., 'The Concept of the Death Drive: A Clinical Perspective', *The International Journal of Psychoanalysis* 90 (2009), 1009–23.

Kieffer, G., 'Chasing Ghosts in the Dark: An Interview with Steve Wilson Regarding Bass Communion': http://archive.today/onUxR (accessed 07 July 2014).

Kilpatrick, N., *The Goth Bible: A Compendium for the Darkly Inclined* (London: Plexus, 2005).

King, C., 'His Truth Goes Marching On: Elvis Presley and the Pilgrimage to Graceland'. In I. Reader & T. Walter (eds), *Pilgrimage in Popular Culture* (Houndmills: Macmillan, 1993), 92–104.

Kristeva, J., *Desire in Language: A Semiotic Approach to Literature and Art* (New York: Columbia University Press, 1980).

Kristeva, J., *Powers of Horror: An Essay on Abjection*. Trans. by L.S. Roudiez (New York: Columbia University Press, 1982).

Lady Gaga, 'Amen Fashion': http://amenfashion.tumblr.com/ (accessed 02 December 2012).

Laing, D., ' "Sadeness", Scorpions and Single Markets: National and Transnational Trends in European Popular Music', *Popular Music* 11 (1992), 127–40.

Larkin, R.W., *Comprehending Columbine* (Philadelphia: Temple University Press, 2007).

Larson, A., 'Fast, Cheap and Out of Control: The Graphic Symbol in Hardcore Punk', *Punk and Post Punk* 2 (2013), 91–106.

Layard, R., *Happiness: Lessons from a New Science* (London: Penguin, 2006).

Leming, M.R. & G.E. Dickinson, *Understanding Dying, Death and Bereavement*, seventh edition (Belmont: Wadsworth, 2011).

Levine, N., *Dharma Punx: A Memoir* (New York: HarperCollins, 2003).

Levy, E., 'A Mix-Tape for Gus' *BBC Radio 4* (12 October 2014): http://emilylevy.co.uk (accessed 12 October 2014).

Lewis, L., 'Introduction'. In L. Lewis (ed.), *The Adoring Audience: Fan Culture and Popular Media* (London: Routledge, 1992), 1–6.

Licht, A., 'Tunnel Vision: Michael Gira', *The Wire* 223 (2003), 30–37.

Lockwood, D., 'Dead Souls: Post-Punk Music as Hauntological Trigger'. In B. Cherry, P. Howell & C. Ruddell (eds), *Twenty-First-Century Gothic* (Newcastle: Cambridge Scholars Publishing, 2010), 99–111.

Long, K.S., 'Rock Lyrics, Advertising, and the Parents' Music Resource Center'. In K.S. Long & M. Nadelhaft (eds), *America Under Construction: Boundaries and Identities in Popular Culture* (New York: Routledge, 1997), 149–68.

Lynch, G., *The Sacred in the Modern World: A Cultural Sociological Approach* (Oxford: Oxford University Press, 2012).

MacDonald, R., D. Hargreaves & D. Miell (eds), *Musical Identities* (Oxford: Oxford University Press, 2002).

Macfarlane, K.E., 'The Monstrous House of Gaga'. In J. Edwards & A.S. Monnet, *The Gothic in Contemporary Literature and Popular Culture: Pop Goth* (New York: Routledge, 2012), 114–34.

MacIntyre, A., *Against the Self-Images of the Age* (Notre Dame: University of Notre Dame Press, 1978).

MacIntyre, A., *After Virtue*, second edition (Notre-Dame: University of Notre Dame Press, 1984).

MacLeod, D., ' "Social Distortion": The Rise of Suburban Punk Rock in Los Angeles'. In K.S. Long & M. Nadelhaft (eds), *America Under Construction: Boundaries and Identities in Popular Culture* (New York: Routledge, 1997), 123–48.

Macmurray, J., *Persons in Relation* (London: Faber & Faber, 1961).

Malinowski, B., *Magic, Science and Religion and Other Essays* (London: Souvenir Press, 1974).

Marcus, G., *Dead Elvis: A Chronicle of a Cultural Obsession* (New York: Viking, 1992).

Margry, P.J., 'Secular Pilgrimage: A Contradiction in Terms?' In P.J. Margry (ed.), *Shrines and Pilgrimage in the Modern World: New Itineraries in the Sacred* (Amsterdam: Amsterdam University Press, 2008), 13–46.

Margry, P.J., 'The Pilgrimage to Jim Morrison's Grave at Père Lachaise Cemetery: The Social Construction of Sacred Space'. In P.J. Margry (ed.), *Shrines and Pilgrimage in the Modern World: New Itineraries into the Sacred* (Amsterdam: Amsterdam University Press, 2008), 143–72.

Marzluff, J.M. & T. Angell, *In the Company of Crows and Ravens* (New Haven: Yale University Press, 2005).

Massey, J.A., 'Introduction'. In L. Feuerbach, *Thoughts on Death and Immortality*, trans. J.A. Massey (Berkeley: University of California Press, 1980), ix–xliii.

McGrath, P., 'Transgression and Decay'. In C. Grunenberg (ed.), *Gothic: Transmutations of Horror in Late Twentieth Century Art* (Boston: The Institute of Contemporary Art/MIT Press, 1997), 152–59.

McMahon, M., *Princess Diana's Message of Peace: An Extraordinary Message of Peace for Our Current World* (La Vergne: Write to Print, 2003).

McMahon, M., *Notes from John: Messages from Across the Universe* (Taylorville: Eternal Rose Publishing, 2012).

McQuillar, T.L. & F. Johnson, *Tupac Shakur: The Life and Times of an American Icon* (Cambridge: Da Capo Press, 2010).

Michaud, S., *Rozz Williams: Le théâtre des douleurs* (Rosières-en-Haye: Camion Blanc, 2010).

Miller, M.R., *Religion and Hip Hop* (New York: Routledge, 2013).

Miller, M.R., A.B. Pinn & B. Freeman, *Religion in Hip Hop: Mapping the New Terrain* (London: Bloomsbury, 2014).

Mintz, R., 'Gothic'. In M. Kehoss & B. Rein (eds), *Gothic* (Santa Ana: Orange County Centre for Contemporary Art, 2012).

Mitford, J., *The American Way of Death Revisited* (London: Virago, 1998).

Mörat, 'Dark Recollections: Sick of It All, *Scratch the Surface*', *Terrorizer* 214 (2011), 72–74.

Morris, C., 'Introduction'. In C. Morris & P. Roberts (eds), *Pilgrimage: The English Experience from Becket to Bunyan* (Cambridge: Cambridge University Press, 2002), 1–11.

Mould, B., *See a Little Light: The Trail of Rage and Melody* (New York: Little Brown & Company, 2011).

Mudrian, A., *Choosing Death: The Improbable History of Death Metal and Grindcore* (Los Angeles: Feral House, 2004).

Myers, B., *American Heretics: Rebel Voices in Music* (Hove: Codex, 2002).

Mullen, B., *Lexicon Devil: The Fast Times and Short Life of Darby Crash and the Germs* (Los Angeles: Feral House, 2002).

Nelson, V., *Gothicka: Vampire Heroes, Human Gods and the New Supernatural* (Cambridge: Harvard University Press, 2012).

Nietzsche, F., *The Will to Power: In Science, Nature, Society and Art*, trans. by W.A. Kaufmann & R.J. Hollingdale (New York: Vintage Books, 1968).

Nobokov, V., *Speak, Memory* (London: Penguin, 2000).

Otto, R., *The Idea of the Holy: An Inquiry into the Non-rational Factor in the Idea of the Divine and Its Relation to the Rational*, trans. by J.W. Harvey (Oxford: Oxford University Press, 1958).

Palmer, S., 'Purity and Danger in the Solar Temple'. In J.R. Lewis (ed.), *The Order of the Solar Temple: The Temple of Death* (Aldershot: Ashgate, 2006), 39–54.

Parisot, E., *Graveyard Poetry: Religion, Aesthetics and the Mid-Eighteenth Century Poetic Condition* (Franham: Ashgate, 2013).

Parker, J., *Turned on: A Biography of Henry Rollins* (New York: Cooper Square Press, 2000).

Partridge, C., *H.H. Farmer's Theological Interpretation of Religion* (Lewiston: Edwin Mellen, 1998).

Partridge, C., *The Re-enchantment of the West: Alternative Spiritualities, Sacralization, Popular Culture and Occulture*, 2 vols. (London: Continuum, 2004, 2005).

Partridge, C., *Dub in Babylon: Understanding the Evolution and Significance of Dub Reggae in Jamaica and Britain from King Tubby to Post-punk* (London: Equinox, 2010).

Partridge, C., 'Popular Music, Affective Space, and Meaning'. In G. Lynch, J. Mitchell & A. Strhan (eds), *Religion, Media and Culture: A Reader* (London: Routledge, 2012), 182–93.

Partridge, C., 'Occulture is Ordinary'. In K. Granholm & E. Asprem (eds), *Contemporary Esotericism* (Sheffield: Equinox, 2013), 113–133

Partridge, C., 'Haunted Culture: The Persistence of Belief in the Paranormal'. In O. Jenzen & S. Munt (eds), *Research Companion to Paranormal Cultures* (Farnham: Ashgate, 2013), 39–50.

Partridge, C., *The Lyre of Orpheus: Popular Music, the Sacred and the Profane* (New York: Oxford University Press, 2014).

Partridge, C., 'Fandom, Pop Devotion, and the Transfiguration of Dead Celebrities'. In F. Metzger & E. Pahud de Mortanges (eds), *Orte und Räume des Religiösen (19–21 Jahrhundert)* (Paderborn: Schöningh Verlag, forthcoming).

Pattison, S., 'Living Relations with Visual and Material Artefacts'. In G. Lynch, J. Mitchell & A. Strhan (eds), *Religion, Media and Culture: A Reader* (London: Routledge, 2012), 194–202.

Perry, I., *Prophets of the Hood: Politics and Poetics in Hip Hop* (Durham: Duke University Press, 2004).

Peterson, R.J., M.A. Safer & D.A. Jobes, 'The Impact of Suicidal Rock Music Lyrics on Youth: An Investigation of Individual Differences', *Archives of Suicide Research* 12 (2008), 161–69.

Phillipov, M., 'Self Harm In Goth Youth Subculture: Study Merely Reinforces Popular Stereotypes', *British Medical Journal* 332 (2006), 1215.

Phillipov, M., *Death Metal and Music Criticism: Analysis at the Limits* (Plymouth: Lexington Books, 2012).

Phillipov, M., 'Extreme Music for Extreme People? Norwegian Black Metal and Transcendent Violence'. In T. Hjelm, K. Kahn-Harris & M. Levine (eds), *Heavy Metal: Controversies and Countercultures* (Sheffield: Equinox, 2013).

Pickering, W.S.F., *Durkheim's Sociology of Religion: Themes and Theories* (London: Routledge & Kegan Paul, 1984).

Pickering, W.S.F. & G. Walford (eds), *Durkheim's Suicide: A Century of Research and Debate* (London: Routledge, 2000).

Pinker, S., *The Better Angels of our Nature: Why Violence Has Decined* (New York: Viking, 2011).

Pirkis, J.E. & R.W. Blood, 'Suicide and the Media: Part I: Reportage in Nonfictional Media', *Crisis: The Journal of Crisis Intervention and Suicide Prevention* 22 (2001),146–54.

Pirkis, J.E., P.M. Burgess, C. Francis, R.W. Blood & D.J. Jolley, 'The Relationship Between Media Reporting of Suicide and Actual Suicide in Australia', *Social Science & Medicine* 62 (2006), 2874–86.

Polanyi, M., *Personal Knowledge: Towards a Post-Critical Philosophy* (Chicago: Chicago University Press, 1962).

Polari, 'From the Fringes of the Milky Way: Tori Amos', *Polari Magazine* (09 May 2009): http://www.polarimagazine.com/interviews/fringes-of-milky-way-interview-tori-amos/ (accessed 07 August 2014).

Porter, D., *Rapcore: The Nu-Metal Rap Fusion* (London: Plexus, 2003).

Porter, R., 'The Hour of Philippe Ariès', *Mortality* 4: 1 (1999), 83–90.

Primack, B.A., M.A. Gold, E.B. Schwarz & M.A. Dalton, 'Degrading and Non-Degrading Sex in Popular Music: A Content Analysis', *Public Health Reports* 123 (2008), 593–600.

Prindle, M., 'Steve Albini: 2005', *Mark's Record Reviews*: http://www.markprindle.com/albini-i.htm (accessed 22 August 2014)

Punter, D., 'The Uncanny'. In C. Spooner & E. McEvoy (eds), *The Routledge Companion to Gothic* (London: Routledge, 2007), 129–36.

Quinn, E., *Nuthin' But a G Thang: The Culture and Commerce of Gangsta* (New York: Columbia University Press, 2005).

Razinsky, L., 'How to Look Death in the Eyes: Freud and Bataille', *SubStance* 38 (2009), 63–88.

Razinsky, L., *Freud, Psychoanalysis and Death* (Cambridge: Cambridge University Press, 2013).

Reader, I. & T. Walter (eds), *Pilgrimage in Popular Culture* (Houndmills: Macmillan, 1993).

Reece, G., *Elvis Religion: The Cult of the King* (London: I.B. Tauris, 2006).

Reed J.D. & M. Miller, *Stairway to Heaven: The Final Resting Places of Rock's Legends* (New York: Wenner Books, 2005).

Reed, L., *The Raven* (New York: Grove Press, 2003).

Reynolds, F.E. & E.H. Waugh (eds), *Religious Encounters with Death: Insights from the History and Anthropology of Religions* (University Park: Pennsylvania State University Press, 1977).

Reynolds, F.E. & E.H. Waugh, 'Introduction'. In F.E. Reynolds & E.H. Waugh (eds), *Religious Encounters with Death: Insights from the History and Anthropology of Religions* (University Park: Pennsylvania State University Press, 1977), 1–10.

Reynolds, S., *Rip It Up and Start Again: Post-punk 1978–1984* (London: Faber and Faber, 2005).

Richards, J., S. Wilson & L. Woodhead (eds), *Diana: The Making of a Media Saint* (London: I.B. Tauris, 1999).

Richardson, N., 'In-between Worlds: Grouper', *The Wire* 334 (December 2011), 26–29.

Riis, O. & L. Woodhead, *A Sociology of Religious Emotion* (Oxford: Oxford University Press, 2010).

Riley, A., ' "Renegade Durkheimianism" and the Transgressive Left Sacred'. In J.C. Alexander & P. Smith (eds), *The Cambridge Companion to Durkheim* (Cambridge: Cambridge University Press, 2005), 274–301.

Rimmer, D., *New Romantics: The Look* (London: Omnibus Press, 2003).

Riordan, J. & J. Prochnicky, *Break on Through: The Life and Death of Jim Morrison* (London: Plexus, 1991).

Robb, J., 'Syd Barrett, the Swinging 60', *The Independent* (07 January 2006): http://www.independent.co.uk/arts-entertainment/music/features/syd-barrett-the-swinging-60-521928.html (accessed 06 August 2014).

Rodman, G.B., *Elvis After Elvis: The Posthumous Career of a Living Legend* (Abingdon: Routledge, 1996).

Rojek, C., *Fame Attack: The Inflation of Celebrity and Its Consequences* (London: Bloomsbury, 2012).

Rojek, C., *Celebrity* (London: Reaktion Books, 2001).

Rollins, H., *Eye Scream* (Los Angeles: 2.13.61, 1996).

Rombes, N., *A Cultural Dictionary of Punk: 1974–1982* (New York: Continuum, 2009).

Rose, T., *Black Noise: Rap Music and Black Culture in Contemporary America* (Middletown: Wesleyan University Press, 1994).

Rose, T., 'Voices from the Margins: Rap Music and Contemporary Cultural Production'. In A. Bennett, B. Shank & J. Toynbee (eds), *The Popular Music Studies Reader* (Abingdon: Routledge, 2006), 216–23.

Rose, T., *The Hip-Hop Wars: What We Talk About When We Talk About Hip-hop and Why It Matters* (New York: Basic Books, 2008).

Royle, R., *The Uncanny* (Manchester: Manchester University Press, 2003).

Sacred Bones Records, 'Pharmakon, *Abandon*': http://www.sacredbonesrecords.com/products/sbr099-pharmakon-abandon (accessed 24 May 2014).

Sampar, M., 'Rock 'n' Roll Suicide: Why Heavy Metal Musicians Cannot Be Held Responsible for the Violent Acts of Their Listeners', *Seton Hall Journal of Sports and Entertainment Law* 15 (2005), 173–96.

Schopen, G., 'Relic'. In Mark C. Taylor (ed.), *Critical Terms for Religious Studies* (Chicago: Chicago University Press, 1998), 256–68.

Schraffenberger, R., 'This Modern Goth (Explains Herself)'. In L. Goodlad & M. Bibby (eds), *Goth: Undead Subculture* (Durham: Yale University Press, 2007), 121–28.

Schulkind, M., 'Is Memory for Music Special?', *Annals of the New York Academy of Sciences* 1169 (2009), 216–24.

Scott, D.B., *From the Erotic to the Demonic: On Critical Musicology* (Oxford: Oxford University Press, 2003).

Segal, R., *Theorizing about Myth* (Amherst: University of Massachusetts Press, 1999).

Sellgren, K., 'Young People "Feel They Have Nothing to Live For"', *BBC News* (2 January 2014): http://www.bbc.co.uk/news/education-25559089 (accessed 28 September 2014).

Shumway, D. & H. Arnet, 'Playing Dress UP: David Bowie and the Roots of Goth'. In L. Goodlad & M. Bibby (eds), Goth: Undead Subculture (Durham: Yale University Press, 2007), 129–42.

Siegel, C., 'The Obscure Object of Desire Revisited: Poppy Z. Brite and the Goth Hero as Masochist'. In L. Goodlad & M. Bibby (eds), *Goth: Undead Subculture* (Durham: Yale University Press, 2007), 335–56.

Sihra, L., 'An Open Casket', *Journal of Palliative Medicine* 14: 2 (2011), 245–45.

Silk, J., 'Open a Vein: Suicidal Black Metal and Enlightenment', *Helvete: A Journal of Black Metal Theory* 1 (Winter 2013), 5–20.

Simpson, D., 'My Favourite Album: *Closer* by Joy Division', *The Guardian: Music Blog* (18 August 2011): http://www.theguardian.com/music/musicblog/2011/aug/18/joy-division-closer (accessed 09 July 2014).

Skerl, J. (ed.), *Reconstructing the Beats* (New York: Palgrave Macmillan, 2004).

Sloboda, J.A. & P.N. Juslin, 'At the Internface between the Inner and the Outer World: Psychological Perpsectives'. In J.A. Sloboda & P.N. Juslin (eds), *Handbook of Music and Emotion: Theory, Research, Applications* (Oxford: Oxford University Press, 2010), 73–98.

Smith, A.L., 'Postmodernism/Gothicism'. In V. Sage & A.L. Smith (eds), *Modern Gothic: A Reader* (Manchester: Manchester University Press, 1996), 6–19.

Smith, C. (ed.), *The Secular Revolution: Power Interests and Conflict in the Secularization of American Public Life* (Berkeley: University of California Press, 2003).

Smith, S., ' "I Felt a Funeral in My Brain": The Politics of Representation in HBO's *Six Feet Under*', *Psychoanalysis, Culture & Society* 14: 2 (2009), 200–06.

Spellman, W.M., *A Brief History of Death* (London: Reaktion Books, 2014).

Spence, L.K., *Stare in the Darkness: The Limits of Hip-hop and Black Politics* (Minneapolis: University of Minnesota Press, 2011).

Spiegel, M. & R. Tristman (eds), *The Grim Reader: Writings on Death, Dying and Living On* (New York: Doubleday, 1997).

Spooner, C., *Fashioning Gothic Bodies* (Manchester: Manchester University Press, 2004).

Spooner, C., *Contemporary Gothic* (London: Reaktion Books, 2006).

Spooner, C., 'Preface'. In B. Cherry, P. Howell & C. Ruddell (eds), *Twenty-First Century Gothic* (Newcastle: Cambridge Scholars Publishing, 2010), ix–xii.

Stack, S., 'Heavy Metal, Religiosity, and Suicide', *Suicide and Life-Threatening Behavior* 28 (1998), 388–94.

Stack, S., J. Gundlach & J.L. Reeves, 'The Heavy Metal Subculture and Suicide', *Suicide and Life-Threatening Behavior* 24 (1994), 15–23.

Stallybrass, P. & A. White, *The Politics and Poetics of Transgression* (London: Methuen & Co, 1986).

Stannard, J., 'The Gathering Storm', *The Wire* 302 (April 2009), 42–47.

Steenstra, S., *Song and Circumstance: The Work of David Byrne from Talking Heads to the Present* (New York: Continuum, 2010).

Stone, A., 'Natality and Mortality: Rethinking Death with Cavarero', *Continental Philosophy Review* 43 (2010), 353–72.

Storck, J., 'Band of Outsiders: Williamsburg's Renegade Artists', *Billburg* (01 January 2002): http://www.billburg.com/community-affairs/archived/band-of-outsiders-williamsburg-s-renegade-artists?id=134 (accessed 18 July 2014).

Stubbs, D., 'Invisible Jukebox: Justin Broadrick', *The Wire* 367 (2014), 22–25.

Stuckrad, K. von, *Western Esotericism: A Brief History of Secret Knowledge*, trans. N. Goodrick-Clarke (London: Equinox, 2005).

Swatos, W.H. (ed.), *On the Road to Being There: Studies in Pilgrimage and Tourism in Late Modernity* (Leiden: Brill, 2006).

Talbot, S., 'Sixties Something', *Mother Jones Magazine* 16: 2 (March-April 1991), 47–49, 69–70.

Taubert, M. & J. Kandasamy, 'Self Harm In Goth Youth Subculture: Conclusion Relates Only to Small Sample', *British Medical Journal* 332 (2006), 1215.

Taylor, C., *Sources of the Self* (Cambridge: Harvard University Press, 1990).

Taylor, C., *The Ethics of Authenticity* (Cambridge: Harvard University Press, 1991).

Taylor, C., *A Secular Age* (Cambridge: Harvard University Press, 2007).

Taylor, S., *People's Instinctive Travels and the Paths of Rhythm* (New York: Continuum, 2007).

The Telegraph, 'Monty Python Classic Tops List of Best Funeral Songs', *The Telegraph* (27 January 2009): http://www.telegraph.co.uk/news/newstopics/ howaboutthat/4352276/Monty-Python-classic-tops-list-of-best-funeral-songs.html (accessed 09 May 2014).

Thaut, M., *Rhythm, Music, and the Brain: Scientific Foundations and Clinical Applications* (New York: Routledge, 2005).

Thompson, H.S., *Fear and Loathing in Las Vegas* (London: Flamingo, 1993).

Thorgerson, S. & A. Powell, *For the Love of Vinyl: The Album Art of Hipgnosis* (New York: PictureBox, 2008).

Thornton, S., *Club Cultures: Music, Media and Subcultural Capital* (Cambridge: Polity, 1995).

Till, R., *Pop Cult: Religion and Popular Music* (London: Continuum, 2010).

Tillich, P., *Dynamics of Faith* (New York: Harper & Row, 1957).

Tillich, P., *Theology of Peace* (Louisville: Westminster/John Knox Press, 1990).

Todestrieb Records, 'Amesoeurs Interview' (03 January 2007): http://label.todestrieb. co.uk/2007/01/03/amesoeurs-interview/ (accessed 12 August 2014).

Tomasi, L., '*Homo Viator*: From Pilgrimage to Religious Tourism via the Journey'. In W.H. Swatos and L. Tomasi (eds), *From Medieval Pilgrimage to Religious Tourism. The Social and Cultural Economics of Piety* (Westport: Praeger, 2002), 1–24.

Tooney, C., *In Her Own Words: The After Death Journal of Princess Diana* (Mt. Pleasant: English Rose Press, 1999).

Toop, D., *Haunted Weather: Music, Silence and Memory* (London: Serpent's Tail, 2004)

Toop, D., *Sinister Resonance: The Mediumship of the Listener* (London: Continuum, 2010).

Townshend, P., *Who I Am* (London: HarperCollins, 2012).

Tsitsos, W., 'Rules of Rebellion: Slamdancing, Moshing, and the American Alternative Scene'. In A. Bennett, B. Shank & J. Toynbee (eds), *The Popular Music Studies Reader* (Abingdon: Routledge, 2006), 121–27.

Turino, T., *Music as Social Life: The Politics of Participation* (Chicago: University of Chicago Press, 2008).

Turner, E., 'The Literary Roots of Victor Turner's Anthopology'. In K. Ashley (ed.), *Victor Turner and the Construction of Cultural Criticism: Between Literature and Anthropology* (Bloomington: Indiana University Press, 1990), 163–69.

Turner, E., *Heart of Lightness: The Life Story of an Anthropologist* (Oxford: Berghahn Books, 2005).

Turner, E., *Communitas: The Anthropology of Collective Joy* (New York: Palgrave Macmillan, 2012).

Turner, V., *The Ritual Process: Structure and Anti-Structure* (Chicago: Aldine, 1969).

Turner, V., 'The Center Out There: Pilgrim's Goal', *History of Religions* 12.3 (1973), 191–230.

Turner, V., *Dramas, Fields and Metaphors* (Ithaca: Cornell University Press, 1974).

Turner, V., 'Variations on a Theme of Liminality'. In S. Moore & B. Myerhoff (eds), *Secular Ritual* (Amsterdam: Van Gorcum, 1977), 36–52.

Turner, V., 'Death and the Dead in the Pilgrimage Process'. In F.E. Reynolds & E.H. Waugh (eds), *Religious Encounters with Death: Insights from the History and Anthropology of Religions* (University Park: Pennsylvania State University Press, 1977), 24–39.

Turner, V. & E. Turner, *Image and Pilgrimage in Christian Culture* (New York: Columbia University Press, 1978).

Turnock, R., 'Death, Liminality and Transformation in *Six Feet Under*'. In K. Akass & J. McCabe (eds), *Reading Six Feet Under: TV to Die for* (London: I.B. Tauris, 2005), 39–49.

Underwood, M. & L. Winters, 'Using the Representation of Grief and Shame in Contemporary Literature and Film to Train Mental Health Professionals'. In J. Kauffman (ed.), *The Shame of Death, Grief, and Trauma* (New York: Routledge, 2010), 155–68.

Vasionytė, I. & G. Madison, 'Musical Intervention for Patients with Dementia: A Meta-analysis', *Journal of Clinical Nursing* 22 (2013), 1203–16.

Walser, R., *Running with the Devil: Power, Gender and Madness in Heavy Metal Music* (Middletown: Wesleyan University Press, 1993).

Walter, T., 'War Grave Pilgrimage'. In I. Reader & T. Walter (eds), *Pilgrimage in Popular Culture* (Houndmills: Macmillan, 1993), 63–91.

Watts, H., 'James Arthur Reveals His Spiral into Drugs and Panic Attacks After *X Factor* Win', *Mirror* (25 October 2013): http://www.mirror.co.uk/3am/celebrity-news/james-arthur-took-drugs-suffered-2528670 (accessed 29 September 2014).

Weinstein, D., *Heavy Metal: The Music and Its Culture*, revised edition (New York: Da Capo Press, 2000).

Weinstock, J., 'Profaning the Sacred: Goth Iconography, Iconoclasm, and Subcultural Resistance'. In A. Grønstad & Ø. Vågnes (eds), *Cover Scaping Discovering Album Aesthetics* (Copenhagen: Museum Tusculanum Press, 2010), 163–78.

Welch, C., 'For Prayers and Pedagogy: Contextualizing English Carved Cadaver Monuments of the Late-Medieval Social Religious Elite', *Fieldwork in Religion* 8 (2013), 133–55.

Whalen, B.E., *Pilgrimage in the Middle Ages: A Reader* (Toronto: University of Toronto Press, 2011).

Wierzbicki, J., 'Psycho-Analysis: Form and Function in Bernard Hermann's Music for Hitchcock's Masterpiece'. In P. Hayward (ed.), *Terror Tracks: Music, Sound and Horror Cinema* (London: Equinox, 2009), 14–46.

Wilkins, R., *The Fireside Book of Death* (London: Robert Hale, 1990).

Williams, R., *The Art of Rozz Williams: From Christian Death to Death*. Ed. by B. Nico (San Franscisco: Last Gasp, 1999).

Wiser, C. & T. Jacks, 'Seasons in the Sun', *Songwriter Interviews*: http://www.songfacts.com/blog/interviews/terry_jacks_seasons_in_the_sun_/ (accessed 10 April 2014).

Wolfe, C., *What is Posthumanism?* (Minneapolis: University of Minnesota Press, 2010).

Woodhead, L., 'Diana and the Religion of the Heart'. In J. Richards, S. Wilson & L. Woodhead (eds), *Diana: The Making of a Media Saint* (London: I.B. Tauris, 1999), 119–39.

Wright, J., 'Rihanna Tells JoJo About Seeing an Exorcism': https://www.youtube.com/watch?v=ZGoNM1wdUnQ (accessed 05 July 2014).

Yang, A., S-J. Tsai, C-H. Yang, B-C. Shia, J-L. Fuh, S-J. Wang, C-K. Peng & N. Huang, 'Suicide and Media Reporting: A Longitudinal and Spatial Analysis', *Social Psychiatry and Psychiatric Epidemiology* 48 (2013), 427–35.

Yglesias, P., *Cocinando!: Fifty Years of Latin Album Cover Art* (New York: Princeton Architectural Press, 2005).

Young, R., H. Sweeting & P. West, 'Prevalence of Deliberate Self Harm and Attempted Suicide Within Contemporary Goth Youth Subculture: Longitudinal Cohort Study', *British Medical Journal* 332 (2006), 1058–61.

Young, R., H. Sweeting & P. West , 'Self Harm In Goth Youth Subculture: Author's Reply', *British Medical Journal* 332 (2006), 1335.

Žižek, S., *The Parallax View* (Cambridge: MIT Press, 2006).

Discography

Albums

2Pac (Tupac Shakur), *RU Still Down? (Remember Me)*. Amaru, 1997.

3 Doors Down, *The Better Life*. Universal Records, 1999.

50 Cent, *Get Rich or Die Tryin'*. Aftermath, 2003.

50 Ways to Kill Me, *50 Ways to Kill Me*. Fecal-Matter Discorporated, 2005.

50 Ways to Kill Me, *Legalize Suicide*. Fecal-Matter Discorporated, 2005.

Tori Amos, *Abnormally Attracted to Sin*. Universal, 2009.

Antlers, *Hospice*. Frenchkiss, 2009.

James Arthur, *James Arthur*. Syco Music, 2013.

AUDiNT, *Martial Hauntology*. AUDiNT, 2014.

Bass Communion, *Ghosts on Magnetic Tape*. Headphone Dust, 2004.

Bass Communion, *Loss*. Soleilmoon Recordings, 2006.

Bauhaus, *The Sky's Gone Out*. Beggars Banquet, 1982.

Between the Trees, *The Story and the Song*. Bonded, 2006.

Big Black, *Atomizer*. Homestead, 1986.

Big Black, *The Hammer Party*. Homestead, 1986.

Biosphere, *Substrata* and *Man With a Movie Camera*. Touch, 2006.

The Birthday Party, 'Release the Bats'. 4AD, 1981.

Black Flag, *Damaged*. SST, 1981.

Black Flag, *Slip It In*. SST, 1984.

Black Sabbath, *Black Sabbath*. Vertigo, 1970.

Black Widow, *Sacrifice*. CBS, 1969.

Blue Öyster Cult, *Agents of Fortune*. Columbia, 1976.

Burial, *Burial*. Hyperdub, 2006.

Cannibal Corpse, *Eaten Back To Life*. Metal Blade, 1990.

Cannibal Corpse, *Butchered at Birth*. Metal Blade, 1991.

Cannibal Corpse, *The Bleeding*. Metal Blade, 1994.

Carcass, *Reek of Putrefaction*. Earache Records, 1988.

Carcass, *Symphonies of Sickness*. Earache Records, 1989.

Johnny Cash, *Hymns from the Heart*. Columbia, 1962.

Johnny Cash, *American IV: The Man Comes Around*. American Recordings, 2002.

Children of Dub, *Chameleon*. Magick Eye, 1996.

Christian Death, *Only Theatre of Pain*. Frontier Records, 1982.

Christian Death, *Sex and Drugs and Jesus Christ*. Jungle Records, 1988.

Christian Death, *Sexy Death God*. Nostradamus Records, 1994.

Christian Death, *Pornographic Messiah*. Sad Eyes, 1998.

Christian Death, *Born Again Anti Christian*. Candlelight Records, 2000.

Circle Jerks, *Group Sex*. Frontier, 1980.

Cloud Cult, *They Live on the Sun*. Earthology, 2003.

Clubroot, *II-MMX*. LoDubs, 2010.

ColdWorld, *The Stars Are Dead Now*. Ancient Dreams, 2006.

Colonize the Rotting, *Composting the Masticated*. Sevared Records, 2010.

Alice Cooper, *Billion Dollar Babies*. Warner Bros, 1973.

Corpus Christi/Decay, *Decadentia Christi* – split album. Hiberica, 2001.

Crass, *The Feeding of the Five Thousand*. Small Wonder Records, 1978.

The Cult, *Love*. Beggars Banquet, 1985.

The Cure, *Pornography*. Fiction, 1982.

The Cure, *4:13 Dream*. Geffen Records, 2008.

Current 93, *All the Pretty Horses*. Durtro, 1996.

Dashboard Confessional, *Dusk and Summer*. Vagrant Records, 2006.

Dead Can Dance, *Within the Realm of a Dying Sun*. 4AD, 1987.

Dead Can Dance, *Aion*. 4AD, 1990.

Death, *Scream Bloody Gore*. Combat Records, 1987.

Death Ride '69, *Elvis Christ*. Little Sister, 1988.

Deathspell Omega, *Si monvmentvm reqvires, circvmspice*. Norma Evangelium Diaboli, 2004.

Demdike Stare, *Tryptych*. Modern Love, 2011.

Depeche Mode, *Violator*. Mute, 1990.

Alela Diane, *To Be Still*. Rough Trade, 2009.

Joy Division, *Unknown Pleasures*. Factory Records, 1979.

Joy Division, *Closer*. Factory Records, 1980.

D.O.A., *Hardcore '81*. Sudden Death, 1981.

The Doors, *The Best of the Doors*. Elektra, 2000.

Nick Drake, *Pink Moon*. Island Records, 1972.

Matt Elliot, *The Mess We Made*. Domino, 2003.

Matt Elliot, *Drinking Songs*. Ici D'ailleurs, 2005.

Matt Elliot, *Failing Songs*. Ici D'ailleurs, 2006.

Matt Elliot, *Howling Songs*. Ici D'ailleurs, 2008.

Matt Elliot, *Failed Songs*. Ici D'ailleurs, 2010.

Emeralds, *Just Feel Anything*. Editions Mego, 2012.

Eminem, *The Marshall Mathers LP*. Interscope, 2000.

Enigma, *MCMXC a.D.* Virgin, 1990.

Brian Eno, *Another Green World*. Island Records, 1975.

Brian Eno & David Byrne, *My Life in the Bush of Ghosts*. Sire, 1981.

Everlast, *Love, War and the Ghost of Whitey Ford*. Martyr Inc., 2008

The Faint, *Danse Macabre*. Saddle Creek/City Slang, 2001.

The Fall, *Cerebral Caustic*. Permanent Records, 1995.

The Fall, *Fall Heads Roll*. Slogan Records, 2005.

Future Sound of London, *Dead Cities*. Virgin, 1996.

Groovie Ghoulies, *Appetite for Adrenochrome*. Crimson Corpse Records, 1989.

Michael Gore, *Fame: The Original Soundtrack from the Motion Picture*. RSO, 1980.

Grouper, *Wide*. Free Porcupine Society, 2006.

Grouper, *Dragging a Dead Dear Up a Hill*. Type, 2008.

Grouper, *The Man Who Died in His Boat*. Kranky, 2013.

George Harrison, *All Things Must Pass*. Apple, 1970.

H.I.M., *Razorblade Romance*. BMG, RCA, 1999.

Iggy and the Stooges, *Raw Power*. Columbia, 1973.

Il Giardino Violetto, *Danse Macabre*. In the Night Time, 2004.

Impaled, *The Last Gasp*. Willowtip, 2007.

Imperial Vengeance, *Black Heart of Empire*. Transcend, 2011.

Incredible String Band, *The 5000 Spirits or the Layers of the Onion*. Elektra, 1967

Inner City Unit, *Maximum Effect*. Avatar Records, 1981.

It's Immaterial, *Life's Hard Then You Die*. Siren, 1986.

The Jimi Hendrix Experience, *Axis Bold as Love*. Track, 1967.

Elton John, *Honky Château*. DJM Records, 1972.

Kansas, *Point of Know Return*. Kirshner, 1977.

Kutless, *Sea of Faces*. BEC Records, 2004.

LA Vampires & Zola Jesus, *LA Vampires Meets Zola Jesus*. Not Not Fun Records, 2010.

Low Brows, *Danse Macabre*. Universal J, 2009.

Lurker of Chalice, *Lurker of Chalice*. Total Holocaust Records, 2005.

Lycia, *A Day in the Stark Corner*. Hyperium Recods, Projekt, 1993.

Johnny Mandel, *M*A*S*H (Original Soundtrack Recording)*. Columbia Masterworks, 1970.

Marilyn Manson, *Antichrist Superstar*. Nothing Records, 1996.

Marilyn Manson, *Lest We Forget: The Best of*. Interscope Records, 2004.

John Martyn, *Solid Air*. Island Records, 1972.

Mayhem, *Dawn of the Black Hearts*. Warmaster Records, 1995.

The Melvins, *Six Songs*. C/Z Records, 1986.

Metallica, *Ride the Lightening*. Megaforce, 1984.

Malcolm Middleton, *A Brighter Beat*. Full Time Hobby, 2006.

Moonspell, *Moon in Mercury*. Steamhammer, 2008.

Moonspell, *Alpha Noir/Omega White*. Napalm, 2012.

Mortician, *Mortal Massacre*. Relapse Records, 1993.

Mortician, *House by the Cemetery*. Relapse Records, 1995.

My Chemical Romance, *Welcome to the Black Parade*. Reprise, 2006.

Naked City, *Grand Guignol*. Avant, 1992.

Napalm Death, *Leaders Not Followers*. Dream Catcher, 2000.

Nick Cave and the Bad Seeds, *The Firstborn is Dead*. Mute, 1985.

Nick Cave and the Bad Seeds, *Murder Ballads*. Mute, 1996.

Nine Inch Nails, *The Downward Spiral*. Interscope Records, 1994.

Nocturnal Depression, *Soundtrack for a Suicide: Opus II*. Sun & Moon Records, 2007.

Nocturnal Depression, *Suicidal Thoughts MMXI*. Sun & Moon Records, 2011.

The Notorious B.I.G, *Ready to Die*. Bad Boy, 1994.

The Notorious B.I.G, *Life After Death*. Bad Boy, 1997.

Ozzy Osbourne, *Blizzard of Oz*. Epic Records, 1980.

Pharmakon, *Abandon*. Sacred Bones, 2013.

Jocelyn Pook, *Flood*. Virgin, 1999.

Iggy Pop, *Skull Ring*. Virgin Records, 2003.

The Prodigy, 'Smack My Bitch Up'. XL Recordings, 1997.

Monty Python, *Monty Python Sings*. Virgin, 1989.

Queen, *The Game*. EMI, 1980.

Lou Reed, *Magic and Loss*. Sire, 1992.

Lou Reed, *The Raven*. Sire, 2003.

MC Ren's, *Shock of the Hour*. Ruthless Records, 1993

Rihanna, *Unapologetic*. Def Jam Recordings, 2012.

Shadow Project, *Shadow Project*. Triple X Records, 1991.

Shaggy, *Intoxication*. VP Records, 2007.

Frank Sinatra, *My Way*. Reprise, 1969.

Siouxsie and the Banshees, *Juju*. Polydor, 1981.

The Sisters of Mercy, *Some Girls Wander by Mistake*. Merciful Release, 1992.

Skream, *Skream!* Tempa, 2006.

Slayer, *God Hates Us All*. American Recordings, 2001.

The Smiths, *The World Won't Listen*. Rough Trade, 1987.

Smog, *Dongs of Sevotion*. Drag City, 2000.

Steel Pulse, *Handsworth Revolution*. Island Records, 1978.

Rod Stewart, *Foot Loose & Fancy Free*. Riva Records, 1977.

Styx, *Edge of the Century*. A&M, 1990.

Suicidal Tendencies, *Suicidal for Life*. Epic, 1994.

Suicide, *Suicide*. Red Star, 1977.

Switchblade Symphony, *The Three Calamities*. Cleopatra Records, 1999

System of a Down, *Steal This Album!* Columbia, 2002.

Talking Heads, *Fear of Music*. Sire, 1979.

Talking Heads, *Remain in Light*. Sire, 1981.

Thievery Corporation, *Culture of Fear*. ESL Music, 2011

The Third Eye Foundation, *I Poo Poo on Your Juju*. Domino, 2001.

The Third Eye Foundation, *Ghost*. Domino, 2006.

The Third Eye Foundation. Domino, *The Dark*, 2010.

Throbbing Gristle, *Heathen Earth*. Industrial Records, 1980.

Type O Negative, *Dead Again*. SPV, 2007.

Uaral, *Sounds of Pain…* Lost Horizon Records, 2005.

Unburied, *Slut Decapitator*. Metabolic Records, 2008.

Unburied, *Murder 101*. Selfmadegod Records, 2012.

Steve Vai, *Sex & Religion*. Relativity, 1993.

Wooden Shjips, *Vol. 2*. Sick Thirst, 2010.

X-Fusion, *Rotten to the Core/Bloody Pictures*. Scanner, 2007.

Years, *Years*. Arts & Crafts, 2009.

Singles and EPs

GG Allin, *The Troubled Troubadour* EP. Mountain Records, 1990.

Bauhaus, 'Bela Lugosi's Dead'. Small Wonder Records, 1979.

Johnny Cash, 'Folsom Prison Blues'. Sun, 1955.

Nick Cave, 'Nature Boy'. Mute, 2004.

Ian Dury, 'Sex & Drugs & Rock & Roll'. Stiff Records, 1976.

Florence and the Machine, 'Kiss With a Fist'. Island, 2008.

Peter Gabriel & Kate Bush, 'Don't Give Up'. Geffen, 1986.

Jimi Hendrix Experience, 'Hey Joe'. Polydor, 1966.

Lauryn Hill, 'Black Rage': https://soundcloud.com/mslaurynhill/black-rage-sketch
(accessed 12 September 2104).

Terry Jacks, 'Seasons in the Sun'. Bell Records, 1973.

Michael Jackson, 'Thriller'. Epic, 1983.

Kansas, 'Dust in the Wind'. Kirshner, 1977.

The Kingston Trio, 'Tom Dooley'. Capitol Records, 1958.

Manic Street Preachers, 'Theme from M.A.S.H. (Suicide is Painless)'. Columbia, 1992.

The Police, 'Can't Stand Losing You'. A&M, 1978.

Elvis Presley, 'That's All Right'. Sun Records, 1954.

Public Image Ltd., 'Death Disco'. Virgin, 1979.

Radiohead, 'Creep'. Parlophone, 1992.

Scouting for Girls, 'Elvis Ain't Dead'. Epic, 2007.

The Sisters of Mercy, 'Temple of Love'. Merciful Release, 1983.

Britney Spears, 'Hold It Against Me'. Jive, 2011.

Donna Summer, 'I Feel Love'. Casablanca, 1977.

Taylor Swift, 'I Knew You Were Trouble'. Big Machine, 2012.

The Who, 'My Generation'. Brunswick, 1965.

Filmography

20,000 Days on Earth (2014). Directed by Iain Forsyth & Jane Pollard.

American Hardcore (2006). Directed by Paul Rachman.

Monty Python and the Holy Grail (1975). Directed by Terry Gilliam and Terry Jones.

Index

Aarseth, Øystein, *see*
    Euronymous (musician)
abjection 5, 57, 88, 97, 98–104, 124, 135
Aborted Christ Childe (band) 44
Aborted Jesus (band) 44
adrenochrome 56, 165
affective space 4, 6, 20, 22, 24, 25, 38, 53,
    54, 57, 58, 62, 64–70, 71, 72, 73, 74,
    75, 76, 78, 80, 83, 86, 87, 93, 94, 95,
    111, 113, 117, 122, 124, 134, 135,
    144, 146, 150, 155
afterlife 12, 14, 51, 69
ageing 12, 50–2, 91, 145, 155
Akita, Masami, *see* Merzbow (musician)
Albini, Steve (musician) 120, 177
Alexander, J. 163, 165
Allin, Kevin Michael 'GG' (musician) 93
Almighty RSO, The (musician) 130
altered states 53, 56
Altheide, D. 173
Altman, Mike (musician) 116
altruistic suicide 106
Amesoeurs (band) 98, 172, 174
Amos, Tori (musician) 113–14, 176
Amputated Christ (band) 44
Anderson, S. 182
androgyny 46, 81
Angell, T. 168
Angels of Light (band) 37
angst 18, 80, 95, 119, 121, 124, 128, 131
anomic suicide 106, 107, 108, 112, 114,
    116, 132
Anso, S.G. 179
antibiotics 11, 51
antiseptic 51
antistructure 45, 56, 151–2
Antlers (band) 21
Antonakakis, N. 175
apocalypticism 84
Appalachian Gothic 94
Aquinas, T. 155
Arab Strap (band) 15

Ariès, P. 9, 10, 11, 12, 158, 159, 160
Armstrong, E.G. 179
Armstrong, J. 4, 157
Arnet, H. 170, 171
Arthur, James (musician) 114, 115, 116
Arya, R. 122–3, 178
Asprem, E. 183
Astbury, Ian (musician) 85
Atkins, M. 83
A Tribe Called Quest (band) 129–30
Augustine 14, 39, 42–4, 57, 155, 163
Aurelius, M. 17, 160
Austin-Broos, D. 140, 182, 186
Autopsy (band) 47, 97
Azerrad, M. 119, 122, 177, 178

Bad Boy Records 130
Bad Brains (band) 107
Baddeley, G. 93–4, 172
Bailey, E. 181
Bakhtin, M. 91–2, 172
Ballard, J.G. 85
Banning, J. 179
Barminski, B. 144
Barrett, Syd (musician) 115
Barth, K. 146, 154–5, 184, 186
Bass Communion (band) 68, 77–9, 146
Bataille, G. 55, 57–8, 91, 122, 124, 160,
    165, 166, 171, 178
Batcave, The 81
Baudelot, C. 106, 174
Baudrillard, J. 50–1, 164, 166
Bauhaus 2, 61, 68, 81, 86
Bauman (band), Z. 3, 15, 26–34, 51, 63,
    91, 92, 102–4, 123, 124, 133, 156,
    157, 159, 161, 162, 166, 171, 174,
    175, 178, 180, 186
Beadle, Lewis, *see* El-B (musician)
Beastie Boys (band) 128
Becker, E. 28, 94, 161, 172
Behead Christ (band) 44
Bemborg, A.D. 149, 184

Bennett, A. 51–2, 164, 177, 179
bereavement 10, 20, 21, 22, 23, 24, 29, 35,
    47, 50, 68, 87, 94, 105, 117, 126,
    134, 158
Bernstein, L. 72, 168
Between the Trees (band) 109
Bevan, William E., *see* Burial (musician)
Bibby, M. 50, 164, 170, 171, 172
Big Black (band) 120, 121
Big L (musician) 130
Biggie Smalls, *see* Notorious B.I.G.
    (musician)
Bikini Kill (band) 119
Binyon, L. 155
Biosphere (musician) 74
Birthday Party, The (band) 81, 86
bisexuality 45, 80
Bivins, J. 38, 162
Black Flag (band) 107, 118, 119, 122, 123
Blacklow, J. 169
black metal 5, 46, 67, 70, 98
Black Sabbath (band) 68–9, 119
Black Widow (band) 70
blasphemy 37
Bloch, M. 20
blood 11, 38, 42, 50, 53, 59, 88, 97, 107,
    109, 119, 123, 125, 127, 130
Blood, R.W. 176, 181
Blue Öyster Cult (band) 23
Blush, S. 119, 174, 177
Boer, R. 57, 164, 166, 172
Bolan, Marc (musician) 81, 142
Bone, B. 163
Bono (musician) 183
Bonvesin de la Riva 11, 88, 158
Book of Common Prayer 9, 14
Boris (band) 54
Bottici, C. 181
Botting, F. 50, 164, 165, 166
Bourdieu, P. 47
Bowie, David (musician) 81, 115
Bowker, J. 159, 166
Brackett, D. 179
Branch, A. 176
Brannigan, P. 178
Brel, Jacques (musician) 23, 160
Bresson, Emilie (musician) 45, 163
Bretthauer, B. 179
Brill, D. 46, 163, 164
Brink, J.T. 172

Broadrick, Justin (musician) 118, 177
Brodsky, J. 144, 184
Brooker, W. 152–3, 185, 186
Brown, J. 180
Brown, M. 171
Browning, R. 187
Brueggemann, W. 43, 163
Bryant, T. 161
Buck Dharma (musician) 23
Bugz (musician) 130
Bultmann, R. 139, 180, 181
Burgess, P.M. 176
Burial (musician) 47, 48, 84
Burke, E. 4–5, 51, 157, 164
Burroughs, W. 91
Bush, Kate (musician) 110
Bynum, C. W. 158
Byrne, David (musician) 27, 33, 78, 115,
    162, 169

Cabaret Voltaire (band) 16
Caillois, R. 55, 121, 123, 178
Calvin, J. 155
Camus, A. 4, 19–21, 28, 35, 83, 91, 129,
    135, 139, 157, 160, 179, 181
cancer 21, 22, 23, 24, 25, 52, 59, 60, 62
Canetti, E. 34, 103, 104
Cannibal Corpse (band) 42, 97, 126
cannibalism 58
canonization 137, 140, 142, 143
cantopop 138
Carcass (band) 58, 93, 97, 124, 129
Cardoso, A. 169
Carroll, L. 152–3
Cash, Johnny (musician) 16, 68, 108
Cate, H. ten 162
Catholicism, Roman 55, 89
Cave, Nick (musician) 13, 31, 47, 57, 58,
    85, 94, 95, 97, 101, 171
Celmins, M. 115, 176
cemeteries 2, 38, 41, 64, 80, 83, 88, 142
Centre for Contemporary Cultural Studies
    39
Cephalic Carnage (band) 97
Chang, J.-C. 181
channeling 140, 155
Chardiet, Margaret, *see* Pharmakon
    (musician)
Charizma 130
Chen, T.H.H. 181

Cheng, A.T.A. 181
Cherry, B. 169, 170
Cheung, Leslie (musician) 138
Children of Dub (band) 56
Chong, M.-Y. 181
Christ Dismembered (band) 44
Christ's Flesh (band) 44
Christgau, R. 22, 160
Christian Death (band) 37, 38, 44, 81
Christianson, E. 172, 178
Chuck D (musician) 128, 179, 180
Church of Jesus Christ 38
Circle Jerks (band) 49, 107, 108
Circle of Dead Children (band) 97
Clack, B. 163
Clark, L.S. 182
Clarke, P.B. 181
Clayton, M. 173
Cloonan, M. 172, 173, 178
Cloud Cult (band) 21
Clubroot (musician) 74
Cobain, Kurt (musician) 116, 141, 156
Cohen, E. 185
ColdWorld (band) 80
Coleman, S. 149, 185
collective effervescence 121, 122, 124
Collège de Sociologie 55
Collins-Kreiner, N. 185
Collins, A. 175, 187
Collins, R. 187
Colonize the Rotting (band) 125, 126
Columbine shootings 98, 172
communitas 46, 52, 122–5, 135, 151–3
Cooke, D. 134, 180
Cooper, Alice (musician) 37, 38, 42
Coorte, A. 76
corpse 1, 10, 11, 18, 19, 41, 44, 50, 56, 58,
     59, 74, 86, 89, 94, 99, 125, 129
Corpse ov Christ (band) 44
Corpus Christi (band) 44
Courson, P. 143
Crash, Darby (musician) 118
Crass (band) 120
Creed, B. 173
Cross, C. 176
crows 69
cryogenics 34
Culler, J. 167
Cult, The (band) 94
Cure, The (band) 18, 81

Current 93 (band) 74
cursed 53, 55
Curtis, D. 82, 170
Curtis, Ian (musician) 81–3, 85, 86,
     90, 94

D-Boy (musician) 130
D.O.A. (band) 107
D12 (band) 130
Dalton, M.A. 178
danse macabre 47
Danse Society (band) 81
Danto, A. 141, 182
darkwave 5, 80
Dashboard Confessional (band) 110
Dastur, F. 14, 17, 25, 159, 160, 161
Davies, D.J. 20, 29, 135, 160, 161, 163
Davis, C. 75, 169
Day of the Dead 5
Day, T. 145–6, 184
de Botton, A. 4, 157
Dead (musician) 105
Dead Baby (band) 47
Dead Can Dance (band) 14, 47, 67, 159
Dead Jesus (band) 44
Dead Kennedys, The (band) 107
Dean, M. 162
Death (band) 41
Death (Gaiman character) 80
death chic 49–52
Death Cult (band) 85
death drive 100–4, 116, 129, 173
death growl 124
death metal 58, 89, 97
Death Ride '69 (band) 184
death rock 37–9, 116
Death Row Records 130, 131
death row 101, 127–33
deathgrind 124
Deathspell Omega (band) 67
decadence 44
decomposition 10, 11, 19, 32, 44, 47, 49,
     88, 90, 165
Definis-Gojanović, M. 175
Demdike Stare (band) 70
demons 17, 40, 51, 95, 99
DeNora, T. 157, 167, 173
Denzin, N.K. 177
DePaoli, G. 182, 183, 184
Depeche Mode (band) 68

depression 5, 50, 80, 83–6, 94, 105–9, 115, 117–19
Derrida, J. 75, 169
DeSpelder, L. A. 158
Diana, Princess of Wales 140–1
Diane, Alela 72
Dickinson, G.E. 159
Digital Mystikz (band) 48
Dismember (band) 47
Dollimore, J. 29, 161
Donne, J. 2, 103, 157, 174
Donnelly, J. 158, 160
Doors, The (band) 144, 184
Doss, E. 182, 183
Douglas, M. 41, 163
Drake, Nick (musician) 141, 154, 156, 186
dread 4, 17, 18, 31, 63, 95
drugs 30, 37, 53, 54, 115
dub reggae 2, 56
dubstep 42, 48, 74, 84
Duffett, M. 183
Dundes, A. 181
Durkheim, É. 39–40, 53, 55, 56, 105, 107, 108, 109, 112, 114, 116, 121, 122, 131, 163, 165, 174, 175, 176, 177, 180
Dury, Ian (musician) 53
Dying Fetus (band) 97
Dyson, M.E. 131, 180

Eade, J. 148, 149, 184, 185
Earles, A. 178
Eck, D. 41
Eco, U. 66
Edelstein, D. 97
Edwards, J. 164
Edwards, P. 158, 160
Edwards, Richey (musician) 116–17, 176
egoistic suicide 106–8, 114, 116
Eide, R. 140, 182
El-B (musician) 48
Eldritch, Andrew (musician) 56, 86
Electronic voice phenomena, *see* EVP
Elferen, I. van 62, 64, 69, 70, 73, 75, 86, 166, 167, 168, 169, 170, 171
Elliot, Matt (musician) 74, 84, 88, 89, 92
Elvis (musician) 30, 137, 141, 142–3, 145–6, 147, 155
Ely Cathedral 1
Emeralds (band) 56

Eminem (musician) 127, 130
emo 109–10
emotion 3, 4–6, 19, 21, 22, 33, 40, 42, 44, 52, 54, 56, 57, 64, 65, 70–3, 91, 98, 108, 109, 110, 111, 112, 118, 119, 122, 125, 129, 131, 134–5, 138, 142, 146, 147, 148, 149, 152, 153, 155, 156
Enigma (band) 67
Eno, Brian (musician) 26, 78, 169
Epicurus 25, 161
eros 37, 50, 101
Establet, R. 106, 174
Euronymous (musician) 105
Evangelicalism 38, 68, 111
Everett, Marcel, *see*, XXYYXX
Everlast (musician) 43
EVP 77
excrement 11, 58, 59, 100, 125
execution 93, 101, 127–33
exorcism 54, 63, 78, 92
Exploding Corpse Action (band) 47
extreme metal 5, 41, 46, 57, 98–9, 120, 123–7

Faint, The (band) 47
Fall, The (band) 2, 83–4
Fall, the 30, 43
fandom 139–56, 183
Farmer, H.H. 15, 35, 106, 159, 162, 174
Farren, M. 118, 177
Fat Pat (musician) 130
fatalistic suicide 106–7, 108
fear 9, 16, 17, 18, 19, 20, 21, 23, 27, 32, 38, 53, 57, 63, 64, 69, 80, 82, 84, 87, 88, 95, 99, 103, 117, 122, 128, 162, 165, 173
Fenimore, R.J. 168
Feuerbach, L. 16
Ffytche, M. 166–7
50 Cent 133
Fish, M. 159
Fish, S. 67, 167
Fisher, M. 83, 85, 169, 170
Fleetwood Mac (band) 115
Flesh for Lulu (band) 81
Florence and the Machine (band) 127
folk music 42, 46, 72, 85, 97, 156, 160
Forsyth, I. 31
45 Grave 81
Foster, Laura 97

Foucault, M. 29, 55, 161, 181
Francis, C. 176
Frankfurt School 39
Frazer, J. 16
Freaky Tah (musician)130
Freedman, P. 158
Freeman, B. 180
Freud, S. 16–17, 20, 63–4, 82, 100–5, 116, 160, 166, 167, 170, 173
Frey, N.L. 151, 185
Fricke, D. 22–3, 160
Frith, S. 70, 126, 163, 168, 173, 178
Fu, K. W. 181
Fugazi (band) 123
Fuh, J-L. 176
funeral 1, 10, 18, 20, 35, 41, 52, 93
Funeral for a Friend (band) 47
funeral songs 35, 162
Future Sound of London (band) 84

Gabriel, Peter (musician) 110
Gabrielsson, A. 42, 163
Gaiman, N. 80, 170
Gaines, D. 107, 108, 114, 174, 176, 177
gangsta rap 128, 132–3
Garces-Foley, K. 10, 158
Garofalo, R. 178
Gawande, A. 158
Geertz, C. 185
Gene Loves Jezebel (band) 81
Germs, The (band) 118
Giddens, A. 159
Gifford Lectures 2
Gilmour, David (musican) 115, 176
Gira, Michael (musician) 20–1, 22, 25, 37, 160
Girard, R. 122–3, 178
Goethe, J.W. 138
Gold, M.A. 178
Goodlad, L. 50, 164, 170, 171, 172
Goodwin, A. 163
Gore Beyond Necropsy (band) 97
gore 5, 38, 41–2, 49, 58, 59, 97, 99, 102, 118–19, 124–7, 129, 135
Gore, Michael (musician) 92
Gorer, G. 176
goth music 5, 6, 50, 52, 57, 61, 62, 67, 68, 70, 73, 79, 81–95, 109–11, 162, 170
Gothic 4, 5, 9, 38, 49, 50–2, 61–95, 97, 98
Graceland 137, 142, 147, 148

Gragnolati, M. 158
Granholm, K. 183
Graveyard poetry 5
Green, J.W. 40, 163
Green, Peter (musician) 115, 116
Gregorian (band) 66
Gregorian chant 65–7, 70, 167
grief 20, 21, 52
grindcore 58, 97, 118
Grønstad, A. 162
Groovie Ghoulies (band) 56
Grossberg, L. 111, 153, 175, 186
grotesque 11, 87–93
Grouper (musician) 70, 168
Grunenberg, C. 166
Gugić, D. 175
Gulf War 102
Gundlach, J. 175
Guy, A. 144

H.I.M. (band) 80
Habermas, J. 65
Haenfler, R. 177
Hagedorn, J. 128, 179
Hagen, C. 90, 171
Halberstam, D. 141, 182
Hall, J.R. 167
Handsome Family, The (band) 94
Hanlan, A. 59, 166
Hannett, Martin (musician) 81, 170
hardcore punk 5, 46, 49–50, 107–8, 117–24, 128, 130, 131
Hargreaves, D. 166, 180
Harkness, G. 179
Harris, Liz, *see* Grouper (musician)
Harrison, E. 182
Harrison, George (musician) 3, 5–6, 140, 146–7
hauntology 73–9, 169
Hawton, K. 181
heavy metal 98–9, 118, 124–7, 166, 175
Hegarty, P. 54, 165
hell 27–8, 34, 40, 51
Hendrix, Jimi (musician) 97, 144, 156
Herbert, T. 173
Herrmann, Bernard (musician) 69, 168
Hesmondhalgh, D. 71, 157, 168
Hibbett, R. 164
Hick, J. 161
Hiley, D. 167

Hill, Lauryn (musician) 138, 179
Hill, S. 76, 169
Hinds, S.S. 179
hip hop 5, 127–34
Hjelm, T. 173
Hobbs, Mary Anne 48
Hobsbawm, E. 159
Hodkinson, P. 163, 164, 170
holocaust, the 163
Hong, Y. 181
Hoover, S.M. 182
Horowitz, Adam (musician) 128, 179
hospices 2, 21
hospitals 1, 21, 49, 130, 131, 138, 143
Houellenbecq, M. 27
Howard, D.N. 169
Howard, G. 172
Howell, P. 169, 170
Hüsker Dü (band) 119, 123, 177
Hutcherson, B. 177
Huxley, A. 165
Hval, Jenny (musician) 111, 117, 175
Hwang, S. 181
hyperreality 51

Idle, Eric 35
Impaled (band) 47, 59, 60, 97
Impaled Christ (band) 44
Impaled Nazarene (band) 44
Imperial Vengeance (band) 166
implicit religion 139
impure sacred 52–7, 58, 61
Incredible String Band (band) 2
industrial music 37, 46, 56, 57, 80, 85, 107,
        120, 172–3
Inner City Unit (band) 137
intertextuality 65–70, 150
invisible death 12
It's Immaterial (band) 3

Jacks, Terry (musician) 23–4, 25, 34, 83
Jackson, Michael (musician) 93
Jacobsen, M.H. 157, 161, 162, 166, 186
Jah, Y. 180
Jalland, P. 158
Jam Master Jay (musician) 130
James, M.R. 76
Jameson, F. 75, 169
jazz 42
Jenks, C. 55, 163

Jensen, J.S. 181
Jenssem, Geir, *see* Biosphere (musican)
Jenzen, O. 161
Jeong, J 181
Jesus 16, 18, 30, 37, 38, 44, 68, 78, 137,
        142–3
Jesus Corpus (band) 44
Jobe, D.A. 175
John, Elton (musician) 110
Johnson, B. 172, 173
Johnson, F. 179
Jolley, D.J. 176
Jones, Brian (musician) 141
Jones, Oliver Dean, *see* Skream (musician)
Jordan-Wrench, J. 177
Joy Division (band) 2, 81–3, 85, 90, 94
Judas Priest (band) 98
Junod, H. 45
Juslin, P.N. 157, 167, 168

Kadafi, Yaki (musician) 130
Kahl, A. 158
Kahn-Harris, K. 173, 178
Kandasamy, J. 175
Kansas (band) 13, 159
Keenan, D. 165
Kehoss, M. 166
Kendrick, J. 172
Kennealy, P. 143
Kernberg, O. 174
Kerouac, J. 46
kerygmatic Christ 137
Kieffer, G. 169
Kilpatrick, N. 164, 165
Kim, H. 181
kinetic ritual 151–4
King, C. 182
Kingston Trio, The (band) 97, 160
Kirk, Richard H. (musician) 16, 159
Knight, Suge 131
Kostenbaum, P. 28, 161
Kristeva, J. 5, 65, 66, 99–100, 101, 104,
        167, 171, 172, 173, 174, 180
Kubrick, S. 66, 67
Kutless (band) 111

Lacan, J. 101
LaCaria, R. 144
Lady Gaga (musician) 50
Laing, D. 167

Lamartine, A. de 25
Landis, J. 93
Larkin, R.W. 173
La Rock, Scott (musician) 130
Larson, A. 177
last enemy 27, 28
LA Vampires (band) 167
Laverne, Lauren 141, 182
Law, R. 144
Layard, R. 103, 114, 115, 174, 176
Lee, E. 181
Lee, Y. 181
Leming, M.R. 159
Lennon, John (musician) 140
Lerner, N. 168
leukemia 24
Levine, M. 173
Levine, N. 177
Levy, E. 72, 168
Lewis Carroll Society 152-3
Lewis, J.R. 167
Lewis, L. 153, 186
Licht, A. 160
Life of Brian 35
liminality 4, 37-9, 41, 42, 45-7, 49, 50,
  52-3, 56-9, 61, 64-5, 70, 72, 91,
  93-4, 97, 98, 100, 109, 119, 120-5,
  132, 135, 148, 151-3
liquid modernity 31
Liu, C.-Y. 181
Livgren, Kerry (musician) 13, 159
Lockwood, D. 81, 170
Long, K.S. 172, 176
Love, Courtney (musician) 116
Lurker of Chalice (musician) 69-70
Luther, M. 155
Lycia (band) 80
Lydon, John (musician) 21-2, 25, 52
Lynch, G. 50, 53, 157, 163, 165, 167, 186

*M*A*S*H* 116, 176
macabre 10, 38, 88, 89, 90, 94
Macabre (band) 97
Macbeth 12
MacDonald, R. 166, 180
Macfarlane, K.E. 50, 164
MacKaye, Ian (musician) 123
MacLeod, D. 176
Macmurray, J. 2, 157
Madison, G. 168

Malinowski, B. 18, 160
Mallinder, Stephen (musician) 16, 159
Mandel, Johnny (musician) 116, 176
Mangled Christ (band) 44
Manic Street Preachers (band) 116-17
Manson, C. 84, 89
Manson, Marilyn (musician) 68
maps of mattering 153
March Violets, The (band) 81
Marcus, G. 180
Margry, P.J. 143, 144, 182, 183, 184, 185
marijuana 54
Marzluff, J.M. 168
masochism 90, 171, 173
Mauss, M. 55
Mayhem (band) 42, 105
MC Ren (musician) 127
McEvoy, E. 164, 166, 171
McGrath, P. 61, 166
McKuen, R. 160
McMahon, M. 140, 182
McQuillar, T.L. 179
McRobbie, A. 126, 163, 178
mediumship 72, 73, 77
melancholy 2, 24, 25, 50, 70, 74, 81, 82,
  84-6, 88, 89, 93, 94, 101, 102,
  109-10, 135
memento mori 1, 3, 5, 6, 13, 20, 24, 34, 39,
  59, 62, 64, 70-3, 83, 90, 95, 100,
  124, 126, 133, 147, 156
memento vivere 24, 35
memory 3, 6, 17, 30-1, 34, 52, 66, 70-3,
  76, 99
Merzbow (musician) 54
mescaline 56, 165
Metallica (band) 114
Metzger, F. 182
Michaud, S. 162
Middleton, Malcolm (musician) 15
Middleton, R. 173, 194
Miell, D. 166, 180
Miller, M. 183, 184
Miller, M.R. 131, 179, 180
Minor Threat (band) 107, 123
Minowa, Craig (musician)v 21
Mintz, R. 166
misanthropy 54, 68, 107
Misfits, The (band) 107
misogyny 120, 126, 127
Mitford, J. 10, 18, 158, 160

Monarch (band) 45, 163
Monnet, A.S. 164
Monroe, M. 141
Monty Python and the Holy Grail 1
Monty Python's Flying Circus 1, 35, 162
Moonspell (band) 93, 94, 95
moral panic 41, 98, 128
Mörat 173, 178
morbidity 2, 3, 11, 76, 80, 81–2, 84–6, 88,
    93, 94, 95, 97–136
Morinis, E.A. 185
Morris, C. 184
Morrison, Jim (musician) 141–4, 156, 183,
    184
Mortician (band) 41, 97, 125
mortuaries 2, 20
moshing 121–2
Mould, Bob (musician) 119, 123, 177
mourning 19, 22, 25, 29, 64, 83, 87, 140
Mozart (musician) 146, 154–5
Mudrian, A. 166
Mullen, B. 176
Munt, S. 161
murder 47, 83, 85, 97, 98, 99, 100, 104,
    120, 127, 130, 132
mutilation 49, 93, 120, 125
My Chemical Romance (band) 24
Myers, B. 179, 180
mysterium trememdum et fascinans 9
myth 28, 55, 57, 93, 115, 137, 138–9, 140,
    141, 143, 144, 145, 148, 150, 153,
    154

Nadelhaft, M. 172, 176
Nailed Nazarene (band) 44
Naked City (band) 89
Napalm Death (band) 47, 59, 97, 118
nausea 55, 60
Nazarene Decomposing (band) 44
Ndembu 46, 58, 59
necrophilia 41, 49
Neige (musician) 102, 174
Nelson, V. 97, 171
new romantics 170
Nietzsche, F. 134, 180
nihilism 46, 86–7, 118, 133
Nine Inch Nails (band) 89, 90, 107, 108
Nirvana (band) 116
nirvana principle 102
Nobokov, V. 33, 162

Nocturnal Depression (band) 80
noise music 54
nostalgia 94, 109
Notorious B.I.G. (musician) 130–2

Oates, Captain L. 106
occult 30, 61, 66, 68, 69, 70, 74, 86, 144
occulture 39, 55, 61, 66, 85, 88, 143, 144,
    183
Ohlin, Per Yngve, *see* Dead (musician)
opiates 54
Oppenheimer, J. 172
Order of the Solar Temple 66
orgasm 53
Osbourne, Ozzy (musician) 42, 49, 69,
    98, 105
Otto, R. 9, 158

Pahud de Mortanges, E. 182
Painter, Roger Alan, *see* Williams,
    Roz (musician)
Palmer, S. 167
paranormal 6, 27, 68, 69, 75, 77
Parents' Music Resource Center,
    see PMRC
Parisot, E. 157
Parker, J. 177
Parsons, Gram (musician) 156
Pascal, B. 10, 15
Pattison, S. 186
Paut, Stéphane, *see* Neige (musician)
Pavarotti, Luciano (musician) 141
Peel, John 48
peregrinus 148
Perry, I. 180
pessimism 84
Peterson, Frank (musician) 66
Peterson, R.J. 175
Pharmakon (musician) 54, 165
Phillipov, M. 98, 125, 173, 175, 178
Pickering, W.S.F. 53, 165, 174
pilgrim-tourist 149
pilgrimage 141, 142, 147–54
Pinker, S. 99
Pinn, A.B. 180
Pirkis, J. E. 176, 181
plainchant 66
Play Dead (band) 81
pleasure principle 100–2
PMRC 98

Poe, E.A. 160
Polanski, R. 66
Polanyi, M. 182
Police, The (band) 110
Pollard, J. 31
pollution 41, 42, 43, 58, 67, 99, 118, 125
Pomus, Doc (musician) 22
Pook, Jocelyn (musician) 66, 167
pornography 37, 49, 54, 59, 117, 126
Porter, D. 179
Porter, R. 158
possession 54, 78–9, 88
post-punk 47, 78, 81, 86
postmodernity 30, 31, 32, 34, 87, 92, 124
postsecular 61, 62
Powell, A. 171
Presley, Elvis, *see* Elvis (musician)
Primack, B.A. 178
Prindle, M. 177
Prochnicky, J. 143, 183
Prodigy, The (band) 127
profane 39–45, 46, 48, 49, 52, 53, 55, 56, 57,
    58, 59, 67–70, 78, 79, 80, 84, 85–6,
    88, 91, 95, 98, 121, 122, 124, 126
prosthetic technology 4, 6, 54, 58, 64, 65,
    99, 110, 165
Prostitute Disfigurement (band) 97
psych-folk 72, 85
psychedelics 54, 56, 115, 165
Psycho 69
Public Enemy (band) 128, 133
Public Image Ltd. (band) 21
punk 46, 56, 57, 81, 98, 107, 118, 119, 120,
    122, 123
Punter, D. 166

Quakers 1
Queen (band) 110
Quinn, E. 179

Radiohead (band) 111
Rammstein (band) 172
Ramsey, Tom (musician) 16
rap 127–34
Rapeman (band) 120
Rapp, Kenneth 22
Rappleye, C. 179
Rathke, Mike (musician) 22
Raudive, K. 77
ravens 69–70, 88

Razinsky, L. 160, 173
Reader, I. 182, 184, 185, 186
Reagan, R. 118
recorded sound 21, 74, 78, 87, 89, 144–7
redemption 43, 47
Reece, G. 143, 183
Reed J.D. 183, 184
Reed, Lou (musician) 21–4, 25, 52, 61–2, 160
Reeves, J.L. 175
Rein, B. 166
reincarnation 6
reposing room 18
resurrection 14, 30, 32, 34
revenants 61, 62, 63–4, 72, 73, 77, 79, 88, 95
revulsion 40, 41, 53, 108
Reynolds, F.E. 166
Reynolds, S. 180
Reznor, Trent (musician) 90–1, 92, 108
Richards, J. 182
Richardson, N. 168
Richmond, Dan, *see* Clubroot (musician)
Rihanna (musician) 78
Riis, O. 183, 184
Riley, A. 165
Rimmer, D. 170
Riordan, J. 143, 183
riot grrrl 119
Robb, J. 176
Rodman, G.B. 181
Roeser, Donald, *see* Buck Dharma
    (musician)
Rojek, C. 138, 144, 145, 181, 184
Rollins, Henry (musician) 118, 119, 123,
    128, 177
Rollins Band (band) 123
Romanek, M. 89, 90, 91, 92
Romanian liturgical chant 66–7
Rombes, N. 177
Rose, T. 128, 132, 133, 179, 180
Rotten Rita, *see* Rapp, Kenneth
Rotten, Johnny, *see* Lydon, John
    (musician)
Rotting Christ (band) 44
Royle, N. 63, 167, 170
Ruddell, C. 169, 170
Run DMC (band) 130

sacer 53, 55
sacred forms 40, 46, 53, 54, 57, 58, 59, 98
sacrifice 38, 56, 65, 106, 123

Sade, Marquis de 67
sadism 97, 99, 120, 173
sadomasochism 90
Safer, M.A. 175
Sallnow, M.J. 148, 184
Sampar, M. 99, 172
Santiago de Compostela 151
Satan 37, 69
Satanism 54, 56, 86
Saville, P. 83
schadenfreude 100–5
Schleiermacher, F.D.E. 155
Schopen, G. 183
Schraffenberger, R. 94, 95, 172
Schuyler, P. 167
Schwarz, E.B. 178
Scott, D.B. 168
Scouting for Girls (band) 146
secular pilgrimage 147, 150
secular religion 139
Segal, R. 181
self harm 105–16
Sellgren, K. 174
Severed Savior (band) 44
sex 14, 28, 39, 41, 43–5, 49, 51, 53–4, 61,
    67, 88, 90–1, 93, 101, 120, 126–7,
    131, 132
Sex Gang Children (band) 81
Shadow Project (band) 87
Shaggy (musician) 67
Shakespeare, W. 12
Shakur, Tupac (musician) 129–31, 141, 156
shamanism 144
Shank, B. 177, 179
Shin, S. 181
Shipman, H. 83
Shroud of Bereavement (band) 47
Shumway, D. 170, 171
Siegel, C. 171
Sihra, L. 158
Silberman, Peter 21, 22, 25
Silk, J. 175
Simpson, D. 83, 170
sin 16, 38–9, 42–4, 57, 95
Sinatra, Frank (musician) 16, 159
Siouxsie and the Banshees (band) 69, 81
Sisters of Mercy, The (band) 56, 81, 86
Sisyphus 28, 34
Six Feet Under 10, 158

Skerl, J. 164
Skinny Puppy (band) 107
Skream (musician) 48
slamdancing 177
Sloboda, J.A. 157, 167, 168
slumber room 18
Smith, A.L. 87, 169, 171
Smith, C. 162
Smith, Mark E. (musician) 83
Smith, P. 165
Smith, Robert (musician) 94
Smith, S. 158
Smiths, The (band) 80
Smithsonian Institution 145
Smog (musician) 37
Southern Baptist 37
Southern Death Cult (band) 81, 85
Spears, Britney (musician) 48
Spellman, W.M. 11–12, 34–5, 159, 162
Spence, L.K. 180
Spinoza, B. 17
spiritualism 77
Spooner, C. 86, 88, 90, 91, 164, 166, 169,
    171
Sprinker, M. 169
Stack, S. 175
Stallybrass, P. 55, 171
Stannard, J. 167
State of Alert (band) 107, 118, 123
steampunk 62, 166
Steel Pulse (band) 72
Steenstra, S. 162
Stekel, W. 101
Stephens, J. 144
Stewart, Rod (musician) 30
Stone, A. 112, 161, 174
Stone, O. 144, 183
Storck, J. 171
Stretch (musician) 130
Strickland, A.L. 158
Stubbs, D. 177
Stuckrad, K. von 170, 181
Styx (band) 102
subcultural capital 47–9, 50–1, 61, 86, 98,
    109, 125
sublime 4–5, 51, 61, 101, 142
Suffocation (band) 97
Sugar (band) 123
suicidal black metal 5

Suicidal Tendencies (band) 107
suicide 5, 38, 46, 47, 66, 80–2, 84, 86–7, 93,
    98, 102, 105–17, 118, 138, 170, 172,
    174, 175, 176, 178, 181, 186, 187
Suicide (band) 113
Sunn O))) (band) 54, 167
Sutlović, D. 175
Swan Lake 21
Swans (band) 37, 54
Swatos, W.H. 184, 185
Sweeting, H. 175
Swift, Taylor (musician) 48
Switchblade Symphony (band) 80
Sylvain, Audrey (musician) 98, 172
symbolic pilgrimage 163

taboo 4, 5, 12, 35, 39, 43, 44, 45, 47, 49, 54,
    57–9, 85, 92, 93, 117, 122, 124, 125
Talbot, S. 183
Talking Heads, The (band) 27, 32, 115
Tartarus 34
Taubert, M. 175
Taylor, C. 13, 30, 159, 161
Taylor, J. 164
Taylor, S. 129–30, 133
Teng, P.R. 181
Teresa, Mother 140
Tester, K. 161, 162, 178
thanatos 34, 37, 100–5
Thaut, M. 71, 168
Theatre of Hate (band) 81
Thievery Corporation (band) 99
Third Eye Foundation, The (musician) 74,
    84, 88
3 Doors Down 110
This Mortal Coil (band) 47
Thompson, H.S. 56, 165
Thorgerson, S. 171
Thornton, S. 47, 48, 164, 172
Throbbing Gristle (band) 81, 84, 85
Tibet, David (musician) 74
Till, R. 182
Tillich, P. 33, 34, 148, 162, 184
Todestrieb, see death drive
Tomasi, L. 184
Tönnies, F. 122
Tooney, C. 140, 182
Toop, D. 71, 73, 75–6, 168, 169
torture porn 97

tourism 148–51, 153
Townsend, Pete (musician) 50
Toynbee, J. 177, 179
transfiguration 138, 139–45, 147, 148, 153,
    154
transgression 35, 37–60, 61, 63, 64, 67, 74,
    76, 80, 86, 88, 89, 93, 98, 106, 107,
    118, 119, 120, 121, 122, 125, 126,
    129, 132, 135
Trigger the Bloodshed (band) 97
Trobriand Islanders 18
Tsitsos, W. 177, 178
Turino, T. 134, 180
turn to the self 12–13
Turner, E. 150–1, 164, 185
Turner, Nik (musician) 137
Turner, V. 45–6, 58, 124–5, 140–1, 151,
    163, 164, 166, 178, 182, 185, 186
Turnock, R. 158
2Pac, *see* Shakur, Tupac
20,000 Days on Earth 13
Type O Negative (band) 80

Uaral (band) 80
Ulcerate (band) 47
ultimate concern 148, 150
ultra-subjectivization 142, 148
Unburied (band) 126
uncanny 62–79, 81, 82, 87, 94, 166–7, 169
undead 51, 61, 62, 69, 78, 86, 94, 95, 102
Underworld 34
unheimliche 63, 64, 69, 73, 87
U.N.L.V. (band) 130

Vågnes, Ø. 162
Vai, Steve (musician) 109
Vail, Tobi (musician) 119
vampires 50, 62, 85, 86, 88, 165
Van Gennep, A. 45
Vania 88–9, 92
Vasionytė, I. 168
Vega, Alan (musician) 113–14
Velez, W. 87, 171
Velvet Underground (band) 22, 62
Vietnam war 46
violence 37, 41, 54, 88, 97–136

Walser, R. 172
Walter, T. 182, 184, 185

waltz 65
Warhol, Andy 22
Watts, H. 176
Waugh, E.H. 166
Way, Gerard (musician) 24–5
Weinstein, D. 173
Weinstock, J. 162
Welch, C. 159
Werther effect 138
West, P. 175
Whalen, B.E. 184
Wheatley, D. 68
white noise 77, 134
White, A. 55, 171
Whitehead, Jeff, *see* Lurker of the
     Chalice (musician)
Who, The (band) 50
Wierzbicki, J. 168
Wilkins, R. 3, 157
Williams, Roz (musician) 37–8, 162
Wilson, S. 165, 166, 182
Wilson, Steve (musician) 77–8
Wiser, C. 160
Witkin, J.-P. 89–92
Wolfe, Cary 78, 169

Wolfe, Charles 137
Wolff, B.P. 83
Wooden Shjips (band) 3
Woodhead, L. 182, 183, 184
words against death 19–25, 135
Wrest, *see* Lurker of the Chalice
     (musician)
Wright, J. 169

X Factor, The 115
X-Fusion (musician) 106
XXYYXX (musician) 74

Years (band) 25
Yella Boy (musician) 130
Yen, A.M.F. 181
Yglesias, P. 171
Yip, P.S.F. 138, 181
Young, R. 175

Zimmerman, T.S. 179
Žižek, S. 101–2, 104, 174
Zola Jesus (musician) 167
Zorn, John (musician) 89
Zouravliov, Vania, *see* Vania

Printed in Great Britain
by Amazon

70015984R00136